D0205437

Rudy Flora

How to Work
with Sex Offenders
A Handbook for
Criminal Justice, Human Service,
and Mental Health Professionals

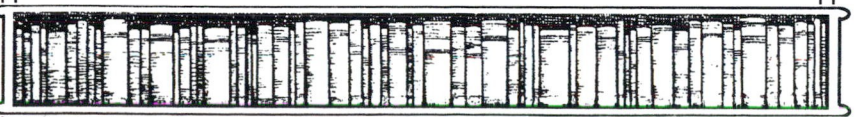

More pre-publication
REVIEWS, COMMENTARIES, EVALUATIONS . . .

"The investigation of child sexual abuse and other sexual offenses requires specialized training of law enforcement, human services, and mental health professionals. However, each of these systems approaches the problem from a different perspective. The effective coordination of the investigation of the allegations, prosecution of the offender and protection of the community, and evaluation and treatment of the offender and victim are not easy matters. Rudy Flora's book brings a much-needed multidisciplinary focus to this complex problem. Each of its fifteen chapters contains valuable information with which investigators, prosecutors, child protective workers, and therapists should be familiar. Professionals new to their roles will find the book very useful, allowing them to understand the protocols and procedures of the other agencies and offices. It also points to those issues that practitioners within each area must become familiar.

Flora shows the reader how each of the three systems performs its own critical role and explains the particular terms and concepts unique to each. The reader can use this fundamental handbook as a springboard for learning about specific issues and procedures in detail. Mr. Flora's book is a welcome addition to the growing literature on the problem of sexual abuse and sexual assault, and will surely be required reading for professionals entering this challenging field."

Mario J. P. Dennis, PhD
Clinical Psychologist,
Harrisonburg, VA

The Haworth Clinical Practice Press
An Imprint of The Haworth Press, Inc.
New York • London • Oxford

How to Work
with Sex Offenders
A Handbook for
Criminal Justice, Human Service,
and Mental Health Professionals

HAWORTH Marriage and the Family
Terry S. Trepper, PhD
Executive Editor

How to Work
with Sex Offenders
A Handbook for
Criminal Justice, Human Service,
and Mental Health Professionals

Rudy Flora

The Haworth Clinical Practice Press®
An Imprint of The Haworth Press, Inc.
New York • London • Oxford

Published by

The Haworth Clinical Practice Press®, an imprint of The Haworth Press, Inc., 10 Alice Street, Binghamton, NY 13904-1580.

Cover design by Marylouise E. Doyle.

Library of Congress Cataloging-in-Publication Data

Flora, Rudy.
  How to work with sex offenders : a handbook for criminal justice, human service, and mental health professionals / Rudy Flora.
      p. cm
  Includes bibliographical references and index.
  ISBN 0-7890-0733-9 (hc. : alk. paper)—ISBN 0-7890-1499-8 (softcover: alk. paper)
  1. Sex offenders—Rehabilitation. 2. Sex offenders—Psychology. 3. Psychotherapy.

HV6556 .H68 2001
616.85'83—dc21   00-069717

This book is dedicated to my wife,
who showed me how to reach for stars
along the Blue Ridge Parkway

ABOUT THE AUTHOR

Rudy Flora, MSW, LCSW, is a clinician in private practice in Virginia, providing individual, family, and group treatment services for sex offenders and their families. He is a Licensed Clinical Social Worker and Certified Sex Offender Treatment Provider. He also serves as an adjunct faculty member at the School of Social Work at Radford University in the Abingdon program. Formerly a probation officer, Flora has worked with sex offenders for over two decades.

CONTENTS

Preface

Sexual offending impacts both victim and offender. The clinical harm experienced by a victim is significant and recovery is long term. Some victims spend a lifetime healing from the trauma of sexual assault. Offenders, too, are often trapped in the tragedy of their deviance. Work with sex offenders is a relatively new science that is now coming to the attention of the public. No longer is sexual abuse being minimized. Still, much more research is merited. On the front line are the men and women in criminal justice, human service, and mental health professions. Usually understaffed, underpaid, and overworked, these professionals continue to intervene, assess, and treat sex offenders in a very effective manner.

The idea for this book started nearly twenty years ago. I was a probation officer and was searching for reference material on sex offenders. I found several articles and books about offenders but experienced difficulty finding one resource that would be of use to me on a daily basis. Later, as a clinician seeking information, I continued to experience the same problem. Realistically, I could not carry around an assortment of articles and books on the subject. Many colleagues reported similar experiences or frustrations.

Globally, a number of specialists in various disciplines have developed assessment, intervention, and treatment techniques that may be considered of value in working with sex offenders. However, no complete manual on sex offenders is available for professionals in the field at the present time. The sharing of learned information about this most special and challenging population appears to be a universal need among system providers. Therefore, I believe that a comprehensive resource is now merited. I am not aware of any book that presents the proposed material for both the beginning and experienced professional in reference handbook form. Most available texts are written for advanced mental health clinicians or for scholars already familiar with this special population. Sexual offending is a worldwide problem impacting many people; all nations report problems of this nature.

This book will serve as a reference guide for criminal justice, human service, and mental health professionals. In the United States, the criminal justice system is now composed of more than 580,000 law enforcement officers and about 220,000 civilians are associated with this field. Such professionals would be represented as police officers, probation and parole officers, correctional staff, and other law enforcement personnel. There are an estimated 560,000 human service and mental health professionals nationwide in all service disciplines. These may include child protective service workers, clinical social workers, psychiatrists, clinical psychologists, marriage and family therapists, licensed professional counselors, and other clinicians.

This text may be a helpful resource for those individuals within the judicial system, including attorneys, judges, prosecutors, and others associated with the court system. Additionally, it can be of help for those in academia and students who are studying the fields of criminal justice, human service, and mental health. Other groups may include schoolteachers, nurses, and other physicians in a health care setting. In addition, this book may serve as a guide to victims and their families who are currently encountering these systems and need basic reference material.

The book is intended to be user-friendly and attempts to offer information about sex offenders in a format that is relevant to the needs of system professionals. Often, those who work with sex offenders have only a limited understanding of what the other practitioner is trying to do. This book will show, in a step-by-step format, how the criminal justice, human service, and mental health systems function. More important, it will give the reader a more in-depth perspective of the various techniques that particular disciplines apply in work with sex offenders. Sex offenders are extremely skillful at avoiding detection, and they will use any confusion displayed by system providers to their advantage. There is no intent to criticize any professional group; we are all still learning. Indeed, it is the belief that we, as professionals, may all benefit by working together in the gathering of knowledge in a joint effort to protect the community and prevent future victims.

Composites of a number of approaches are reviewed. No one single approach is endorsed or recommended. However, I have included one treatment modality that I have found personally useful in my work with sex offenders. This treatment approach does not discount the many other effective therapies in existence.

The book is easy to read and is not overly theoretical. Jargon and terminology have been kept to a minimum and are used only within the framework of the systems now in place. Emphasis is placed on the etiology, identification, intervention, and treatment methodologies of sexual offenders. This work does contain some essential theory, but provides a balance between principle and application. In order for the reader to fully comprehend the seriousness of this social problem, certain sections of the text are presented in a graphic but not sensational context; generally, there has been a tendency in research to sanitize the information about sexual offenders and the physical and psychological damage done to their victims.

Rudy Flora

Acknowledgments

For the production of this work, I feel a deep sense of gratitude and appreciation for a number of people. First, for my family, who were encouraging, helpful, supportive, and willing to listen; for my mother, a teacher of life and people, always an inspiration to me; to the memory of my father, I miss you; for my uncles and aunts for caring; for some very special friends through the years who have had an impact on me: Thanks, Doug and Patty, Homer and Beverly, Jean, Beverly, Bob, Colin, Sean, Lois, JoAnn, Rhoda, Kalmal, Stitch, Vincent, Buddy, and Sean; for Eva and Jack, who literally walked me through this project. In addition, Teenia, your typing never ceases to amaze me. Josh, thanks for mowing. I know you both are probably glad the project is over. Other friends of support are in Greenbrier, Monroe, and Washington counties. I am especially thankful to the Smyth-Bland Regional Library staff for their time and assistance in locating research articles and books, particularly the work completed by Brenda. Your efforts to help were outstanding. Also, to the Washington County Public Library staff for your services and the wonderful places to write in peace and comfort. And all the best to Ward H staff, past and present. I have been extremely fortunate to have found a publisher in The Haworth Press, whose staff has given me much support and encouragement in this work. All authors should be so lucky to be surrounded by such a group of dedicated professionals. Finally, to Terry Trepper, my editor, who believed in this work, and for his invaluable advice, assistance, counsel, clinical integrity, direction, insight, and wisdom.

Chapter 1

The Sex Offender: An Introduction

An emerging patient population that is receiving increasing public and media attention is sex offenders. Sex offenders present difficult clinical problems in our society that challenge accustomed methods of intervention and treatment.

A fast-growing trend now exists in social policy to render services to this new patient phenomenon. However, many criminal justice, human service, and mental health professionals are unfamiliar with this population due to limitations of experience or specialized training. Meanwhile, more sex offenders are encountering these systems and requiring services at a rapid rate.

Therefore, as sex offenders grow as an identified patient population, the need for more skilled professionals is expected to increase. However, the criminal justice, human service, and mental health systems have only recently started to respond. As a result, only a limited number of experienced professionals can now offer help.

Sexual crimes impact the victim, families, and the community in a psychological manner that other crimes or mental disorders do not. Many offenders were early victims of sexual abuse themselves. Incarceration alone has not alleviated the problem, and other methods to prevent offenses or recidivism appear to be merited. To address the complexities of the sexual offender, a knowledge base is needed. Encountering offenders requires certain skills in order to properly protect the public while working with the perpetrators.

In many instances, criminal justice, human service, and mental health professionals operate in isolation from one another. Transfer of knowledge is often limited and impaired by interagency regulations. A more unified approach is required. Many sex offenders are able to avoid detection, prosecution, treatment, and incarceration as the result of system conflict. Overall, there appears to be a lack of information sharing and networking among disciplines about sexual offenders at the present time. Such situations lead to confusion and, worse, inappropriate methods of intervention. Communities and future victims remain at risk as additional solutions are sought.

The purpose of this book is to serve as a reference guide for persons planning to work, or now working with sex offenders in the criminal justice, human service, and mental health professions. This book explores those systems that offer services and how they function. Also, this book provides information about assessment, intervention, and treatment of sex offenders.

DEFINITIONS

To begin, a sexual offense may be defined as a criminal action that occurs against another individual. Such sexual behavior may be used to display anger, control, domination, hostility, and power upon a person. Victims may be coerced, forced, or manipulated into engaging in sexual activity. Individuals who are unable to render informed consent as the result of mental incompetency or who are deemed minors may be considered victims of a sexual offense.

O'Connell, Leberg, and Donaldson (1990) define a sex offense as a criminal action involving inappropriate sexual behavior that occurs when one party does not give, or is incapable of giving, informed consent. Incidents may range from acts of rape to voyeurism in which the victim has not given consent. Other situations may include children sexually used, in a passive or forcible manner, by another minor or an adult.

In some circumstances, the victim may sustain a physical injury. A weapon may have been a part of the attack, used to threaten or harm the victim. Sexual assault may include vaginal, oral, or anal penetration. Other sexual offenses may include inappropriate acts of touching, fondling, or indecent exposure situations. Males and females of all race and age groups have been reported victims.

Coleman and colleagues (1996) report that a sex offender is an individual who commits a sexual crime that violates cultural morals or laws. Laws may vary by locality, but most cultures have certain sexual behaviors they define as inappropriate and unacceptable.

Sex offenders may be preadolescent, adolescent, or adult. The majority of offenders are male, although more female offenders are now being reported. Throughout this book, offenders will be referred to in a gender-neutral manner whenever possible.

Sex offenders are found among most races, cultures, age groups, and religious faiths. Offenders exist among both the employed and unemployed and within all income groups. Some sex offenders may be college educated while others may be high school dropouts. Sex offenders may be married, involved in a relationship, or single at the time of the reported offense. Offenders may be known to the victims or strangers to them. Some offenders are members of the victim's immediate family; others have been a friend or acquaintance. Many sex offenders have a paraphilia disturbance. Many have offended on multiple occasions.

STATISTICAL INFORMATION

Sexual violence against women and children is currently witnessing a dramatic increase in public awareness. Sexual crimes are now being treated in a serious manner, which is promoting new research, knowledge development, and clinical expertise.

Statistical data sometimes fail to capture the extent of a social problem or crime and its impacts upon the victim and the surrounding community. However, the sheer volume of reported sexual offenses and the estimated number of victims are alarming and not easily discounted.

Globally, South Africa appears to have the highest reported rate of rape in the world. Hawthorne (1999) reports that more than 1.6 million incidents of rape or sexual assault (estimated) occur yearly in South Africa. During 1998 alone approximately 104.1 rapes per 100,000 persons occurred. Yet, only one in thirty-five is reported.

Salholz and colleagues (1990) report that the United States has a rape rate nearly four times higher than Germany's, thirteen times higher than Britain's, and more than twenty times higher than Japan's.

In the United States, it is estimated that a woman is raped every six minutes, and every hour sixteen women confront a rapist. More than 12 million women are raped at least once in their lifetime, and three out of four are expected to be victims of at least one violent crime. About 61 percent of rape victims were said to be younger than eighteen years of age at the time of the assault, three out of ten had not yet reached their eleventh birthday, and almost 80 percent knew their offender. Only about 16 percent of sexual assaults are reported by victims to the police, however.

In 1990, rape was increasing at four times the rate of other crimes (Salholz, 1990). A survey conducted by the National Victim Center found that 683,000 women had been forcibly raped in the United States during that year. This total exceeds U.S. Justice Department reports by five times (*Time,* 1992). Some experts have suggested, however, that since many rapes often go unreported, the number of victims may have actually been in the millions.

Equally disturbing is the number of child victims reported. Abel and colleagues (1987), in a landmark study, found that the average female-oriented pedophile had nearly twenty different child victims, while the male-oriented pedophile had victimized as many as 150 children. Approximately 561 persons participated in this survey, with offenders ranging from exhibitionists to rapists. More than 291,000 acts of paraphilic behaviors were reported in this survey.

SEX OFFENDERS AND SOCIAL POLICY

Through the years, sex offenders have been impacted by social policy changes in the United States. Laws for the special commitment of sex offenders first appeared during the 1930s. Offenders were believed to be at a high risk for relapse; at the same time, they were seen as good candidates for treatment services.

The American Psychiatric Association (1999) reports the first laws were designed to accomplish two goals: (1) cure sex offenders in a shorter time than if incarcerated and (2) protect the community from persons believed to be sexually dangerous.

More than half of all states enacted sex offender commitment laws in some form, known as "sexual psychopath laws," "sexually dangerous persons acts," and "mentally disordered sex offender acts." However, by the 1970s, many of these laws had lost endorsement as hope of curing sex offenders declined. All but twelve states and the District of Columbia, by 1990, had changed or reversed earlier sex offender commitment laws.

The desire to commit sex offenders has resurfaced. Several states have adopted new indeterminate commitment statutes; several other states have similar laws pending. A different policy has evolved within these new laws that is slanted toward the commitment of a sex offender only after incarceration in prison.

These new laws do not reflect the earlier belief that sex offenders can be successfully treated and cured. As a result, a shift has started to occur in which offenders are now being referred to the mental health system for inpatient treatment services. Sex offenders are now being involuntarily committed to state psychiatric facilities upon the completion of their prison sentences if they are believed to be a danger to others.

Sex offenders may appear as a clinical paradox for criminal justice, human service, and mental health professionals. It is questioned by some system providers if sex offenders deserve or even merit treatment. This question, although challenging in concept, does not address the rising cost of services, the recidivism rate, and the tragic toll sexual deviance creates upon those victimized. A number of complex physical and mental disorders can be present that are difficult to treat or resolve.

Mental health is not and never has been a perfect science. As a discipline, it should be noted that the treatment of sex offenders is in the early infancy stages of development. Social policymakers may desire to withhold assumptions until more empirical data is obtained. All treatment programs are said to possess failures; substance abuse programs may be cited as an example in which relapse may occur in many cases, while others refrain from further drug and alcohol abuse.

Communities are requesting more comprehensive services that address safety concerns. Advocate rights' groups have impacted the way both offenders and victims are treated. Victims are more likely to report a sexual offense now than in the past. Parole boards are becoming more reluctant to discharge a sex offender back to the community if they have the option to continue incarceration and will withhold release. Offenders who refuse treatment may serve longer sentences.

Treatment is mandatory in some states prior to parole. Duty-to-report laws now require doctors, nurses, school counselors, teachers, and therapists to report cases of suspected sexual abuse; professionals in general are now more alert to the signs of sexual abuse. Courts are giving longer sentences to persons convicted of a sexual offense. In May 1996, the Violent Crime Control and Law Enforcement Act of 1994 was amended to require the release of relevant information to protect the public from sexually violent offenders. This act, also known as Megan's Law, mandates community notification of sex offenders released from prison. In addition, in more than half of the fifty states, certain sex crimes now require offenders to register with law enforcement agencies.

Several states are also requesting state law enforcement departments maintain and update a Web page on the Internet of sex offenders convicted of certain sexual crimes. The offender's name, address, and sexual conviction are listed and a recent photograph is included. Several states are also defining offenders as violent sexual predators if convicted of certain crimes. In addition, several states have established licensure requirements for sex offender treatment providers with certification requirements for training and clinical experience.

However, criminal justice, human service, and mental health professionals remain somewhat mired down in debate about sex offenders and who should provide services to them. Many sex offenders have been referred to corrections for care in the past. Correctional facilities have attempted to offer help, but remain concerned about their role in working with this population on a clinical basis. Some earlier programs started in correctional facilities have been closed; others remain in place. Psychiatric facilities express concern about placing sex offenders among the mentally ill, who possess less intrusive disorders. Social policy still continues to struggle with determining what system is best equipped to serve the sex offender while protecting the community.

HOW THE CURRENT SYSTEM WORKS

Usually a sex offender is able to victimize a number of individuals before first encountering the criminal justice, human service, or mental health systems. As a result, it is important for all agency professionals to have a protocol in place that quickly identifies possible sex offenders or allegations of sexual abuse.

For child sexual abuse, the initial child abuse report is routinely filed with the local department of human or social services. Child protection service workers will evaluate the complaint, then make a determination if an investigation should be conducted. Often, social service departments are among the first agencies contacted.

Child abuse complaints may come from a variety of sources, including family members, neighbors, or other acquaintances. Other reports or complaints may be filed by physicians, nurses, schoolteachers, guidance counselors, and mental health workers prompted, in part, by duty-to-report laws. Sources sometimes request that their identities remain undisclosed.

Cumming and Buell (1997) note that most social service agencies have an established policy for the investigation of child sexual abuse allegations. A child protective service (CPS) worker is assigned to investigate the report (such titles vary by state). A CPS worker will inform law enforcement officers, the district prosecuting attorney, and the child sexual abuse team (if one exists in that locality) of the complaint. Human service agencies are mandated by law to ensure the protection of the child. In addition, human service agencies share the burden of responsibility in the investigation of the allegation, as well as preparing the case for court. Some children found to be at risk may need to be removed from the home. A CPS worker usually coordinates this process. In cases where the an allegation is found to be serious and perhaps life threatening, a police officer may be asked to accompany the CPS worker to the residence. An officer may remain active in the case.

Cumming and Buell (1997) note that in the sexual abuse complaints of a child, the primary role of the law enforcement officer is to prevent additional incidents of harm and to provide protection if warranted. The officer also is expected to investigate the allegation for possible criminal prosecution, gather evidence, and notify the prosecuting or district attorney of the incident. Referrals of child sexual abuse to police departments usually come from CPS workers. Police and CPS workers share the responsibility of arranging the investigation and may conduct joint interviews. In the event that the complaint is filed first with law enforcement, police officers are responsible for notifying social services of an allegation. Police officers must establish probable cause of a criminal offense to take action. Cooperation with other agencies is important. Such agencies may include the district attorney's office, hospital, probation department, mental health center, and the local school. Using proper evidence gathering procedures is encouraged.

Typically, most adult victims report sexual abuse first to a police officer. Adult protection services (APS) may become involved in cases in which the victim may not be legally competent, as well as with someone who has a mental illness. Victims often are in shock, appear disoriented, and are confused. Shame and embarrassment are influential factors to consider when interviewing a victim of sexual assault. As a result, to avoid additional trauma, many law enforcement departments assign male and female teams or have access to a rape counselor for assistance. In some cases, adult sexual assault cases are first encountered by health care professionals.

All reported victims are referred to a physician for a medical examination. Most hospital staff are well versed in rape and sexual assault situations. A chain of custody of any medical evidence is required. The physician will attempt to establish the possibility of sexual abuse, diagnose, and treat the victim. The medical examination should occur as soon as possible after the report.

The district attorney is responsible for the possible prosecution of the sex offender and the protection of the child or adult victim. Most district attorneys work closely with CPS and APS workers and police officers during the investigation of a sexual abuse complaint. A district attorney well versed in sex crimes may meet with members of a sexual assault team and the victim several times during an investigation. Evidence is reviewed; potential witnesses are interviewed if an arrest is expected.

Sex offenders usually elect by this point, if they have not already done so, to engage the services of a defense attorney. In some situations, an offender will employ an attorney during the interview and investigation stage, prior to the filing of a possible warrant for arrest. This is a difficult time for both the victim and the offender. Stress levels during this period can be exceptionally high. Most offenders initially will deny the offense, display defense behaviors that connote innocence, and be the image of a law-abiding citizen. Professionals associated with the investigation process may be confronted with a number of behaviors, including anger, attack, denial, minimization, personalization, rage, and rationalization.

Some offenders will blame the victim; others will attempt to organize family and friends in an effort to protect their welfare. Victims may sometimes be exposed to the offender's denial of the incident. Both offender and victim often will display fear and withdrawal during this period. Some victims will become confused, blame themselves, and may recant their testimony. Offenders will sometimes attempt to threaten, manipulate victims, or control information about the crime to police. Police officers should carefully limit the offender's access to the victim during the investigation process.

Commonly, the last individual to be interviewed in a sexual abuse complaint is the sex offender; this is a part of most agency protocol when investigating sexual abuse situations. All available information should be obtained before confronting the offender. An informal meeting may be agreed upon with the suspect. The district attorney is consulted prior to such a session.

In child abuse cases, after the interview and related investigation, the human service agency will then rule if the complaint is founded, if there is reason to suspect, or if the allegation is unfounded. The wording of these rulings varies by state. Evidence indicating a founded ruling results in the case being referred to law enforcement. During this period, the situation usually increases in intensity; if the child is believed to be in danger, his or her safety may be evaluated. Law enforcement officers will continue to gather information and share their findings with the district or prosecuting attorney.

A warrant for arrest may be filed against the offender if law enforcement officers believe there is sufficient evidence. The offender is then formally arrested and can be incarcerated. A bail or bond hearing or arraignment is then held, depending upon the laws of the particular locality; the suspect may be released pending a court hearing.

Child and adult victims are often referred to mental health professionals for treatment services after an allegation of sexual assault. A variety of behaviors may be exhibited by the victim. Victims may not seek therapy until after the shock of the event has subsided. Some victims may seek clinical services immediately; others never enter therapy. Victims sometimes are reluctant to enter treatment. Some may protest or resist help. Mental health professionals who offer clinical services to a victim may expect to be summoned to court to provide testimony. Most courts need to hear the extent of the psychological harm experienced by the victim. Other professionals may be summoned to offer testimony in court regarding sexual assault cases.

In most states, an arraignment is usually held after the arrest. During this process, the arrest warrant is reviewed with the defendant. In cases in which the accused is unable to obtain the services of an attorney, a public defender is appointed by the court. A district attorney will usually request that the offender not be permitted to have contact with the victim. In cases where the victim is a child and a family member is the suspect, the district attorney may ask the court to order the accused out of the home. In emergency situations, a child may be taken into temporary custody and placed in a foster home.

A court hearing is scheduled for the defendant. In many cases, the offender has been released from jail prior to the hearing. Many sex crime cases are continued before a hearing is actually held. This situation is fairly commonplace across the United States, as the result of crowded court dockets, scheduling of witnesses, and the particular nuances of sex crime cases. Unfortunately, this is upsetting for the victim and his or her family and sometimes impairs testimony. Defense attorneys are aware of this issue and will attempt to delay a hearing, if possible.

Initially, a lower court will first hear a case involving a sexual abuse complaint. Child sexual abuse cases are first heard in a family court before a judge; the courtroom is closed and the public cannot attend such proceedings. Adult sexual crime offenses are referred to a general or district court. These courts are open to the public unless the presiding judge requests that the hearing be closed. Witnesses may be asked to remain outside of the courtroom until their testimony is required. Many lower courts do not keep a record of testimony unless requested.

Both the prosecution and defense are permitted to present witnesses. Usual witnesses may include the CPS or APS worker, police officer, physician, mental health professional, and other collateral witnesses. Family members, friends, co-workers, and possible witnesses to the crime may also be summoned to testify. Both the victim and the accused offender are permitted to present information. Lower court proceedings tend to be informal and permit attorneys, offenders, victims, and witnesses a certain amount of latitude in an effort to present evidence for an adjudication or finding. Most courts will permit child and adult victims to be questioned in detail but are careful that the behavior of counsel is not overly harmful to any party. The defendant is usually questioned at length, unless he or she declines to offer testimony. A victim's prior sexual history is not allowed to be addressed in court proceedings in most states.

In the event that the case is adjudicated and a verdict is found, sentencing sometimes may be withheld pending additional information. The court may order an evaluation of the offender by a mental health professional. A report by a probation officer may also be requested. Misdemeanor sex crime cases may be resolved by the lower court. Some felony offenses are reduced to a misdemeanor or are plea-bargained to a lesser charge by the prosecuting attorney and defense counsel. Offenders may be sentenced to jail or committed to an inpatient psychiatric hospital for treatment. Others may be placed on probation with a suspended jail sentence and ordered to attend outpatient therapy. Court fines, costs, and victim restitution may be requested. An offender has the right to appeal a sentence, which then is referred to a higher court.

A felony offense is referred to a higher court for final adjudication and sentencing. These venues include a judge and a jury, if requested; they are considered to be courts of record, with all testimony transcribed or recorded in some fashion. Most higher courts are in session for several months at a time, with a prospective list of possible jurors. Higher courts are more formal in their proceedings. Again, all witnesses, the victim, and the offender are summoned to appear again to offer testimony. Sentencing, on a finding of guilt, is usually more severe for a felony. Incarceration is usually ordered. However, in certain cases only probation supervision is requested. A presentence report by a probation officer may be ordered. Mental health evaluations are sometimes sought. Final adjudication can include treatment on an inpatient or outpatient basis by the court. An offender can be committed to a psychiatric facility. Federal and state laws will impact the type of sentencing imposed.

Normally, sex offenders who are incarcerated will be referred first to a type of holding center for an assessment before placement in a correctional facility. Staff evaluate each new inmate for placement. Eventually, the offender is placed in a correctional institution. Some states offer treatment for sexual offenders during incarceration. Other correctional facilities possess only limited services and prefer that clinical treatment options be managed by mental health providers after parole occurs. Some states place sex offenders at specialized facilities.

Parole expectations for sex offenders have changed. Several states now request sex offenders to attend treatment programs while in prison. Early release may be used as an incentive. Offenders who do not volunteer to participate in treatment programs usually are required to complete their full sentence. Many sex offenders are now serving all or most of their complete sentence as the result of changes in parole standards. Sex offenders who are paroled are referred to probation and parole departments for follow-up services. Parole conditions may include a mandate that the offender participate in a sex offender treatment program. Offenders who resist treatment services may be returned to prison.

Certain offenders who have completed their prison sentence are now being committed involuntarily to state psychiatric hospitals for a period of time. Such offenders are viewed as dangerous and a risk to the community. This form of treatment is still being debated. A review hearing is required on a regular basis. Discharge is dependent upon the individual's clinical status.

Chapter 2

The Criminal Justice System

This chapter is about the criminal justice system and those who work with sex offenders. Primarily, three professional cluster groups are most likely to deal with persons accused or convicted of sexual crimes, aside from those in the judicial system. These groups may include those in direct law enforcement services, correctional staff, and probation and parole officers. Typically, sex offenders gain the attention of the criminal justice system after a report has been filed that some type of sexual misconduct has occurred.

Sex crime reports have increased, although criminal offenses are dropping. This may be attributed, in part, to active victim groups, community safety issues, changes in parole board criteria, duty-to-report laws, new legislation impacting law, increased media attention, professional awareness of sexual abuse, public concern, stronger court sentences, and the societal emotional factors associated with sexual crime today (Schwartz and Cellini, 1995).

According to Greenfeld (1997), in the United States, on a given day, about 234,000 sex offenders may be found in care, custody, or other form of correctional monitoring. Such a population, if grouped in one area, would constitute a medium-sized city. About 60 percent of these offenders are said to reside in the community and are on either probation or parole status. However, current law requires tracking of some offenders to be terminated by the criminal justice system upon completion of their supervision.

Approximately 906,000 offenders were confined in state prisons in 1994, of which 88,000 persons or 9.7 percent were classified as violent sex offenders. The number of persons sentenced for violent sexual assault, other than rape, has grown by an annual rate of nearly 15 percent, an increase that exceeds any other category of violent crime; it also exceeds any other category except drug trafficking.

Police, in 1995, made 34,650 arrests for rape, and 94,500 arrests for other sexually related offenses. During 1994 and 1995, one-third of all victims of sexual assault reported the offense to a law enforcement agency. During 1992, approximately one in twenty reported complaints of a violent felony in the seventy-five largest counties were the result of a rape assault. Alarmingly, about 50 percent of rape defendants are released prior to trial. The average bond for a rape defendant is listed at $23,500. Yet eight of ten defendants accused of rape pleaded guilty. About two-thirds of those found guilty were eventually incarcerated.

LAW ENFORCEMENT

Sex crime cases are difficult cases to investigate. The investigation of a sex crime involves special techniques that are unique and different in approach as compared to other types of criminal offenses. The victim is often extremely upset and/or emotionally distraught.

The Initial Investigation

Bennett and Hess (1998) report the most important phase of any investigation occurs at the preliminary stage; certain decisions are made that will impact the possible outcome of a case. A specific protocol is recommended when investigating a sexual crime. A format used for adult female victims is outlined but may be modified for child victims. These procedures, in part, are recommended as follows:

1. Record the arrival time at the crime scene.
2. Determine the whereabouts of the victim.
3. Learn the physical condition of the victim.
4. Immediate medical assistance may be merited.
5. Close the crime scene area.
6. Attempt to identify the offender.
7. Determine, if possible, if the perpetrator is in the area.
8. All witnesses should be interviewed.
9. A radio report may be useful if the suspect has escaped.

The Crime Scene

According to Moreau and Bigbee (1995), there are several stages to the search of the crime scene that are appropriate to the investigation. This may differ from the initial or preliminary investigation. The basic steps are listed as follows as provided by Moreau and Bigbee (1995, p. 68):

1. Approach scene
2. Secure and protect
3. Preliminary survey eventuality that does not fall into a preplanned sequence [Both planned and unplanned surveys usually occur]
4. Narrative description
5. Photograph scene
6. Sketch scene
7. Evaluation of latent fingerprint evidence and other evidence
8 Detailed search for evidence collection, preservation and documentation of evidence
9. Final survey
10. Release of scene

Victim Interview

Bennett and Hess (1998) recommend that a supportive style interview first be conducted for a victim of rape or sexual assault. A sexual assault is a humiliating event; even the retelling of the incident to others can be emotionally painful. Although police officers need to obtain the facts in regard to the offense, it is important to remember the physical and psychological stress that the victim has experienced. The incident may lead a victim to appear uncooperative, hostile, or fearful. Others may seem confused, disoriented, and reluctant at times to offer details regarding the incident. It is appropriate for both male and female staff to be present during the interview.

The interview should be conducted in a "sympathetic" and "understanding" manner. Immediate information collection should be limited to the victim's full name, home residence, place of employment, and telephone number. Details of the actual sexual assault can be postponed. The initial interview should be completed in a private setting away from others. The physical appearance of the victim may need to be documented by a photograph. Bruises, cuts, lacerations, marks or torn clothing should be noted. The behavior of the victim will need to be recorded. The relationship between victim and offender, if any, should be determined during the session.

Burgess and Hazelwood (1995) suggest the following guidelines, summarized in part, for the actual interview of the victim.

1. Always involve the victim in the interview, explain each step of the process, and leave a telephone number.
2. Give the victim freedom to talk or vent during the interview; the victim's first name should not be used without permission.
3. The interview location should be comfortable and secure.
4. Ask the victim if he or she would rather tell about the incident in his or her own words or be questioned.
5. Use active listening skills.
6. Be attentive to what the victim is expressing; be watchful for behaviors such as guilt, fear, humiliation, or unnecessary attempts to convince.
7. Investigators should offer reassurance to the victim that he or she is now safe and was not responsible for the assault.
8. Questions about humiliating acts or specific sexual behaviors of the offense should be carefully presented. Inapproriate words, such as *climax,* should be avoided.
9. Use professional terminology whenever possible in the interview. Language can be adjusted for the victim if needed.
10. Language that is used during the interview should not be judgmental or threatening to the victim.
11. Officers should make it clear to the victim that issues of power, control, anger, and aggression are the important elements of the crime, not sex.
12. Investigators should focus on the fact that the crime was an act of violence; any sexual aspects of the incident should not dominate the interview.
13. Investigators should obtain the facts of the crime in as detailed or accurate manner as possible.
14. Investigators should take precautions to ensure the victim does not believe the process is "voyeuristic."
15. Before the interview, an introduction is critical, and the officers should introduce themselves in a professional, confident, and sincere manner.
16. In ending the interview, the investigators should let the victim know that he or she will be given periodic updates.

17. The victim should be referred to a therapist or social service program for issues of trauma.
18. Before concluding, the victim should be asked if he or she has any questions the investigators can answer.
19. The victim should always be thanked by the investigators for the time he or she has given.

A "behavioral-oriented" style interview is recommended for gathering information from the victim about the sexual assault. Such details about the attack will assist police in preparing a profile of the offender. This session usually occurs during the second interview of a victim. Specific sexual and nonsexual behavior should be reviewed during such a meeting. Hazelwood and Burgess (1995) report that the information obtained, summarized in part, should include:

1. Method of contact
2. Level of control
3. Use of physical force
4. Victim resistance
5. Reaction to resistance by offender
6. Offender sexual dysfunction
7. Type of sexual acts
8. Offender interaction
9. Victim interaction
10. Any behavioral changes during assault by offender
11. Precautions used by offender
12. Items removed
13. Prior victim contact
14. Personality traits exhibited by attacker

Interviewing Sex Offenders

Bennett and Hess (1998) suggest that the suspect should be the last person interviewed in the investigative process. Such an approach allows investigators to collect all available information possible by the time the interview occurs. However, police are encouraged to remain nonjudgmental and objective during the interview, and not to demonstrate preconceived feelings about an offender. There are many different interview styles.

One key element is the development of rapport. This should be approached in a nonconfrontational manner. An investigator may begin by building a working relationship with the suspect by asking about his or her family, job, and/or personal interests. The investigator will then want to ask the offender or suspect to tell his or her side of the story in a detailed fashion from start to finish. It is important not to interrupt the suspect in his or her retelling of the incident. Police investigators are encouraged to show interest and to keep the interview an interactive process. The objective of the interview is to obtain the truth, including the information necessary for proving guilt or innocence. Officers are encouraged to remember the importance of the offense and the dramatic impact it will have upon the suspect. Also, the offense must be proven; all parts of the story must support the allegation.

One technique is to direct the conversation toward eliciting the subject's emotions, if the victim and offender had a relationship prior to the offense. For example, the investigator may explain to the suspect that the victim explained that he or she cared for the offender. Although the victim wanted the sexual relations to end, he or she did not want anything harmful to happen to the offender. The subject will be reminded of how much he or she also cares for the victim and how he or she could spare the victim the harm of further investigation into the incident or a court proceeding. (This style of interview also may be effective in child incest cases.)

Another approach is to request that the subject go to police headquarters independently to help clarify a situation in which he or she may be suspected of a crime. Some sex offenders, who are upset or anxious about being discovered, may agree to such a meeting. (This type of meeting may merit a review with a district attorney.)

Another example of interviewing sex offenders is to ask the suspect to explain why the victim would have lied about the incident. Many offenders will have difficulty answering this question (Bennett and Hess, 1998; Hertica, 1991).

Another example of an interview process is known as "fantasy-based interviewing." This approach is recommended particularly for predatory sex offenders. This style of interview is based upon the fact that, although everyone has fantasies, the sex offender's fantasy behavior includes mental rehearsals for actual enactment of sexually aggressive incidents. Investigators who interview predatory sex offenders should assertively seek the suspect's fantasy/masturbatory type of behavior (Bennett and Hess, 1998; Mann, 1996).

The "fantasy-based interview" consists of six steps:

1. Provide a relaxed environment that is comfortable for the offender.
2. Encourage the discussion of fantasy, noting that all persons fantasize.
3. Use a therapy-like format that includes terms such as *disclosure, deviant thoughts, sexual urges,* and *masturbatory fantasy.*
4. The interviewer will need to help the subject to feel secure in order to reveal his or her fantasy system.
5. The subject should be encouraged to discuss his or her fantasy system in detail.
6. Determine if fantasies resemble the crime.

Evidence Recovery

In many cases, medical and forensic staff may assist in the evidence recovery process. However, all staff in criminal justice, human service, and mental health professions need to possess a basic understanding of how such evidence is obtained. It is important to have a sexual assault evidence collection protocol initiated for all victims. Moreau and Bigbee (1995) report that this examination normally involves several areas that will have a potential impact on evidence recovery and investigation. These are listed as follows:

1. A medical history should be completed.
2. Discretion should be used in obtaining history, which must include information concerning the last time the victim had consensual sexual relations with another partner.
3. A blood sample should be obtained from the victim's partner for elimination as a potential subject.
4. An inquiry regarding the nature of the assault itself should be a part of this process.
5. A physical examination including the identification of areas of trauma or injury attributed to the assault should be completed.

6. An evidence recovery protocol should be a part of the investigation process.
7. A chain of custody format should exist.

The methods and procedures in gathering sexual assault evidence are important for the apprehension and prosecution of an offender. As a result, a sexual assault evidence collection kit is viewed as a key component to the investigative process. The following is an outline of the process:

1. The victim's clothing should be obtained and placed in a sealed secure package.
2. The head hair of the victim should be combed or brushed for evidence.
3. The pubic hair of the victim should be combed or brushed for evidence.
4. Combing/brushing of body hair regions other than head and pubic should be done on the victim for evidence.
5. For female victims, the vaginal cavity should be swabbed to detect the presence of spermatozoa and/or other seminal fluid as part of the protocol process.
6. The oral cavity is to be swabbed for detection of spermatozoa or seminal fluid in regard to this process.
7. The anal cavity is to be swabbed to detect the presence of spermatozoa and/or seminal fluid.
8. Microscope slides or smears are to be made from vaginal, oral, and anal swabbing.
9. A swabbing of the penis should be completed for evidence.
10. Aspiration of the vaginal region should be completed.
11. An oral rinse of the mouth should be completed.
12. A nasal mucus sample should be obtained.
13. The fingernails should be scraped for any findings.

Profiling Sex Offenders

According to Hazelwood and colleagues (1995), criminal investigation analysis and profiling was first started by the Federal Bureau of Investigation Academy, Behavioral Science Unit, on an informal basis in 1972. This program is said to have been "formalized" in 1978; then the FBI was specifically assigned the task of assisting law enforcement agencies. In 1984, President Reagan approved the creation of the National Center for the Analysis of Violent Crime (NCAVC), which is said to have replaced the Behavioral Science Unit at the FBI Academy. However, this profile training was terminated in 1991. NCAVC continues to provide services at no cost to criminal justice organizations; other agencies may submit requests for services on a fee basis.

The criteria for a case to be reviewed are minimal and may include the following: the case must involve a crime or succession of crimes; there is a component of violence; the offender is unknown; all investigative leads have been exhausted. Sex crimes that include rapes, lust/murder situations, mutilations, displacement of sexual areas of the body, serial murders, child molestations, and ritualistic crimes are some offenses that are particularly appropriate for profiling. In analyzing a case for profiling purposes, victimology is important. Victims are determined by categories of low, moderate, and high risk of being assaulted. Low-risk victims are those who have personal, professional, and social lives that do not normally expose them to threatening situations. Moderate-risk victims are those persons who are generally of good reputation, have advanced the possibility of becoming a victim of a criminal action by working late, changing lifestyles (such as meeting dates through advertisements), or by other personal habits. High-risk victims are those whose lifestyles or employment regularly exposes them to dangerous encounters with persons with criminal histories, such as drug dealing, residential location, and excessive sexual behavior (Hazelwood, 1995).

Also, in profiling a sex offender, the following factors may be considered (Hazelwood, 1995, pp. 171-176):

1. Victimology (as outlined by levels)
2. Method of approach
3. Method of control
4. Amount of force
5. Victim resistance
6. Reaction to resistance
7. Sexual dysfunction

8. Type and sequence of sexual acts
9. Offender verbal activity
10. Attitudinal change
11. What preceded the attitudinal change
12. Precautionary actions
13. Items taken
14. Purpose of assault

It is understood, of course, that particular information is not available at the time which in part necessitates the need for the profile. In addition, the profile will be influenced by the following factors (Hazelwood, 1995, pp. 177-180):

1. Personality characteristics
2. Race
3. Age
4. Arrest history
5. Marital status
6. Residence
7. Education
8. Military history
9. Employment
10. Transportation
11. Appearance and grooming

[A disclaimer is given on each profile.]

THE SEX OFFENDER AND CORRECTIONS

Steele (1995) reports that the number of incarcerated sex offenders has steadily risen in the United States. Between 1998 and 1990, the total number of sex offenders imprisoned increased by 48 percent, while during that same period the total prison population rose only 20 percent.

Greenfeld (1997) notes that in 1980 state prisons held 295,819 individuals, an estimated 20,500 or 6.9 percent of whom had been convicted of rape or sexual assault. The prison population has now increased by 206 percent from 1980 to 1994, while the number of sex offenders in prison during that same period of time grew by 330 percent. The largest group of sex offenders in prison committed offenses that included molestation, fondling, and other related kinds of sexual assault. Additionally, persons incarcerated for sexual crimes were more likely to be male and Caucasian, as compared to other violent offenders. A significant finding is that sex offenders were substantially more likely than other incarcerated persons to report having been a victim of childhood physical or sexual abuse.

INCARCERATION AND INPATIENT AND OUTPATIENT TREATMENT COSTS

Monetary costs for the life sentencing of a sex offender are high. A sex offender who is given a life sentence at age thirty and dies at age seventy would cost a state about $1,000,000 over the course of his lifetime (Steele, 1995; McGrath, 1994; Prentky and Burgess, 1990; Pithers, 1987).

Greenfeld (1997) reports that approximately 14 percent of sex offenders are mandated by the court to receive psychological or specialized sex offender treatment services. Steele (1995) notes that treatment does not deter all offenders from reoffending. Current estimates indicate that the recidivism rate drops by 10 to 30 percent if a treatment component is included. The total cost for an investigation, arrest, prosecution, and incarceration for seven years with no treatment for a sex offender is averaged at $169,029. Victim expenses, which include treatment, are estimated at $14,304. However, many offenders assault more than one victim. The cost of a new sex offense, arrest, investigation, prosecution, confinement, and parole was listed at $152,000.

Remarkably, the cost for treating a sex offender in an inpatient psychiatric facility actually may be lower. One example is a program in Bridgewater, Massachusetts. The cost of treatment for one offender over a five-year period was listed at $118,146. However, a correctional program in Minnesota for sex offenders that lasts ten months was found to be higher, with a cost over a two-year period (between 1989 and 1991) of an estimated $115,591. The cost per day for services in the prison was found to be $67.21; the inmate cost per day for treatment was found to be $7.73. However, the cost of a new sex offense was listed at $183,333.

A Vermont outpatient treatment program was found to cost $103,800. Offender treatment is reported to be subsidized at a rate of $345 per year for three years for up to 100 sex offenders. It is estimated that if recidivism is only reduced by 1 percent, Vermont saves $35,000 over the cost of the program. An 8 percent recidivism rate would produce a savings of about $1,000,000.

The Virginia Statistical Abstract (1994) reports that the annual operating expenditure for any inmate in the United States during 1990 was estimated at $15,604. In a survey of several states, the annual operating expenditures per inmate for 1990 were listed as follows: Virginia, $16,145; Delaware, $11,208; District of Columbia, $13,894; Florida, $13,902; Georgia, $12,930; Kentucky, $11,118; Maryland, $17,214; North Carolina, $18,496; South Carolina, $10,268; Tennessee, $20,048; and West Virginia, $11,699.

Across the United States, it appears correctional departments have taken the lead in providing inmate/inpatient and outpatient treatment services for sex offenders. Currently, the largest proportion of sex offender treatment occurring in the United States appears to be sponsored, in part, through funding by state and federal correctional agencies. In 2000, the cost of many outpatient treatment services for adults was relatively inexpensive. Some fees begin for as little as $1,200 per patient to $2,800 per patient annually, for group treatment services only. Assessment and individual and family service costs can vary.

CORRECTIONAL TREATMENT PROGRAMS

Various treatment programs for sex offenders are offered by correctional facilities throughout the United States and abroad. One innovative program for sex offenders was created by the Vermont legislature in 1982. The Vermont Treatment Program for Sexual Aggressors was also the first therapy program to employ relapse prevention with sexual offenders (Pithers, Martin, and Cumming, 1989).

Both individual and group therapies are utilized by the Vermont system. As a result of treatment efficiency and efficacy, the program emphasized group therapy. Marital and family therapy are also utilized by this treatment program when found to be appropriate for the particular offender. The program currently encompasses three residential sites and twenty outpatient treatment programs.

Therapy groups at the Vermont program focus upon the following (Pithers, Martin, and Cumming, 1989, pp. 296-298):

1. Victim empathy
2. Personal victimization
3. Emotional recognition
4. Anger management
5. Communication skills
6. Knowledge of sex
7. Cognitive distortions
8. Behavioral therapy for sexual arousal disorders
9. Relapse prevention
10. Transition
11. Problem-solving techniques

Criteria for admission to the Vermont program include the following:

1. Offenders must desire to enter treatment.
2. The candidate's sentence must be of adequate duration for appropriate inpatient treatment services to be offered.
3. Clients must be willing to participate in a comprehensive assessment process.
4. Individuals who have a history of sadistic aggression or who are career criminals may not be considered appropriate candidates for this residential treatment program.

Criteria for transition from the Vermont residential program to outpatient treatment services, in addition to a patient's sentence, may include the following:

1. The offender must be able to describe high-risk situations.
2. For each high-risk situation, the patient must be able to verbalize coping responses.
3. The offender must be able to anticipate possible new risk situations.
4. Offenders must be able to demonstrate the ability to express anger, frustration, and stress in nonsexual ways.

5. Each offender must demonstrate his or her understanding that every person has a right to determine his or her own sex role, providing that such a role is not in conflict with the law.
6. All offenders must demonstrate decreased arousal to disordered patterns of sexual interests.

Persons referred to outpatient treatment will continue to be monitored by probation and parole services. The Vermont Department of Corrections provides funding for all outpatient treatment for sex offenders. Contracts with local vendors in the public and private sectors are offered. All sex offenders are expected to pay a portion of the cost of treatment. A condition of a patient's probation and parole conditions includes a requirement that the patient be involved in the payment fees in Vermont.

PROBATION AND PAROLE SUPERVISION

Supervising sex offenders is an arduous and exacting assignment for probation and parole officers. Unlike in other criminal populations, when a sex offender relapses another person is always harmed. Sexual abuse impacts victims in a manner that is extremely destructive. As the result, there is a certain underlying stress for officers who monitor sex offenders. Yet public, state, and federal legislators in many localities have failed to comprehend the importance of the position the probation and parole officers occupy. Community safety and the very success of a sex offender may depend upon the quality of services rendered by a probation and parole department. Many probation and parole officers carry caseloads so large that they are almost impossible to manage.

Cumming and Buell (1997) recommend a defined supervision strategy for probation and parole officers working with sex offenders. This approach or philosophy, modeled from a relapse prevention styled format, is listed as follows:

1. Most sex offenders can learn self-regulation skills. Sexual misconduct behavior can be reduced.
2. Psychotherapy should be court ordered. Such therapy should be considered "essential and effective." Probation and parole rules should require treatment services.

3. Some sex offenders are not receptive to or appropriate for treatment services and should not be referred to an outpatient program.
4. Sex offenders should be held responsible for their actions. Those who continue their sexual aggression need to be jailed or returned to prison.
5. Treatment is an important method of prevention, limiting the number of additional victims.

Presentence Investigation Report

Cumming and Buell (1997) report that a presentence report is ordered by a judge after a sex offender has been found guilty by a court. Generally, probation and parole officers are assigned by the courts to gather the appropriate information. Sometimes there are special occasions in which a report is requested prior to adjudication. The presentence report serves as a critical link in providing information to the court about a sex offender. Also, these reports may impact disposition, sentencing, or the type of supervision a sex offender may be ordered to follow.

A presentence report for a sex offender usually includes the following information:

1. A description of the crime
2. The victim's statement
3. The defendant's statement
4. The offender's childhood, family, marital, and personal background
5. Current living situation
6. Education
7. Employment and financial history
8. Medical history
9. Military experience
10. Religion
11. Substance abuse history
12. Previous mental health or psychiatric treatment services
13. Criminal history
14. Any prior periods of probation and parole supervision
15. Other incidents of sexual aggression
16. Prior periods of imprisonment or incarceration

The National Crime Information Center (NCIC) should be contacted for previous records. Essential for the report is the interview with the offender. Such an interview may involve several hours over a period of several sessions. If possible, at least two separate meetings with the offender should take place to obtain information.

Interview Strategies

Certain strategies may elicit more information than other interview techniques. As a result, the following techniques are recommended when interviewing a sex offender (Cumming and Buell, 1997; McGrath, 1990; Pithers et al., 1989):

1. Use words or terms that are easily understood.
2. Questions should be direct, specific, but nonjudgmental.
3. Avoid words that connote a particular sexual disturbance, such as *exhibitionist, pedophile,* or *rapist.* Terms such as *touching, stroking,* or *penetration* may be appropriate reference words.
4. Obtain details about the offense, not why it occurred. Offenders sometimes desire to understand their deviancy in order to limit additional aggression. Developing insight by the offender is not useful for the presentence investigation.
5. Develop questions that require a "yes" response. More difficult questions may be asked during an interview with less resistance.
6. Denial is found in many offenders. Such behavior or defense tactics should not be made easy for the offender who refuses to acknowledge his or her crime.
7. Be prepared to repeat questions to obtain needed information.
8. Avoid reducing anxiety. A certain amount of tension can produce important details about the crime.
9. Do not permit religion to qualify a sexual action or limit the responsibility of the offender.
10. Do not reveal information early in the interview. Encourage the offender to provide details about the incident.
11. Almost all offenders will limit information, qualify behavior, and rationalize their sexual aggression. Be prepared that some minimization will occur during the session.
12. Confrontation is sometimes needed during an interview to obtain merited information.

13. Encouragement and support may be rendered when appropriate.
14. Questions should occur in a "successive-approximation" format. Police and victim statements may differ from the offender's version. Details can be gathered more easily when the crime is reviewed in a step-by-step fashion.

Sexual History Gathering

Sexual history gathering is an important part of the presentence report. Questions may include the following:

1. Where did the sexual assault occur?
2. How was the victim selected?
3. Was force used in regard to the offense?
4. What was the victim's reaction?
5. Was the sexual crime arousing to the offender?
6. What did the offender say to the victim?
7. Did alcohol or drug use occur prior to the offense?
8. What acts did the offender want to do but did not do? Why not?
9. Were there any acts that the offender wanted to do but was unable to perform?
10. Was a weapon used or visible?
11. How did the offender feel after the sexual offense occurred?
12. Has the offender ever attempted to stop sexual aggression in the past?

Presentence Summary and Recommendation

Cumming and Buell (1997) note that the summary and recommendation portion of the presentence investigation should address the level of risk the offender will present to the community. In addition, the report will need to examine amenability to treatment services.

Amenability to treatment may be based upon the following factors:

1. Does the offender admit to the sexual offense?
2. Does the offender accept responsibility for his or her actions?
3. Does the offender demonstrate victim empathy or remorse?
4. Does the offender identify or acknowledge that his or her behavior is a problem?
5. Does the offender display a sincere interest in change?

6. Does the offender agree to attend a specialized treatment program?
7. Does offender display a willingness to abide by all probation and parole conditions?

Supervision of Sex Offenders

Special knowledge is required by probation and parole officers who supervise sex offenders. In urban areas, a number of probation and parole departments have developed special units where officers provide supervision only for sex offenders. This can be more difficult in rural areas, in which a probation and parole officer may be expected to be more of a generalist and carry a wide variety of cases, including offenders who have committed a sexual crime. Some techniques to consider in working with a sex offender may include the following:

1. A sex offender should remain with one probation and parole officer, if possible, throughout his or her period of supervision.
2. Training should be available to all officers.
3. Large caseloads should be avoided when supervising sex offenders.
4. Officers should have a basic understanding of sexual disorders and behaviors associated with offenders.
5. A protocol for home visits; ideally, visit in a team of two persons.
6. Office visits should be conducted near support staff.
7. Access to home telephone numbers, residences, photographs of family of officers is not permitted.
8. Transfer of sex offenders out of the locality or state should be evaluated carefully.
9. No sex offender should be released from supervision if a risk to reoffend remains present without a notice to the court of origin or consultation with the district attorney or both.
10. Offenders who carry a psychiatric disorder merit other services, as medication compliance.
11. Intensive supervision status may be merited at times.
12. Random urine and drugs screenings should be used.
13. Travel permits should be evaluated carefully.

14. Offenders with a history of substance abuse should not be allowed to use alcohol or drugs.
15. Sex offenders who reside with minor children should be monitored.
16. Sex offender treatment should be required (many on federal probation are required to remain in treatment during their entire supervision).
17. Electronic monitoring is helpful if available.
18. House arrest and curfew periods may be appropriate.
19. Use surveillance staff if available
20. Probation and parole conditions need to be specific and detailed, with concrete expectations regarding supervision.

Probation and Parole Violations

Sometimes it can be difficult to determine if a violation should be issued for a sex offender. Close monitoring of offenders may be helpful and prevent the necessity for a formal violation to be issued. Revocation is usually appropriate when a new sexual offense has occurred. Behavior that is considered a technical violation is sometimes more difficult for an officer to ascertain. Should the offender be charged for a rule infraction?

Cumming and Buell (1997) suggest that officers may use the following guidelines:

1. Did the offender have contact with a victim or his or her identified target population?
2. Did the offender fail to avoid high-risk situations that could influence the likelihood of a new sexual offense?
3. Has the offender resisted treatment services in a mandated outpatient program?
4. Has the offender used drugs or alcohol or failed a random screen test?
5. Does the offender fail to reside in a living environment that is safe and that endorses his or her recovery program?
6. Does the offender refuse to offer information in treatment about behavior or lifestyle?
7. Has the sex offender violated specific special conditions of probation or parole?

Chapter 3

The Human Services System

Sex offenders cost society a great deal of money. The economic burden of this population has been quoted at the staggering amount of $2,055,528,000 in 1990 alone in the United States. Unfortunately, the vast majority of this money is presently directed toward the incarceration of offenders, an approach resembling the old farm analogy of closing the barn gate after the horse has escaped. Significant funding for the prevention of sexual abuse and treatment of offenders remains a low priority in many states (Bradford, 1998; Pithers et al., 1995).

Mandated with the daunting duty of monitoring child welfare in this country is the human services system. As a result, human services is one of three social systems that regularly encounters and intervenes with sexual offenders. Human services is often called when an allegation of sexual misconduct has been reported.

A part of each human services department are the units of adult and child protective services. These two units receive most sexual abuse reports filed by victims, family members, concerned citizens, police, or other area professionals. Often overworked with large caseloads, understaffed and underfunded, human services continues to make a valiant effort nationwide to investigate complaints of adult and child sexual abuse, while supervising other situations of concern.

In working with a sex offender it is important for the reader to possess some knowledge about human services and how sexual abuse complaints are processed. Therefore, some of the more important aspects of the human service system are outlined, as well as its role in investigating abuse allegations. To avoid repetition, the focus of this chapter will be upon child sexual abuse and human services. It should be noted that most human service agencies have adult protective service units that follow similar procedural guidelines as child protective services. Adults monitored by an adult protection unit may include the elderly and the mentally or physically disabled.

CHILD PROTECTIVE SERVICES

Waldfogel (1998) defines child protective services as a group of laws, funding sources, and agencies that have been developed by state and federal governments in an effort to respond to the child abuse situation. Similar laws, funding sources, and agencies also exist for adult protection services.

All states and the District of Columbia have established laws requiring the investigation of suspected cases of child abuse. Each county or city has a local human service department. The size of an agency may depend upon funding from local, state, and federal sources. An agency budget usually determines the staffing ratios and salaries of caseworkers assigned to a child protective service unit. However, most human service departments report ongoing struggles in providing merited services of allocated funding. All too often human service departments are stretched to provide only the basic services to those in need. Most human service departments provide a multitude of assistance programs for a wide array of special populations from infant care to assistance for the elderly. The number of staff and salaries of caseworkers are often impacted by the volume of services expected from the agency.

DEMOGRAPHICS

Victims of child sexual abuse are infants, toddlers, children under the age of twelve, and adolescents. Victims are both female and male. Boys are more likely to be sexually abused outside of the home; girls have a higher incident rate of sexual abuse inside the home. Children who are sexually abused at home are more likely to be victimized repeatedly by the offender.

According to reports, during 1996 in the United States, CPS units received more than 3 million complaints of alleged child abuse or neglect situations, representing a rate between 43 and 47 reports per 1,000 children, depending upon survey results. Such surveys, although the summary totals vary slightly, are indicative that the reporting rates are high in the United States as compared to other countries. Usually, child neglect and physical abuse are the most frequent types of complaints received by CPS units. Sexual abuse reports involving children were found to be the third most frequent complaint, but have declined in the last decade (Waldfogel, 1998; Wang and Daro, 1997).

Lower-income children are the most likely candidates for a report to be filed with a CPS Unit. The majority of child sexual abuse allegations tend to involve Caucasian children. Ethnic and minority children were most often reported for physical abuse or neglect situations (Waldfogel, 1998; Cappelleri, Eckenrode, and Powers, 1993; Jones and McCurdy, 1992; Spearly and Lauderdale, 1983).

Poverty places immense pressures upon families and children. Chronic stress may lead to destructive acts of anger and rage by a parent. Children in homes with limited financial resources may be without adequate clothing, food, or shelter. As in most circumstances, money impacts a family system; a child can become a target of misplaced hostility as the result of anxiety, despair, and hopelessness. Parents may be without family or community support or resources. Addiction, marital discord, and spousal abuse are sometimes clinical features of a family in crisis. Sadly, sometimes child sexual abuse is also found.

However, income and race should not be the only measurements in evaluating a family for child sexual abuse. Many low-income families demonstrate excellent parenting skills. Conversely, many cases of child sexual abuse are found in homes with all available material and financial opportunities.

Sex offenders themselves offer a great deal of demographic data about their selection of child victims. Incarcerated sex offenders reported that two-thirds of their victims were minors at the time of the crime—or about four in ten persons reported that their victims were twelve years of age or younger (Greenfeld, 1997).

Poulos and Greenfield (1994) report that in Virginia, for instance, four of every five convicted sex offenders knew their adult or child victims prior to the incident. One in three offenders were related to the child victim. Children were much more likely to be sexually assaulted by acquaintances, relatives, or people they knew. Four of five child victims knew their offender, compared to only half of assaulted adults. The victim and offender were found to be related in almost half of all sexual offenses involving children, as compared to only 12 percent of all incidents of assault against adults. Also, in sexual exploitation cases, the sex offender was more likely to be a friend to the child or their family, followed by a parent or stepparent.

INTERVENTION

The investigation of a complaint of child sexual abuse can be a difficult process for even the most seasoned worker. Child sexual abuse is often a covert and secret action, sometimes with little or no collaborating testimony or physical evidence.

Appropriate evidence is difficult to obtain. Usually the only witness is a minor child—the victim. In cases of incest, the family may be in denial about the event. The victim may experience a variety of defense mechanisms in an effort to cope with his or her violation. Acting out, anger, denial, dissociation, depression, isolation, repression, or rationalization are often common features found in a sexually abused child. The horror that a child experiences as the result of a sexual offense committed by an adult for pleasure forever marks the ego. Such selfish pleasure-seeking by an offender may only last a few moments or can occur on a repeated basis, but leaves a lasting psychological scar. Many offenders were sexually abused as children as well.

Professionals may experience emotional reactions, because such cases produce strong feelings. Countertransference issues can arise. The alleged offender will often challenge a caseworker. A defense attorney may be quickly employed. Human service workers may find themselves quickly placed in the defensive position of justifying the investigation.

Waldfogel (1998) states that three stages of intervention are employed by child protective services in responding to a report of neglect or abuse. In the first stage, a complaint is filed with a CPS unit alleging that a child is being abused or neglected. The complaint is submitted for review. In the second stage, an evaluation process occurs, and a decision is made as to whether the report should be investigated by staff. Some reports are screened out at this stage if insufficient information exists or the complaint does not meet agency mandate guidelines. In the third stage, an investigation is initiated by the agency, and a staff member will follow through on the report. A part of this stage requires that the CPS staff meet with the alleged victim of abuse or neglect and all other appropriate collateral individuals. In cases of child sexual abuse, the offender may be one of the last persons interviewed after sufficient evidence is gathered.

The primary purpose of the investigation is to determine if the child in question has actually experienced some type of maltreatment. If evidence is obtained that the child has been sexually abused, the case may be ruled as founded, supported, or substantiated. In certain situations, only a limited amount of evidence can be obtained, but there is suitable concern that the child may be at risk. As a result, the case may be ruled by CPS as a finding of a reason to suspect with additional involvement by agency staff and the police if merited. In investigations in which there is no finding of child sexual abuse, the matter will be ruled as unfounded, unsupported, or unsubstantiated; the case is closed. In cases in which child sexual abuse is founded, the matter usually is then referred to law enforcement for additional investigation and possible prosecution of the offender.

Marshall and Barrett (1990) note that the system fails to adequately address the psychological needs of victims during an investigation of child sexual abuse. In many incest cases, the child, rather than the perpetrator, is removed from the home during an investigation. Such a policy conveys a confusing message to the child that he or she has done something wrong. A child already traumatized by sexual abuse can be revictimized by such procedures.

Child protection service workers are often expected to juggle the demands of the investigation while working with the both the offender and the victim. These roles do not always easily mesh. In cases in which there is a founded finding of suspected child abuse, a caseworker will report evidence to the local police. However, many CPS units regularly work with police during an investigation prior to a ruling to minimize a child's risk for further sexual exploitation. The local district attorney is usually alerted when a case appears to support a finding of sexual abuse.

The CPS worker and police may interview a number of individuals prior to the determination of a ruling. The complainant is usually the first witness to be interviewed by the CPS unit. Sometimes, the complainant's creditability is of question. Workers are encouraged to keep detailed notes or tape record interviews (depending upon law) of sessions. Interviews may include other collateral individuals. The interview process should include the child. The alleged offender is usually the last person to be questioned. This permits the caseworker to assemble as much evidence as possible before confronting the perpetrator. In the event that the interview process is expected to take time and there is reasonable doubt of the child's safety, an emergency removal order may be obtained.

In a number of communities, CPS teams have been developed to offer caseworkers support and guidance during an investigation. Such teams may include the caseworker, several other CPS workers, and the unit supervisor. Also, a part of these teams may include a district attorney (usually an assistant), a law enforcement officer, a mental health professional, and a physician. These teams are able to offer a more comprehensive assessment of a suspected child abuse situation and ways to intervene quickly, lessening the risk of further abuse to the child.

When a case of child sexual abuse is suspected to exist, information regarding the offense is then referred to the local law enforcement agency of that community. If sufficient evidence is obtained, an arrest warrant is filed. The offender is then arrested, and the matter is referred to the court for a hearing. The human service worker will be expected to testify for the prosecution about the sexual abuse allegation and the reason for the findings. CPS workers need to have gathered documented evidence that has been reviewed by police and the district attorney.

Child abuse cases are usually heard first in a family or juvenile court setting. Such courts are closed to the public and usually are not courts of record, unless testimony is requested to be stenographed or taped. In the event of a finding when the offense is considered a felony, the matter is then referred to a higher court, depending upon the state statutes. The child usually is expected to offer testimony during a court hearing in most states. However, in certain states, to lessen the trauma for the child, a videotaped testimony of the child describing the sexual abuse is admitted as an acceptable form of evidence. Anatomical dolls are used by many CPS workers to allow the child to reenact the sexual abuse.

CLINICAL FEATURES IN CHILD SEXUAL ABUSE

Child sexual abuse may be identified by a number of clinical behaviors of physical symptoms. However, each child victim is unique and may reveal elements of sexual abuse in a special way.

Swann (1993) reports three ways in which the question of child sexual abuse may arise. First, a disclosure may be made by a child who has experienced some form of sexual abuse. Second, the behavior of a child may reflect the possibility that sexual abuse has occurred. Third, there is physical evidence of abuse.

Behavioral manifestations include a variety of symptoms which alert workers that sexual abuse may have occurred in a child. Swann (1993) refers to the following behaviors:

 1. Alcohol abuse
 2. Aggression
 3. Clinging
 4. Delinquency or criminal activity
 5. Depression
 6. Fear of being alone with a particular adult
 7. Flashbacks
 8. Isolation
 9. Nightmares
10. Phobias
11. Promiscuity
12. Problems with intimacy
13. Sexual preoccupation
14. Sexual aggression
15. School problems or truancy
16. Somatic complaints
17. Sleeping and eating disorders
18. Suicide attempts
19. Running away
20 Unwilling to go home after school
21. Unwilling to undress in physical education classes
22. Vulnerability to sexual victimization

James and Nasjleti (1983) report that incest victims may reveal their abuse through one or more symptoms:

1. Excessive masturbation
2. Overt sexual acting
3. Simulation of sexual activity with other or younger children
4. Fear of being alone with a particular male or female adult
5. Violence or physical aggression
6. Self-mutilation, such as cutting
7. Bruising, marks about the face, neck, groin, buttocks, or inner thighs
8. Unusual fear of restrooms, baths, or showers
9. Advanced knowledge about sex
10. Artwork that has a sexual content
11. Written schoolwork with sexual overtones
12. Language that includes sexual references
13. Play that involves sexuality
14. A reaction or repulsion to physical contact or touch

Other clinical symptoms may include having anger outbursts, being accident prone or unusually awkward, acting compulsive or expressing a need to control situations, exhibiting cruelty to animals and people, having crying spells, experiencing dissociation, destroying property, wearing excessive clothing in warm weather, being fearful, setting fires, showing hostility, hopelessness, impulsiveness, issues of poor self-esteem, lying, maintaining poor eye contact, having problems of concentration and attention, being reckless, and expressing uncontrolled rage.

Physical signs of child sexual abuse may include abrasions in genital or anal area, bruises, erythema, wearing heavy makeup, lacerations, penile swelling or discharge, pregnancy, sexual dysfunction, urination pain, vaginal discharge, or infections.

OTHER BEHAVIORAL AND DEVELOPMENTAL ISSUES

Victims of sexual abuse experience both physical and psychological trauma. Sexual assault is a violation that has long-term consequences.

James and Nasjleti (1983) report that sexually abusive behavior is extremely harmful to a child's development. As a result, the following may be expected:

1. A loss of one's childhood innocence, which cannot be regained
2. A feeling of alienation as the ego struggles to cope with the offense
3. An inability to cope with an adult in a sexual manner, producing conflict and role confusion
4. Anxiety and difficulty in feeling singled out from other siblings and the peer group
5. The terrible burden of keeping sexual abuse a secret
6. A clinical disturbance as the result of the child's inability to cope with the trauma
7. The overloading of stimulation and insufficient tension relief, impacting ego functioning
8. In incest cases, the development of an inappropriate and misguided alliance with one parent over another

Male incest victims are reported to experience the following developmental problems:

1. He fears being identified as being unmanly and ashamed because he was unable to protect himself.
2. If molested by a male, he may fear others will believe he is a homosexual.
3. If he was sexually abused by a female adult, he will be reluctant to report the offense and challenge society's standard of masculinity.
4. Boys molested by their mothers assume responsibility for the action.
5. Male victims fear no one will believe their report of sexual assault.
6. Male victims fear nothing will be done if the sexual abuse is committed by a woman.
7. Boys fear that they may be harmed again if they report the assault, since the offender has threatened them and warned them not to tell.

Female child victims also experience a number of problems if they report their sexual assault. However, in terms of appearance, development, and behavior, their abuse is more difficult to detect. The following characteristics are noted:

1. Female child victims in incest cases are reluctant to report the offense for fear of upsetting the family structure.
2. Some female victims will occupy a dominant role within the family system.
3. Some female victims will present a passive affect.
4. Female victims may attempt to nurture or parent their parents, repressing their own emotional pain.
5. An attempt to appear unkempt to ward off male attention, believing they somehow are the cause of sexual interest.
6. Some will overcompensate by grooming themselves in a meticulous fashion because they believe that their bodies are unclean.
7. A child female victim will often attempt to minimize her trauma to CPS workers, police, schoolteachers, or therapists.
8. Guilt and shame occurs if some pleasure was experienced during the sexual event.
9. Acting out behavior can be displayed.
10. Running away can be an alternative.

THE CHILD PROTECTIVE SERVICE WORKER

Moore (1992) reports that investigating complaints of child abuse is extremely stressful work that impacts the caseworker in a unique manner. The turnover rate among caseworkers is high. Burnout is often cited as a reason for leaving child protective services. Caseworkers regularly encounter difficult situations in which children are suspected to be at risk.

Most caseworkers possess a college degree in social sciences; many have bachelor degrees in counseling, psychology, social work, or other related human service degrees. Standards for the employment of a caseworker differ from state to state. Few caseworkers have any prior clinical training in work with sex offenders or child sexual abuse. Presently, only a few institutions provide their students with any in-depth studies about sexual abuse and sex offenders.

Appropriate education, training, and supportive supervision are important issues for the validation and maintenance of caseworkers.

Newly employed caseworkers are most likely unprepared to enter the arena of child sexual abuse. In some states, it is not uncommon to find inexperienced caseworkers assigned to complicated and difficult cases as a part of their "in-service" training. To properly document an allegation and present the evidence to the court is a difficult process and not quickly learned. An analogy would be to place a police officer with no training in the field with a gun. A similar program appears to be merited for caseworkers assigned to child abuse units—particularly those involved in working with sexual abuse complaints. A caseworker's lack of knowledge can be equally harmful to the victim.

The very epicenter of the prevention and early intervention of child sexual abuse is dependent upon, in many circumstances, a system that is overburdened. *NASW News* (2000) reported that salary issues and large caseloads were an issue for Maryland child welfare workers, who had expected assistance from a bill passed in 1998. Such problems are characteristic for the staffs of many units who are selected to oversee a very precious commodity—a child.

A CPS Case in Court

A CPS investigation can be a grueling experience for a beginning caseworker. This may be illustrated in the case of the suspected child sexual abuse reported involving a twelve-year-old Caucasian male from an upper-middle-class home. The parents of the victim are divorced, and the child lives with his mother, who is employed in a nearby city. She holds an executive-level position and works long hours. The child's contact with his biological father, who lives in another state, is limited to holiday and occasional weekend visits. The mother is dating and has a male companion. An allegation is made that the mother's companion has had oral sex with the child. The prosecuting attorney is informed of the status of the case. The complaint is determined to be founded. The police become involved and an arrest warrant is filed against the adult male. The mother of the child reports that she does not believe the incident occurred. The male companion denies the allegation. However, the child is very detailed in his description of the offense. Nonetheless, no physical evidence is found by a consulting physician. A mental health professional for the state is unable to substantiate any claims of abuse. An attorney is employed by the mother and the companion. Eventually, a court date is set. Witnesses for the prosecution include the child, the caseworker, investigating police officer, a teacher, physician, and the clinician. The defense attorney summons a number of friends, colleagues, co-workers, and supervisors of the mother and the companion, all of whom testify favorably on the part of the defendant. Also, the defense attorney has employed a mental health professional to evaluate the child. The caseworker has had little prior court experience and has never testified in a child sexual abuse case. He or she has had no special training in sexual abuse or about sex offenders. The prosecuting attorney and supervisor may have prepared the caseworker in regard to testimony, but this is of only limited help to the new caseworker. A skilled defense attorney will quickly attempt to discredit the caseworker's findings. Questions by a defense attorney can be rather intimidating to a newly hired caseworker. The caseworker becomes anxious at the hearing and presents a confusing account of the investigation. Evidence is revealed that challenges part of the information gathering process conducted by the caseworker. Documentation is lacking. Certain questions by the caseworker during the interview with the victim are found to be leading. Will the court find suitable proof for an adjudication of guilt of the defendant? Will the child be returned to the home where he claims he has been sexually assaulted? A courtroom, at times, appears to be an unkind and difficult environment for a beginning caseworker. Sometimes justice can be enacted only when evidence and related testimony is presented in an appropriate form.

Preparing for Court

A CPS worker should prepare in advance for court. A professional case presentation may have a strong impact upon a court ruling. The stakes can be very high in founded case situations in which the very life and protection of a child are of concern. Preparation for a child sexual abuse court hearing should include the following:

1. Outline the case presentation.
2. Documentation should reflect time, date, and a description of the offense.
3. Details of the offense are important.

4. Always staff, in advance, pending court cases with a supervisor.
5. Review the case and specific testimony.
6. Seek support from other CPS staff and consulting professionals within the confines of state confidentiality law.
7. Review all documents and evidence before a hearing.
8. Role-play the pending hearing.
9. Review skills in offering testimony.
10 Visit the courtroom in advance.
11. Be prepared to offer credentials and experience in court.
12. Actual testimony should be specific, concise; do not offer unsolicited information.
13 Prepare a notepad with information related to the case.
14. Be polite, professional, and courteous.
15. Dress in a conservative manner.

Conducting a CPS Investigation

A great deal of literature is available for review regarding sexual abuse. However, little information exists for a CPS worker who is expected to investigate a sex offender as the result of a reported complaint. The following protocol may be followed:

1. Review the complaint information prior to starting an investigation.
2. Staff the case with the CPS supervisor, if the case requires investigation.
3. Use a team approach of two caseworkers if the case merits a site visit.
4. Personal safety is an issue.
5. Take a cell telephone.
6. Have a call-in check system arranged in advance.
7. Always inform staff of the location of any visit.
8. Assess the level of danger: Will alcohol, drugs, or weapons be present?
9. High-risk situations should merit the presence of a police officer.
10. Always take notes during interviews and use tape recorders if permitted by state law.
11. Interview the individual who filed the complaint first.

12. Be well versed in state law and the investigation of CPS complaints involving child sexual abuse allegations.
13. Follow the chain of evidence and adhere to departmental guidelines at all times during investigations.
14. Interview collateral persons, if possible.
15. Interview the child victim.
16. Gather as much evidence and related information as possible.
17. However, time and the safety of the minor is an issue.
18. A case in which evidence appears to indicate child sexual abuse should include the involvement of a law enforcement officer.
19. Evidence indicating sexual abuse may merit review with the prosecuting attorney.
20. Interview the alleged offender last, if possible, after all data has been collected.
21. The interview may occur in the home, but be alert to safety issues.
22. Evaluate the condition of the home.
23. Are any sexually inappropriate behaviors displayed during the interview?
24. Are any sexual toys or pornography in evidence?
25. Be versed in the assessment of a sex offender.
26. Be versed in sexual disorders.
27. Expect defense techniques, such as anger, control, denial, manipulation, and rationalization.
28. Establish rapport.
29. Use a structured interview method; be polite and informal.

Chapter 4

The Mental Health Professional

Sex offenders are now being referred to the mental health community in large numbers for treatment services. This may be attributed, in part, to a rise in sexual crime reports, community safety issues, active victim groups, stronger court sentences, and changes in parole board criteria.

In addition, criminal justice and human service professionals are being encouraged to find other solutions for managing this growing population. Judges, prosecutors, defense attorneys, child protective service workers, and probation officers are unable to rely upon incarceration as the sole source of care for sex offenders. Prisons and jails alone appear unable to serve as an amenable solution for the care of all offenders.

Most sex offenders are eventually released upon completion of their sentences. As a result, more comprehensive services are being requested by communities to address safety concerns. The criminal justice and human service systems have begun to seek mental health professionals on an active basis for assistance and guidance.

Probation and parole now often include conditions to attend outpatient therapy. Sex offenders placed on probation or being paroled are regularly being ordered to participate in therapy. Probation departments are contracting the services of qualified sex offender therapists in order to offer additional safeguards for communities. Several states are now committing sex offenders to state psychiatric facilities upon completion of their prison sentences. Individuals believed to be at risk to reoffend are being referred to inpatient programs for additional treatment services. Such patients may be placed on a civil commitment status in order to prevent their return to the community. Other states are limiting parole options for sex offenders, requiring them to complete a program of treatment while still incarcerated. Many offenders are being held the full length of their sentence in prison rather than qualifying for early parole release.

This chapter explores the mental health system and those professionals who work with sex offenders. This patient population can be difficult to treat. Only a limited number of experienced clinicians are qualified to provide treatment services to sex offenders at the present time. Those who do provide treatment for sex offenders require certain specialized skills and abilities. Many clinicians, in both the public and private sectors, are often reported to be inexperienced, unfamiliar, or even uncomfortable in providing therapy for sex offenders.

As a group, mental health professionals represent a wide spectrum of disciplines and educational backgrounds. Various state code and regulation statutes usually define the requirements for a practicing clinician. Generally, most practitioners providing services for sex offenders in a given state usually are found among psychiatrists, psychologists, clinical social workers, licensed professional counselors, marriage and family therapists, and other similarly titled clinicians. Several states are adopting regulations that require therapists who work with sex offenders to be credentialed in some form in addition to standard licensure.

THE ROLE OF THE THERAPIST

Sex offenders present unique and special problems when involved in psychotherapy. The role of the therapist differs for this patient group. However, many of these issues have not yet been addressed in depth by research.

A key element for clinicians to consider when working with sex offenders is the ability to accept the patient as an individual while acknowledging his or her behavior as being deviant. Most sex offenders have experienced a form of rationalization or depersonalization toward their victims to allow themselves permission to commit acts of deviancy. The offender may be opposed to treatment, is reluctant to admit to the sexual offense, and displays only limited victim empathy. As a result, the therapist is presented with the task of treating and attempting to change the behavior of an individual who has committed acts of sexual harm against another, which can be a rather overwhelming assignment for a therapist.

Kottler (1993) reports that, in general, a therapist who is sincere and self-disciplined can have a dramatic impact upon a patient and his or her presenting problem behavior. Most clients can distinguish a mental health professional who displays genuine interest in their welfare. Almost all patients respond in some manner when treated with respect and dignity. These same qualities can also be applied in therapy—even with sex offenders. There are exceptions, of course, with certain disordered individuals. The art of engaging sex offender patients in a goal to change their behavior can be challenging. Sex offenders are usually initially unwilling or reluctant to stop behaviors that have been a source of pleasure for a number of years.

Sex offenders possess the same anxieties, behaviors, and fears that are representative of all patients. A number of defense mechanisms can be expected to occur for the sex offender as a patient during psychotherapy. Such defense mechanisms may include acting out, affiliation, anticipation, denial, devaluation, displacement, dissociation, help-rejecting, complaining, inappropriate humor, intellectualization, passive aggression, projection, rationalization, repression, splitting, suppression, and other related behaviors. The treatment provider who is unwilling or unable to address these behaviors in therapy will be impaired in his or her efforts to change the offender's behavior. Offenders who continue to present distracting behaviors in psychotherapy remain at risk to reoffend.

Countertransference issues may occur for therapists when working with sex offenders. Clinicians can also display defense mechanisms when confronted with a difficult patient or behavior. Such responses are not atypical, but merit attention if the clinician is unable to resolve his or her feelings. Providers often benefit from a professional support network of other mental health clinicians. The therapist must display a high level of professionalism when interacting with a sex offender.

Gender may also be an issue when working with sex offenders. This may be especially true when offering treatment services to this particular patient population group. A primary concern for programs should be the emotional and physical safety of the therapists. Many offenders have a history that includes a distorted belief system regarding sex. Present treatment programs offer a variety of compositions that include individual and co-therapy teams. Certain patients may respond only to a particular gender. Some patients may be distracted or threatened by a male therapist and may benefit from work with a female clinician; the reverse may also occur. The offender's background, crime, level of threat, and masturbatory history should be variables taken into consideration when a specific therapist is chosen.

STANDARDS IN TREATMENT

Licensing and certification have started to emerge at the state level for those working with sex offenders. Several states now require practicing clinicians to demonstrate a level of competency to qualify as a sex offender treatment provider.

Coleman and colleagues (1996) report that treatment is viewed as an opportunity to offer protection to the public while reducing the number of future additional offenses. Although the cost of treatment may be an obstacle for some, the decision not to treat can be far more costly both emotionally and psychologically for the offender, present and future victims, and the community. As a result, certain guidelines and standards are recommended in the treatment of sex offenders. The standards are listed as follows.

Statement of Purpose

Although each profession has its own standards of care, the following are minimal recommendations for standards of care. It is recommended that professionals involved in the treatment of sex offenders use the following minimal criteria for the evaluation of their work. It is recommended that the reasons for exceptions to these standards, in the management of any individual case, be very carefully documented.

Definitions

Standards of Care

Standards of Care are exactly what is implied: standards for caring for patients. In this case, care and treatment of sex offenders.

Paraphilia

Paraphilia is an erotosexual condition occurring in men and women who are responsive to, or dependent upon, an unusual or socially unacceptable stimulus in the imagery or fantasy for optimal initiation and maintenance of erotic-sexual arousal and the facilitation or attainment of orgasm.

Sex Offense

If paraphilia is enacted in actual behavior rather than in erotic fantasy or dream, it may qualify as a criminal sex offense. There is great discrepancy throughout the world as to what constitutes a sex offense (Pallone, 1990).

Sexual Offender

An individual who commits a sexual crime as legally defined in his own culture or legal jurisdiction.

Psychological Treatment

Psychological treatment refers to the array of therapies which have been designed to treat sex offenders. Different treatments are based on different psychological and psychiatric theories regarding the origin of the paraphilic sex offending, for example, psychoanalytic, cognitive, behavioral, social learning, and family systems theories. Psychological or psychiatric care can be provided in individual, couple, family, or group settings. The purpose of treatment is an attempt to prevent further offending behavior and further victimization of others.

Biomedical Treatment

Biomedical treatment refers to the use of pharmacological treatment or neurosurgery for the purpose of alternating sexual fantasies, impulses, and behavior. Pharmacologic therapy has included (but is not limited to) the use of antiandrogens, antidepressants, and antianxiety, antiepileptic, antipsychotic, or other medications.

Surgical treatment might involve brain surgery to correct temporal lobe seizures. With the advent of effective chemotherapies which alter the erotosexual response, the necessity of psychosurgery in the absence of epileptic foci has been rendered inappropriate.

Professional Competence

Possession of an academic degree in a behavioral science, medicine, or for the provision of psychosocial clinical services does not necessarily attest to the possession of sufficient competence to conduct assessment or treatment of paraphilic or sex offending problems. Persons assessing and/or treating sex offenders should have clinical training and experience in the diagnosis and treatment of a range of psychiatric and psychological conditions and also specialized training and experience in the assessment and treatment of paraphilic and sex offender problems. This would generally be reflected by appropriate licensure as a psychiatrist, psychologist, or clinical therapist and by documentation of training and experience in the diagnosis and treatment of a broad range of sexual conditions, including paraphilic disorders and sex offenses. Treatment providers must be competent in making a differential diagnosis. The following are minimal standards a professional should adhere to:

1. A minimum of a master's degree or its equivalent or medical degree in a clinical field granted by an institution of education accredited by a national/regional accrediting board
2. Demonstrated competence in therapy as indicated by a license (or its equivalent from a certifying body) to practice medicine, psychology, clinical social work, professional counseling, or marriage and family counseling
3. Demonstrated specialized competence in counseling and diagnosis of sexual disorders and sex offending behaviors as documentable by training or supervised clinical experience, along with continuing education

Antecedents to Sex Offender Treatment

1. Prospective patients should receive an extensive evaluation of their sex offending behavior which would include appropriate-

ness for treatment, amenability for treatment, psychological/psychiatric diagnoses, evaluation for safety and protection for the community.

2. A thorough physical examination is recommended especially when physical problems are suspected that might require specific treatments, i.e., heart problems, high blood pressure, liver damage, brain lesions, and epilepsy.

3. Prospective patients should receive a psychological and/or psychiatric examination which would rule out other psychological/psychiatric disorders. If any other psychological/psychiatric disorders are found, treatment of such disorder requires separate (appropriate) treatment prior to treatment for paraphilic or sex offending behavior.

4. If medication is deemed necessary or requested by the patient, the patient must be given information regarding the benefits and potential side effects or disadvantages of biomedical treatment.

The Principles of Standards of Care

Principle 1: While treatment effectiveness of adult sex offenders has not been clearly demonstrated, there are indications that some kinds of treatment may be effective in managing and reducing recidivism with some types of sex offenders.

Principle 2: Sex offender treatment is viewed by offenders as an elective process (the choice is theirs), since individuals may not view their sex offending behavior as psychologically or medically pathological.

Principle 3: The evaluation of treatment of sex offenders requires specialized skills not usually associated with the professional training of clinical therapists or medical professionals.

Principle 4: Sex offender treatment is performed for the purpose of improving quality of life and is considered a humane treatment for people who have committed a sex offense and to prevent the patient from engaging in further sex offending behavior.

Principle 5: The patient with a documented biomedical abnormality is first treated by procedures commonly accepted as appropriate for any such medical conditions before beginning, or in conjunction with, psychotherapy.

Principle 6: The patient having a psychiatric diagnosis (e.g., schizophrenia) is first treated by procedures commonly accepted as appropriate for the psychiatric diagnosis, or, if appropriate, for both simultaneously.

Principle 7: Sex offender treatment may involve a variety of therapeutic approaches. It is important for professionals to keep abreast of this growing and developing field and provide the most efficacious treatments which have been demonstrated through outcome studies. Some of the most effective approaches available today involve cognitive and behavioral therapies which include increase in victim empathy, control over offending urges, and relapse prevention.

Principle 8: A treatment plan may involve the use of pharmacotherapy which typically relieves some sexual arousal and fantasy. Impulse control is thereby increased and individuals feel less driven by their sexual compulsion or their paraphilic fantasy imagery.

Principle 9: The current treatment of sex offenders often causes special legal problems for the professionals offering such care and treatment. Therefore, the professional should work with the criminal justice system in a professional and cooperative manner.

Principle 10: Sex offenders often have a need for follow-up treatment/visits, and this should be encouraged or possibly required.

Principle 11: It is unethical to charge patients for services which are essentially for research and which do not directly benefit the patient.

Principle 12: In order to effectively persuade the professionals in the legal community as well as society in general about the efficacy of sex offender treatment, professionals should cooperate with and carry out scientifically sound treatment outcome research.

Principle 13: Sex offenders often must face legal proceedings, and professionals treating these individuals must be prepared to appear in court if necessary.

Principle 14: Sex offenders are given the same rights to medical and psychological privacies as any other patient group, with the exception of where the law requires otherwise, i.e., reporting laws, subpoenaing of records. (Coleman et al., 1996, pp. 7-10)

THERAPIST QUALIFICATIONS AND SKILLS

People enter psychotherapy in order to change. Most have experienced some type of individual, family, social, or occupational problem that has caused some psychological conflict in their lives.

Usually, most individuals seek treatment on a voluntary basis. However, a number of patient populations are court ordered to receive treatment as the result of a criminal violation. Some persons may be hospitalized involuntarily for treatment; others may be referred to an outpatient program as an intervention. Incarceration may first occur followed by parole or probation with a referral to an outpatient treatment program. Such a patient population may include sex offenders who have in recent times become much more visible to the professional community.

James and Nasjleti (1983) report that therapists providing treatment services to families involved in sexual abuse situations must be both accepting and direct. A permissive or lax attitude is not considered appropriate for the therapeutic interaction with such clients. In addition, it is important that therapists are comfortable with all aspects of human sexuality in order to convey an atmosphere that permits discussion of sexually abusive behaviors. (Many of these same techniques may be applied when working only with the sex offender.) A number of characteristics are noted to be essential to this work, which are listed (in part) as follows:

1. Comfort in relating to a cotherapist of the opposite sex as an equal, if a male and female team is used
2. Ability to deal with feelings of pain, helplessness, fear, vulnerability, and grief—a necessary skill for clinicians
3. If therapists are uncomfortable in expressing vulnerability, patients will be unable to voice their vulnerability and fears
4. Capability in open discussions of any issues relating to human sexuality
5. Ability to communicate in an open, honest, and nurturing manner, which is effective in working with sexually abusive family systems
6. Comfort in being assertive and vocally intense when merited, to assume power and control during certain periods in treatment, when feelings and tensions are high
7. Being aware that many of these offenders possess dysfunctional interactional histories that involve emotional, physical, and sexual abuse

8. Competence in relating in an emotionally intimate but nonsexual manner with a cotherapist
9. Need a good sense of humor—resistance and tension can sometimes be managed effectively with levity.

O'Connell, Leberg, and Donaldson (1990) suggest that therapists should possess certain professional qualifications. These are summarized as follows:

1. A formal education with a professional degree at the master or doctorate level, or medical degree.
2. Clinical experience is considered to be the single most important qualification for a sex offender therapist.
3. Such prior clinical experience should include work with involuntary patients.
4. Background should include knowledge of sexual deviancy and offender issues.
5. A therapist must be aware of the psychological impact sexual abuse has had upon victims.
6. A sex offender therapist must be knowledgeable of the criminal justice system, as in law enforcement, corrections, and probation and parole.
7. Clinicians should have an understanding of the dynamics of the court system.
8. Clinicians should have knowledge of available resources in the community.
9. Clinicians should display the ability to be assertive and direct at times.
10. Clinicians should be alert to manipulation by a sex offender.
11. Therapists must have the ability to question an offender about his or her sexually inappropriate behaviors in a very detailed manner.

O'Connell, Leberg, and Donaldson (1990) cite several personal traits and abilities as important when working with sex offenders. These are summarized as follows:

1. The ability to cope with stress is needed because work with sex offenders can be especially demanding.

2. The ability to discuss sexual matters openly and without reservation is a must, for often the information will be of a graphic nature.
3. Sexual deviancy can be unpleasant to hear about, and many skilled clinicians are often deterred by this situation.
4. Be alert to issues of countertransference.
5. The ability to be precise, show attention to details, be accurate and a desire to seek out information are important.
6. A therapist must be aware of certain sexual misconduct behaviors in an effort to be alert to a possible relapse situation.
7. The ability to be objective is necessary.
8. A therapist must be willing to work with a patient on a long-term basis.
9. The ability to be realistic is needed, because sex offenders do not easily give up their sexual deviant interests.
10. Clinical insight is essential as some offenders will oppose therapy, resist change, are not amenable to treatment, and remain a threat to community safety.
11. The clinician must have no sexual deviant or criminal history, for a therapist must serve as a role model; relapse can be extremely destructive for patients in care.

CLINICAL ASSESSMENT

A clinical assessment should be completed for each sex offender referred to treatment. These assessments may vary widely among programs. A comprehensive assessment may include an psychiatric evaluation, psychological examination, and an interview by a clinical social worker. A battery of sexual inventory and psychological tests may be completed for each offender.

The plethysmograph and polygraph are used in some inpatient or residential centers but are often found to be utilized more in community-based programs. Many inpatient psychiatric settings and correctional treatment programs rely heavily only upon the interview and assessment components in order to determine a prescribed course of treatment services. Unfortunately, time demands, cost of testing, and staffing levels are realistic factors influencing the assessment of sex offenders. Formal time studies have not yet been completed on the assessment process for sex offenders as compared to other patient populations receiving treatment services. It is suspected, however, that many sex offenders receive a more detailed evaluation now than many other disordered individuals.

Maletzky (1998) has reviewed the assessment process for sex offenders and notes the following:

1. "No single instrument, psychological, social, or physiological, has been proven to be definitive in the assessment of sexual offenders" (Maletzky, 1998, p. 478).

2. An unstructured interview appears to be favored more by clinicians in obtaining information from the sex offender. Sessions may be two or three hours in length and separated over a period of several sessions.

3. A mental status examination will need to be completed with the sex offender. Clinicians will want to know the offender's level of awareness and orientation, attitude regarding victim empathy, acceptance of responsibility for their behavior, and any psychiatric impairment.

4. Clinicians may want to encourage the use of a journal or record. This self-report method is sometimes an effective tool in gathering information about sexual behavior, thoughts, urges, and masturbatory fantasies. Tape recorders can also be used.

5. A review of the case history is recommended. Sources may include the arrest warrant, the court order and related documents, child protection service investigation, police report, victim's statement, probation presentence history and any other information significant to the case. Any previous criminal, medical, sexual, psychiatric, or substance abuse history is of value. Childhood, family, marital, educational, and social history information is important. Biological and organic factors are very relevant.

6. Collateral interviews with family members or professionals familiar with the case may be of help. Offenders will lie or will present distorted or untruthful information during the interview process. Therefore, contact with other information sources is of help when working with a sex offender.

7. No one single psychological instrument has been found to be distinctive for the testing of sex offenders. However, psychological

testing may determine intelligence, level of functioning, and related diagnostic information. Any testing should be conducted prior to the clinical interview.

8. The plethysmograph has been used in the evaluation of sex offenders. This form of assessment can determine arousal and attraction to certain sexual behaviors, age groups, and genders. Most important, a majority of sex offenders will display a deviant sexual arousal reaction during testing. Evaluators are encouraged to be aware that there are limitations with this form of assessment. Standardization is merited. Additional research appears to be warranted with use on other larger populations. No control studies of significance have been completed. The test itself is expensive to purchase and costly to administer. Some offenders do not respond to the test, will resist, find the examination to be intrusive, and sometimes refuse to cooperate. The instrument cannot prove or disprove that sex offending has occurred. Evaluations are performed only on offenders who have been caught. Sexual reaction reflects only the arousal (at the time) of the test stimuli. (Still, this type of examination is found to be of value for clinicians and helpful during the assessment process. Examinations are usually held twice: once before entry into a treatment program and then prior to a possible discharge. Some programs may use the test on a selected basis to be more cost-effective.)

9. The polygraph test has been used with sex offenders. Scores are not admitted as evidence in most courts in the United States at present. Such an examination, like all tests, possesses a margin of error and false readings can occur. Clinicians need to be aware that the polygraph is still a subject of debate. (However, many clinicians consider the polygraph a helpful barometer in the assessment and treatment process of sex offenders, in addition to the plethysmograph. Such examinations can be revealing of truthful or deceptive behaviors. Also, this examination does elicit extensive information in certain offenders and is seen as an effective tool in work with offenders. A full self-disclosure examination may be used prior to entry into a therapy program, with at least yearly maintenance reviews. Some programs may elect to use the exam as needed to limit costs.)

Groth (1990) recommends the following summarized sections for use in the clinical assessment of an offender's sexual behavior:

Premeditation. The offender's version of the events leading up to the offense, including whether a victim was sought out intentionally for the purpose of sexual assault or the incident was opportunistic and spontaneous.

Victim selection. The offender should be questioned in detail about his or her selection of the victim including age, race, sex, social relationship, situation, and physical characteristics.

Style of attack. The offender should be questioned in how he or she achieved control over the victim in order to carry out the offense including the use of deception, entrapment, threat, intimidation, physical force, or violence.

Accompanying fantasies. The interviewer should question the offender about his or her fantasies and if any sexual thoughts had preceded the incident. Questions should explore the offender's fantasy system, content, and development.

Role of aggression. Questions about physical force should be explored with the offender, as well as whether the victim was harmed. How was the sexual assault initiated and did the offender resort to physical force only when the victim resisted? Did the offender use more physical force than was necessary, and was the aggression eroticized?

Conversation. During the incident, did the offender talk to his or her victim and was the dialogue hostile, instructional, or inquisitive?

Sexual behavior. What was the nature of the offender's sexual activity with the victim? Did the offender demand from and/or perform on his or her victim kissing, fondling, masturbating, breast sucking, oral sex, anal or vaginal penetration? The duration of the assault will need to be discussed. Additionally, did the offender experience any sexual dysfunction and what was the sexual response to the assault?

Mood state. The interviewer should explore the offender's mood at the time of the offense. How did the offender feel at the time of the offense? Were the offender's emotions of anger, fear, depression, frustration, sexual arousal, excitement, or other related emotions?

Contributing factors. The interviewer should explore in detail what psychosocial factors or precipitating stressors occurred prior to the offense. Also, does the offender have a mental illness? Is he or she mentally retarded, or does the offender have organic problems, a head injury, or substance abuse problems?

Responsibility. Does the offender acknowledge the offense and accept responsibility for his or her actions? Does the offender qualify his or her behavior or deny the offense?

Recidivism. The interviewer will need to explore the offender's sexual development, paraphilia onset, frequency of sexual assault, past interventions, and any change or progression in the sexual action.

Deterrence. The interviewer will need to explore any incidents that may have deterred the offender from committing an act of sexual assault.

Sexual development. The interview should include a history of the offender's past sexual education, childhood, and behavior, unconventional sexual experiences, marital relations, sexual lifestyle, fantasies, concerns, and any traumatic events, including any history of victimization.

CONFIDENTIALITY

The issues involving confidentiality and the therapeutic relationship may be more complicated when working with sex offenders. Usually, privacy is a part of the treatment agreement between the therapist and patient. The therapy encounter permits the patient to present his or her worst fears and related behaviors in a setting free of judgment and the fear of exposure. The therapist becomes a trusted confidant. An integral part of therapy is the dynamic exchange of transference between therapist and patient. This form of interaction sometimes parallels even the most intimate of relationships, such as parent and child, husband and wife, attorney and client, or priest or minister and church member.

Cohen (1995) observes that the need for confidentiality and professional ethics is based upon the individual's expectations of privacy and nondisclosure and the recognition that treatment outweighs the demands of disclosure. The promise of confidentiality is made within a privileged relationship; then the patient may prevent the release of information to others. Privilege is a matter of law and varies by state and provider. The right of privilege belongs to the patient and may be invoked to keep the therapist from releasing information. A past crime, for example, may not be released if a court rules that the matter is privileged.

As a result, clinicians should be very clear with a sex offender as to what information may or may not be released. Many treatment providers inform sex offenders during the initial intake that not all information shared will be considered privileged, dependent upon the jurisdiction. An informed consent or a waiver of confidentiality release is sought during this session. Clinicians should be versed with the state laws of their locality.

O'Connell, Leberg, and Donaldson (1990) note that confidentiality may not always be possible when treating a sex offender. The therapist is sometimes confronted with situations in which the duty to warn the public exceeds the patient's right to privacy. Several states have enacted laws in which a therapist is bound to report privileged information when a sexual abuse or criminal action is discovered. Also, law exists in some states as a part of duty-to-report situations in which possible impending harm of an individual by another may occur. This information should be shared with an offender at the time of the initial intake. A therapist working with sex offenders must be willing to adhere to community safety issues.

SERVING AS AN EXPERT WITNESS

A sex offender treatment provider is often requested to appear in court in regards to a patient. An expert witness is determined by the court and the trial judge. Education, training, licensure, certification, experience, and scholarship are often factors that qualify therapists to appear in court as expert witnesses. Equally important is the therapist's skill, reputation, and history as an expert witness in previous court hearings.

Kennedy (1986), in citing courtroom conduct for psychologists, states that six characteristics are important in serving as an expert witness. These attributes may be used for almost all clinical professionals who are summoned to the court to offer testimony. They are as follows:

1. Prepared
2. Exact

3. Brief
4. Coherent
5. Responsive
6. Controlled

The expert witness must be prepared to offer to the court testimony about a patient. As a result, the therapist should review the case in detail prior to the presentation at the court. It is often helpful to write a summary of the patient, in addition to taking the case file to court. Equally important is the need to be exact in testifying, rather than giving general and vague answers. Also, being able to report answers to questions in a brief, coherent, and responsive manner without a lot of jargon is helpful. The information may be clinical in context but must be understandable to the lay professional. To illustrate this point, a therapist can offer the court a diagnosis, but should explain the features and general behaviors of a pedophile.

There are often pitfalls for expert witnesses in a courtroom setting. These may include:

1. Poor scholarship
2. Poor clinical work
3. Poor preparation
4. Poor control
5. Poor grasp of issues
6. Poor presentation

Chapter 5

Clinical Classification
of Sexual Disorders

Sexual offenders often possess behaviors that meet the criteria for some type of clinical disorder. Numerous studies have demonstrated findings of the existence of a psychosexual disturbance in certain individuals.

Coleman and colleagues (1996) report that research has revealed that many sexually related behaviors can be attributed, in part, to manifestations of a biomedical/psychiatric/psychological type of illness or disorder. Other research has demonstrated that certain sexual behaviors are related to early childhood and family events, developmental factors, behavioral experiences, and trauma.

However, evidence of a type of impairment does not necessarily excuse the actions of a sexual offender, or lessen the psychological impact that a victim experiences. Such clinical information does provide those in the criminal justice, human service, and mental health professions with an opportunity to provide appropriate interventions to victim and abuser.

This chapter offers readers a review of current recognized disorders, features of each diagnosis, and examples of how these problems impact individuals.

SEXUAL DISORDER

The *Diagnostic and Statistical Manual of Mental Disorders,* Fourth Edition is a reference guide used by clinicians. This text was last updated in July 2000 by the American Psychiatric Association, and is more commonly referred by those in mental health as the DSM-IV-TR. The discussion in this text refers to information found in the 1994 edition, DSM-IV. Specific features and behaviors are listed as guidelines to determine a type of disorder.

Sexual problem behaviors may be found in the Sexual and Gender Identity Disorders section of the DSM-IV. This section includes Sexual Dysfunctions, Paraphilias, Gender Identity Disorders, Gender Identity Disorder Not Otherwise Specified, and Sexual Disorder Not Otherwise Specified.

Actually, more than forty types of paraphilias have been found to exist but are not included in the DSM-IV (Money, 1993) (please refer to Chapter 6 for further discussion on paraphilias).

The DSM-IV lists ten specific sexual disorders that are clinical in nature and can be found in sex offenders. Eight of these disorders fall under the category of paraphilias. The remaining are listed under the section Paraphilia Not Otherwise Specified, and Sexual Disorder Not Otherwise Specified.

The eight individual paraphilias are identified as exhibitionism, fetishism, frotteurism, pedophilia, sexual masochism, sexual sadism, transvestic fetishism, and voyeurism.

PARAPHILIAS

Paraphilia is a condition that involves sexual behaviors that are dependent upon certain actions or fantasies for arousal and orgasm. Such behaviors may be performed alone or with a consenting or nonconsenting adult partner or child. Certain acts may be considered unusual, socially unacceptable, or harmful to others.

According to the American Psychiatric Association (1994), a paraphiliac disturbance may include intense, recurring, and sexually arousing fantasies and urges. The behavior may incorporate nonhuman objects. In some cases, humiliation of a companion is a part of the conduct. The problem must have persisted for six months, and the actions have caused clinical distress or impairment in social, family, or occupational functioning.

Paraphilias may be divided further into three separate categories. *Paraphilia* is found when a certain target object is sexualized such as a child, article of clothing, or even an animal. *Sexual deviation* is present when behavior occurs that is not commonplace to a particular culture, as in men who cross-dress for erotic arousal. *Perversion* is a behavior in which a central theme is enhanced and eroticized, leading to sexual gratification, as in partialism, where the focus is on a particular body part, as in a foot fetish (Meyer, 1995).

Some individuals feel compelled always to include perversion fantasies as a part of their sexual expression. These persons are dependent upon a fantasy and ritual system of behaviors that is paraphiliac in content, with related stimuli that activate their erotic arousal system. An example of this type of behavior is an adult male who is sexually aroused only by pornographic magazines of nude preadolescent girls. Such a person is extremely dependent upon this specific stimuli in order to achieve arousal by viewing materials that portray children in a sexual form. This person may engage in sexual intercourse with a consenting female adult partner, but can be stimulated first only by viewing magazines relating to child pornography.

Others may experience a sexually deviant preference only on an occasional basis. These incidents may be only episodic in occurrence, whereas at other times the individual may function in an acceptable manner. Such persons are said to maintain a sexual relationship that does not include paraphiliac fantasies or related inappropriate sexual stimuli. Stress can trigger a regression in behavior, as well as other psychosocial factors. A man who has experienced recent marital conflict with his wife may enter a period of heavy drinking. During this period, his social and psychological inhibitions may change, and he will engage in an incident in which he exposes himself to someone.

Kaplan and Sadock (1998c) report that a number of theories may be attributed to a paraphilia dysfunction. These may include castration anxiety, childhood sexual abuse, developmental impairment, narcissism, trauma, oedipal conflict issues, overly strong identification with the opposite sex, and powerlessness with issues of control (please refer to Chapter 9).

Other theories have included behavioral and biological problems, courtship and intimacy deficits, medical difficulties, and personality and psychiatric pathology.

Some related information about paraphilia may include:

- Approximately 10 to 20 percent of all children have been molested by age eighteen (Meyer, 1995).
- More than 50 percent of all paraphilias have their onset before age eighteen (Abel, Rouleau, and Cunningham-Rathner, 1986).

- Most persons who suffer from one paraphilia disorder are likely to possess at least two or three other paraphiliac disorders (Abel et al., 1988).
- Individuals with a paraphilia problem rarely seek help on their own without intervention by criminal justice, human service, or mental health (American Psychiatric Association, 1994).
- The majority of children molested by sexual offenders were found to fall into two significant categories: young boys outside the home by strangers and young girls inside the home by family members. More offenses occur against boys than girls (Abel et al., 1987).

Exhibitionism

Exhibitionism is a disorder that involves the recurring urge and desire to expose one's genitals to another person. Usually the victim is a stranger or an unsuspecting person (American Psychiatric Association, 1994).

Diagnostic criteria for 302.4 Exhibitionism

A. Over a period of at least 6 months, recurrent, intense sexually arousing fantasies, sexual urges, or behaviors involving the exposure of one's genitals to an unsuspecting stranger.

B. The fantasies, sexual urges, or behaviors cause clinically significant distress or impairment in social, occupational, or other important areas of functioning (p. 526). (Reprinted with permission from the *Diagnostic and Statistical Manual of Mental Disorders,* Fourth Edition. Copyright 1994 American Psychiatric Association.)

Usually, exhibitionists have a desired target population and location as a part of the offending cycle. Such places may include public areas such as mall parking lots, public parks, or playgrounds where the intended victims may be found, all with easy access to escape. Many exhibitionists will use a car; they drive about hunting for potential victims.

A middle-aged, Caucasian married male, father of two preadolescent daughters, has a history of exposing his penis to adult women. His target population may be slender, brunette Caucasian females in their early twenties. Such an offender will fantasize about exposing his genitals to a potential victim prior to the offense. His cycle of offending may include cruising in his car during the evening hours after work, searching for victims outside of his own community.

The sexual excitement occurs in the anticipation of the exposure. Masturbation may occur prior to, during, or after the event has occurred. Usually no attempt at further sexual activity with the victim is made. There is a desire to shock, frighten, or surprise a victim. Some offenders experience a fantasy in which the victim will also become sexually aroused.

Other information about exhibitionism may include:

- This disorder is found mainly in males (Kaplan and Sadock, 1998c).
- Exhibitionism is the most common of paraphilias leading to contact with the criminal justice system. One-third to two-thirds of all reported sexual crimes involve some form of exhibitionistic behavior (Marshall, Eccles, and Barbaree, 1991).
- Exhibitionists are extremely diverse in the methods of exposing themselves to victims. Some operate vehicles, driving while exposing their genitals. Others will use an elevator or walk on a street with a portion of their pants open. Reports occur in which some individuals will leave curtains or blinds open or doors to bedrooms and bathrooms ajar (Carnes, 1983).
- Exhibitionists account for approximately one-third of sex offenders who relapse (Rooth, 1973).
- A lack of aggressive behavior displayed by exhibitionists may be linked to their passive personality styles. The opportunity for such men to expose themselves reduces the potential for them to resort to a more harmful type of sexual dysfunction (Rooth, 1973).
- Exhibitionists are believed to be the most treatable of the paraphilias (Marshall et al., 1991).

Fetishism

A fetishism disorder exists when a person is sexually aroused on a recurrent basis by certain nonliving objects. These objects represent a special meaning to the subject and evoke strong sexual feelings. Sexual activity is associated with particular objects that have been eroticized (American Psychiatric Association, 1994).

Diagnostic criteria for 302.81 Fetishism

A. Over a period of at least 6 months, recurrent, intense sexually arousing fantasies, sexual urges, or behaviors involving the use of nonliving objects (e.g., female undergarments).

B. The fantasies, sexual urges, or behaviors cause clinically significant distress or impairment in social, occupational, or other important areas of functioning.

C. The fetish objects are not limited to articles of female clothing used in cross-dressing (as in Transvestic Fetishism) or devices designed for the purpose of tactile genital stimulation (e.g., a vibrator) (p. 526). (Reprinted with permission from the *Diagnostic and Statistical Manual of Mental Disorders,* Fourth Edition. Copyright 1994 American Psychiatric Association.)

In some reported cases, the fetish disorder can be acted out in a passive manner by the individual, such as working in a shoe store, selling female lingerie, styling hair, or through other socially acceptable forms of behavior. The identified object of sexual attraction will play a role in the individual's fantasy process. Such a person may masturbate with the object, observe the item while masturbating, or use the object in some fashion during a sexual encounter. Sometimes such individuals will relive a fantasy, replaying the event (e.g., selling a pair of shoes to a woman, touching her foot, then later masturbating while thinking of the experience).

Other fetish behavior can be acted upon with a consenting sexual partner. A man who has sexual intercourse with his wife only if she wears black high heels may suffer from a fetish disorder. Such behaviors should not be confused with typical fantasy behavior and sexual play. For the behavior to be deemed a fetish level disorder, the person has recurrent urges, fantasy, to experience a particular sexual event in a certain way. Sexual gratification, when a fetish is present, is often linked with the object that has special erotic meaning. Behaviors or thoughts can be incorporated into a fetish system.

Clinical information about fetishism may include:

- Fetishism is primarily a disorder found in males and is rare in females (Kunjukrishnan, Pawlak, and Varan, 1988).
- The sexual focus of fetishism is on nonliving objects, such as shoes, underwear, panty hose, or stockings, that are in some fashion intimately associated with the human body (Kaplan and Sadock, 1998c).
- Usually, this disorder is said to have started in adolescence, although in some cases as early as childhood. This disorder is chronic in duration (Kaplan and Sadock, 1998c).
- The fetish object is somehow linked to someone from the offender's past or childhood. This person may have been someone the offender loved or cared for in a significant manner. In other instances, the individual may have experienced some type of traumatizing event that is sexualized (Kaplan and Sadock, 1998c).
- Fetishism is often found in men who practice autoerotic activities, bondage, and transvestism behaviors (Byard, Hucker, and Hazelwood, 1990).
- Fetishism is considered to be a displacement behavior. A symbol is eroticized (Kunjukrishnan, Pawlak, and Varan, 1988).
- Persons who practice fetishism usually do not encounter problems with the criminal justice system (Meyer, 1995).

Frotteurism

Frotteurism is a disorder in which an individual is sexually stimulated by touching, rubbing, or having physical body contact with another individual. Usually, the victim is a nonconsenting stranger. The offender will attempt to have their body or genital area touch or rub against the victim (American Psychiatric Association, 1994).

Diagnostic criteria for 302.89 Frotteurism

A. Over a period of at least 6 months, recurrent, intense sexually arousing fantasies, sexual urges, or behaviors involving touching and rubbing against a nonconsenting person.

B. The fantasies, sexual urges, or behaviors cause clinically significant distress or impairment in social, occupational, or other important areas of functioning (p. 527). (Reprinted with permission from the *Diagnostic and Statistical Manual of Mental Disorders,* Fourth Edition. Copyright 1994 American Psychiatric Association.)

A case of frotteurism may be illustrated by an adult male who selects elevators in high-rise office buildings to act out his sexual need. This individual will place himself near potential victims in an elevator that is crowded and intentionally bump or touch passengers. Incidents appear to be accidental, and the perpetrator will often offer an excuse for the clumsy behavior. Victims are sometimes unaware of the offense.

Clinical information about frotteurism may include:

- This disorder is found mostly in male offenders (Kaplan and Sadock, 1998c).
- The event is usually carried out in a public location where victims are fairly easy to access, such as a crowded room, mall, or subway. Victims are nonconsenting and usually unknown to the offender. The perpetrator will fantasize that he has a special relationship with the victim during the encounter. Most acts of frottage are believed to start during adolescence and early adulthood; they then will decline in frequency as the offender becomes older. Escape is important to avoid detection, and to avoid possible prosecution (American Psychiatric Association, 1994).
- Victims often do not report the crime for fear of reprisal or that their complaint will not be taken seriously (Meyer, 1995).
- Frotteurs are rarely arrested because the act often goes without notice by the victim (Meyer, 1995).

Pedophilia

Pedophilia is a disorder characterized by sexual attraction to and/or sexual activity with a child. Features include fantasies, sexual urges, and possible sexual behavior with a youth. Persons suffering from this disorder must be sixteen years of age or older and at least five years older than the child. For individuals in late adolescence with such a problem, no age difference is specified, and clinical judgment in assessment is encouraged (American Psychiatric Association, 1994).

Diagnostic criteria for 302.2 Pedophilia

A. Over a period of at least 6 months, recurrent, intense sexually arousing fantasies, sexual urges, or behaviors involving sexual activity with a prepubescent child or children (generally age 13 years or younger).

B. The fantasies, sexual urges, or behaviors cause clinically significant distress or impairment in social, occupational, or other important areas of functioning.

C. The person is at least age 16 years and at least 5 years older than the child or children in Criterion A.

Note: Do not include an individual in late adolescence involved in an ongoing sexual relationship with a 12- or 13-year-old.

Specify if:
Sexually attracted to Males
Sexually attracted to Females
Sexually attracted to Both

Specify if:
Limited to Incest

Specify if:
Exclusive Type (attracted only to children)
Nonexclusive Type (p. 528)

(Reprinted with permission from the *Diagnostic and Statistical Manual of Mental Disorders,* Fourth Edition. Copyright 1994 American Psychiatric Association.)

Pedophilia behavior may differ in action depending upon the individual. Certain persons may meet their sexual needs by viewing child pornography videos while maintaining a sexual relationship with an adult. Others may find sexual gratification only through actual sexual encounters with children. The sexual behavior may appear rather passive in manner and consensual by bribery. More severe forms of this disorder may result in threats of force, coercion, or actual physical assault of victims, including rape.

An illustration of a pedophile may be a single male who is active in church youth groups. He is a college graduate and works full time in addition to his volunteer services. He is sexually attracted to preadolescent females and seeks out this target population in locations that young girls frequent. The sexual abuse may be displayed first in a covert manner, with the offender only engaging in frottage behaviors in which his body accidentally touches the girls during church youth volleyball games. Later, a potential target victim is selected and a more premeditated form of sexual offending behavior is initiated with the offender offering to transport a young girl home after games, befriending both the victim and her parents. As the relationship develops, a more seductive and aggressive approach is started by the offender, such as fondling the victim's breasts. This sexual behavior advances; soon the offender is regularly fondling the child, which includes genital contact while she is clothed, oral sex, and unclothed vaginal activity. The girl may have first been informed by the offender that the behavior was appropriate. Later, the girl may be subjected to forms of manipulation and bribery or to threats of harm, such as that she or her parents would be killed if she exposed the situation. Such offenders often take part in positions in a community in which they will have an opportunity to encounter potential victims.

Other clinical information about pedophilia:

- Approximately 20 percent of all females and 10 percent of all males have been sexually molested prior to eighteen years of age (Abel and Osborn, 1995).
- Sexual activity with female victims is reported more than pedophilia involving male victims. However, homosexual pedophiles tend to have more victims than heterosexual pedophiles. Victims for a heterosexual pedophile may number as many as twenty separate children, while a homosexual pedophile may molest as many as 150 victims (Kaplan and Sadock, 1998b; Abel et al., 1987).

- Sexual interest is not limited to one sex. Some offenders may prefer males while others prefer females. Some offenders may be attracted to both sexes (American Psychiatric Association, 1994).
- Most cases of actual child molestation involve genital fondling or oral sex. Vaginal or anal sexual activity is infrequent except in cases of incest (Kaplan and Sadock, 1998c).
- Those with a pedophilia disorder may report a sexual attraction to children of a specific age range and gender. Those found to be attracted to females usually report an interest in young girls between the ages of eight to ten years, while those who are sexually aroused by males are more inclined to select children that are slightly older (American Psychiatric Association, 1994).
- A large portion of adolescents committing sexual crimes, including acts of pedophilia, are often victims of sexual abuse themselves. Many also experienced physical violence in the home (Becker, 1989).
- Those persons who are sexually attracted to children have usually experienced some interruption in their own developmental growth. Such persons may be at the same developmental level socially as the child (Carnes, 1983).

Sexual Masochism

Sexual masochism involves the recurrent act of being humiliated, beaten, bound, or otherwise made to suffer in some way to achieve arousal and orgasm. Fantasies may include being raped while being held or bound by others without means of escape. More aggressive forms of this disorder may be found in persons who will bind themselves, use pins to stick oneself for the purpose of inflicting pain, commit acts of self-mutilation, or endure forms of electric shock, alone or with a partner. Masochistic acts that may be sought with a partner include bondage, blindfolding, paddling, spanking, whipping, beating, electrical shocking, cutting, and other forms of humiliation, both verbal or physical (American Psychiatric Association, 1994).

Diagnostic criteria for 302.83 Sexual Masochism

A.   Over a period of at least 6 months, recurrent, intense sexually arousing fantasies, sexual urges, or behaviors involving the act (real, not simulated) of being humiliated, beaten, bound, or otherwise made to suffer.

B. The fantasies, sexual urges, or behaviors cause clinically significant distress or impairment in social, occupational, or other important areas of functioning (p. 529). (Reprinted with permission from the *Diagnostic and Statistical Manual of Mental Disorders,* Fourth Edition. Copyright 1994 American Psychiatric Association.)

This disorder may be evidenced by a male who requests that his partner humiliate him by using profane and derogatory language while striking his buttocks with a leather belt. Another example of this type of problem may be evidenced by a woman who requests to be tied to her bed and blindfolded with a scarf by a consenting partner during sexual intercourse. More severe forms of this behavior may include self-mutilation with a razor, encouraging a partner to batter him or her in an aggressive manner, or hanging.

Clinical information on sexual masochism may include:

- Sexual masochism is found in both males and females.
- Most masochistic behavior begins in adolescence.
- Females are more likely to be introduced to sexual masochism, while males appear to discover this interest on their own.
- There is a hypothesis or probability that individuals engaging in sexually masochistic behaviors do not do as well in relationships where the partner does not share the interest.
- A survey of 182 persons with sadomasochistic interests revealed the following: 52.5 percent of men and 57.5 percent of women were married; 31.4 percent of men, 20 percent of women were college graduates; 38.5 percent of men, 13.3 percent of women had monthly incomes between $1,001 and $2,000.
- Preferences of sadomasochistic interests have included the following for both sexes: spanking, master-slave relationships, oral sex, masturbation, bondage, humiliation, erotic lingerie, restraints, anal sex, pain, whipping, rubber and leather clothing, boots and shoes, stringent bondage, enemas, torture, golden showers by urine, transvestism, petticoat punishment, and toilet activities (Breslow, Evans, and Langley, 1985).

Sexual Sadism

Sexual sadism is a disorder that is characterized by individuals who obtain sexual pleasure through the psychological and physical suffering of others. The behavior involves the desire to control, devalue others, and/or the infliction of pain. Severe forms of this disorder may lead to emotional trauma, physical harm, or death for consenting and non-consenting partners (American Psychiatric Association, 1994).

Diagnostic criteria for 302.84 Sexual Sadism

A.   Over a period of at least 6 months, recurrent, intense sexually arousing fantasies, sexual urges, or behaviors involving acts (real, not simulated) in which the psychological or physical suffering (including humiliation) of the victim is sexually exciting to the person.

B.   The fantasies, sexual urges, or behaviors cause clinically significant distress or impairment in social, occupational, or other important areas of functioning (p. 530). (Reprinted with permission from the *Diagnostic and Statistical Manual of Mental Disorders,* Fourth Edition. Copyright 1994 American Psychiatric Association.)

This disorder may be found to be expressed in a mild form when an individual is sexually aroused by acts in which a consenting partner is punished, spanked, whipped, or pinched. More serious forms of this disorder may lead to excessive features of brutality, inflicting serious physical harm to a victim as sexual assault and rape.

Other clinical data concerning sexual sadism may include:

* The disorder was named after Marquis de Sade, an eighteenth-century French writer and military officer who committed violent acts of sexual behavior against women. He was imprisoned several times (Kaplan and Sadock, 1998c).
* Sexual sadism may include the use of restraints, whipping, blindfolding, paddling, spanking, pinching, beating, burning, electrical shocking, rape, cutting, strangulation, torture, mutilation, or killing (American Psychiatric Association, 1994).

- Sadistic rape is aggressive, eroticized with ritualistic acts involving the victim. The offender's mood state is often one of intense excitement and depersonalization. Sadistic rape may include language that is commanding, degrading, or alternately reassuring and threatening. Weapons can be used to capture the victim, along with methods of restraint and possible forms of torture. Victim selection for sadistic rape is determined by specific features or symbolic representation (Groth, 1990).
- Characteristics found to be associated with sexual sadism include childhood physical abuse, history of cross-dressing, peeping, obscene telephone calling, or indecent exposure incidents. Clinical history may include: marriage, military experience, education beyond high school, established reputation as a solid citizen, and an incestuous relationship with a son or daughter. Sexual sadism and offending characteristics have included careful planning of the offense, victim taken to preselected location, unemotional or detached affect during the offense, intentional torture, victim beaten, and sexual dysfunction during the offense (Gratzer and Bradford, 1995).

Transvestic Fetishism

Transvestic fetishism is a disorder that is revealed by a recurrent desire to cross-dress in female attire. This disorder is found only in heterosexual males. Men who cross-dress will masturbate while fantasizing about themselves and a certain female or related object of sexual interest. The male will imagine himself to be in both roles of man and woman in the sexual fantasy. This disorder does not occur in individuals with a gender identity problem (American Psychiatric Association, 1994).

Diagnostic criteria for 302.3 Transvestic Fetishism

A. Over a period of at least 6 months, in a heterosexual male, recurrent, intense sexually arousing fantasies, sexual urges, or behaviors involving cross-dressing.

B. The fantasies, sexual urges, or behaviors cause clinically significant distress or impairment in social, occupational, or other important areas of functioning.

Specify if:

> **With Gender Dysphoria:** if the person has persistent discomfort with gender role or identity (p. 531)

(Reprinted with permission from the *Diagnostic and Statistical Manual of Mental Disorder,* Fourth Edition. Copyright 1994 American Psychiatric Association.)

An example of this disorder may be a man who will on occasion cross-dress in women's clothing, including a dress, underwear, and stockings. While masturbating, he will fantasize about himself and a woman in a sexual situation. He may be married and on occasion act out his fantasy with his sexual partner. A small number of individuals may experience gender dysphoria and attempt to live permanently as a female or seek surgery. This disorder begins in adolescence or childhood.

More information about transvestic fetishism may include:

- The male, when not cross-dressed, is usually masculine in manner. Some men may wear female attire that is hidden or concealed (American Psychiatric Association, 1994).
- Transvestic fetishism occasionally leads individuals into conflict with the criminal justice system in disturbing the peace situations if cross-dressing in a public area (Meyer, 1995).
- Only a small percentage of men with transvestic fetishism disorders seek treatment (Wise, 1990).
- The majority of those seeking treatment and/or volunteering for research studies with transvestic fetishism problems were found to be Caucasian, well educated, married or previously married, had started cross-dressing before age twelve, highly successful, and well-integrated members of the community. Marital problems are most often the contributing psychosocial stressor leading patients into treatment. Transvestic fetishism is a chronic disorder (Brown, 1995).

Voyeurism

Voyeurism is a disorder in which a person obtains sexual pleasure by observing unsuspecting individuals, usually strangers, who are disrobing, unclothed, naked or engaging in some form of sexual activity. The disorder is found most often in males (American Psychiatric Association, 1994).

Diagnostic criteria for 302.82 Voyeurism

A. Over a period of at least 6 months, recurrent, intense sexually arousing fantasies, sexual urges, or behaviors involving the act of observing an unsuspecting person who is naked, in the process of disrobing, or engaging in sexual activity.

B. The fantasies, sexual urges, or behaviors cause clinically significant distress or impairment in social, occupational, or other important areas of functioning (p. 532). (Reprinted with permission from the *Diagnostic and Statistical Manual of Mental Disorders,* Fourth Edition. Copyright 1994 American Psychiatric Association.)

This disorder may be expressed, for instance, in the form of peeping in a window and viewing a couple who are engaged in sexual intercourse. Another form can be found in individuals who find sexual pleasure in viewing others who are disrobing, partially unclothed, or naked. Pools and public rest areas are opportunity areas for voyeurs.

Other information regarding voyeurism may include:

- The act is limited to looking, with no other sexual activity sought. The individual may masturbate and orgasm during or after the incident. The onset of voyeuristic behavior is before age fifteen. The course tends to be chronic (American Psychiatric Association, 1994).
- Voyeurs who are arrested are usually charged with trespassing. Voyeurs enjoy their behavior and enter treatment only if arrested, fear of being caught, or the behavior is impacting other areas of their lives (Smith, 1976).

PARAPHILIA NOT OTHERWISE SPECIFIED

According to the American Psychiatric Association (1994), a coding of "Paraphilia Not Otherwise Specified" may be used for paraphiliac disturbances that do not meet the criteria for other disorders. This disorder is identified as 302.9. Such problem behaviors may include obscene telephone calling, known as telephone scatologia, necrophilia, which includes having sexual relations and/or attraction to a corpse, and others (please refer to Chapter 6).

SEXUAL DISORDER NOT OTHERWISE SPECIFIED

This section is used for clinicians when the sexual disturbance does not meet the criteria features of a specific sexual disorder. Neither sexual dysfunction nor a paraphilia would appear to be appropriate for diagnosis.

According to the American Psychiatric Association (1994), the diagnostic criteria for 302.9 "Sexual Disorder Not Otherwise Specified" is as follows:

1. Marked feeling of inadequacy about sexual performance that is self-imposed regarding masculine or feminine behaviors or features.
2. Clinical distress in having a number of sexual partners without intimacy.
3. Significant distress about sexual orientation.

Chapter 6

The Paraphilias

BACKGROUND AND HISTORY

The word paraphilia is defined as a type of mental disorder characterized by an obsession with unusual sexual practices (*Random House Dictionary,* 1987). Also, the term is believed to have evolved from two separate Greek words referring to "the side of " and "love" (Kaplan and Sadock, 1998c).

Current research appears to be divided into several different camps as to whether paraphilia behaviors are exclusive or nonexclusive. In the exclusive form, only paraphiliac behaviors would promote arousal, while in the nonexclusive form, the patient may be stimulated by both paraphilia and other types of stimuli. Some researchers believe most paraphiliacs can perform other sexual acts without the associated behaviors. Those who cannot experience sexual gratification without paraphilia behaviors are few in number.

Abel (1989) reports that paraphilia behavior is the extreme exaggerated form of sexual activity. For instance, many persons may seek out erotic forms of entertainment in literature, theater, movies, and television without problem. Individuals will, on occasion, experiment sexually and may involve fantasy to enhance a relationship. Self-help books in any bookstore display a variety of suggestions for those seeking to express an erotic or romantic fantasy in a relationship. A woman may wear lingerie or a man may wear a robe during a sexual encounter. This type of behavior should not be confused with paraphilia action that includes recurring rituals and fantasies in order to achieve sexual gratification or the involvement of a child or unwilling partner.

Meyer (1995) reports that paraphilia behavior may include erotosexual fantasies, masturbatory practices, props, and a possible partner. The fantasy is believed to occupy the thought process in both a conscious and unconscious manner. Individuals who possess a paraphilia condition usually depend upon a particular and specialized fantasy for sexual arousal. Certain articles of clothing or other objects may be a part of the fantasy, which may or may not include a sexual companion. The partner can be consenting or nonconsenting depending upon the act. Rituals may be a part of the imagery.

Paraphilias are also identified as a sexual deviation and perversion. Meyer (1995) suggests the severity of a paraphilia problem is usually dependent on the degree of enactment and level of distress. A mild condition may produce some distress for an individual who fantasizes but chooses not to act out their sexual imagery. Persons who suffer from a moderate form of paraphilia may occasionally act upon their fantasy and may experience some social or occupational problems. In the most severe cases of paraphilia, individuals will act out their fantasies on a regular basis with possible social, family, and occupational difficulties.

Paraphilia itself refers to the unusual sexual response to a particular object or behaviors. An example may include a sexual response to an article of clothing, certain female attire, a child, or an animal. Sexual deviation refers to abnormal sexual action that conflicts with normal cultural behaviors. Men who cross-dress in women's clothing to achieve sexual orgasm and persons who require bondage arrangements to experience gratification represent such situations. Perversion refers to a developmental change or way of reacting to eroticism in which a form of sexual activity takes on a significant role. Sexual attraction to a corpse (necrophilia) may be considered an illustration in which a psychosocial crisis somehow impacts an individual's erotic developmental growth.

Males appear to represent the majority of reported individuals suffering from a paraphilia. However, both men and women are known to possess paraphilias. Such practices are considered unusual or socially unacceptable (Coleman et al., 1996).

The onset for a paraphiliac disorder occurs before the age of eighteen for more than 50 percent afflicted by the dysfunction. The rate of occurrence of paraphiliac behavior appears to peak for individuals between the ages of fifteen and twenty-five, then a decline will most likely occur. Paraphiliac action can reoccur during psychosocial events that are stressful for an individual throughout life.

Marital conflict, job loss, or death of a significant other can produce the reemergence of paraphilia behaviors. It is estimated that approximately one-third to one-half of all child molesters were sexually abused themselves as children. As many as 10 to 20 percent of all children are estimated to have been molested in some manner by age eighteen (Meyer, 1995).

SOME CLINICAL STUDIES

Sex offenders can possess a clinical history of paraphilias that is extensive. Certain acts can be passive in manner, while other actions cause harm to another. (As listed in Chapter 5, there are eight primary disorders now recognized by the American Psychiatric Association.)

A landmark study in 1987 was conducted on paraphiliac behaviors in sex offenders. A total of 561 subjects were interviewed for the project. The study involved individuals who were not incarcerated. High frequency acts were found to include exhibitionism, frottage, masochism, transvestitism, and voyeurism (Abel et al., 1987).

Many stereotypical assumptions were found to be challenged. The majority of sex offenders surveyed were found to possess a moderate amount of education and were usually employed. About 40 percent of the respondents had completed one year of college, 64 percent were fully employed or enrolled in school. Approximately one-half of the subjects in the study had a relationship with another adult partner involving marriage or significant relationship in some form (Abel et al., 1987).

Child molestation results were found to be of significant interest. Pedophiles who abused female targets in nonincest situations had a mean average offense rate of 23.2 acts, and a median average of 1.4 offenses. Pedophiles who abused male targets had a mean average offense rate of 281.7 in nonincest situations, and a median average of 10.1 offenses. The study found that paraphiliacs who offended young boys outside the home committed the highest number of crimes in this category. Pedophiles involved with children outside the home were found occasionally to reoffend the same victim, particularly men who molest boys.

Pedophiles who commit incest involving female victims had a mean average of 81.3 acts and a median of 4.4 acts. Pedophiles who commit incest crimes involving male victims had a mean average of 62.3 acts, 5.2 median average of acts.

Rapists involved in the study were reported to commit an mean average of 7.2 offenses, median average of 0.9 offenses. Approximately 126 rapists were involved in the study.

Exhibitionists had a reported mean average of 504.9 offenses and a median average of 50.9 offenses. Additionally, it was reported that exhibitionists and rapists usually commit one act per victim.

Voyeurs, with 62 respondents, committed a mean average of 469.9 offenses and a median average of 16.5 acts. Voyeurs were found to sometimes reoffend the same individual.

Also, in a separate study in 1988, it was found that only 10.1 percent of the paraphilia respondents possessed only one diagnosis. Most were found to have two or more diagnoses of some type of paraphilia dysfunction. Approximately 19.2 percent of the respondents were found with two diagnoses of paraphilia, 20.6 percent had three diagnoses, and 11.5 percent had four diagnoses. The other 37.6 percent surveyed were found to possess five to ten different types of paraphilia behaviors (Abel et al., 1988).

In another clinical study, Dietz, Cox, and Wegener (1986) report some significant findings for exhibitionists. Based upon arrest records, it was found that the highest number of exposure incidents occurred in the spring during the months of April, May, and June. Exposure incidents occurred less often during the months of December, January, and February. Most incidents of indecent exposure occurred during the daylight hours and in public outdoor places. Exhibitionists rarely repeat their crime with the same victim.

Several similar clinical features appear to exist in these disorder groupings. Paraphilias are often found to be intrusive, involuntarily repetitive with a compulsive component. Comparable features are found to exist in impulse control disorders, and obsessive-compulsive disorder. A biological explanation for sexual offending behavior is being explored.

Bradford and Gratzer (1995) report that a possible relationship or parallel features may exist between impulse control disorders and paraphilias as a part of the obsessive-compulsive behavior groupings.

Many sexual offenders often report problems that include compulsive urges, obsessive-like thoughts about sex, and difficulty in managing their desires and impulses. A sex offender may be seen now as not only an individual who desires to harm another, but also as someone who is impaired and acts out those sexual urges and needs as the result of impulse control problems and obsessive-compulsive behaviors. Available findings may help lessen offending incidents, which in turn reduces the number of individuals assaulted. Additional studies are being continued in the area by a number of researchers.

THE CRIMINAL JUSTICE SYSTEM AND PARAPHILIAS

Abel (1989) notes that the criminal justice system (including the judicial system) tends to be uncomfortable with some aspects of paraphilia sex crimes, such as exhibitionism, and will minimize or fail to explore the offense behavior, permitting the offender to escape prosecution. Offenders who can afford legal representation often avoid prosecution or incarceration or receive a lesser sentence during a plea-bargaining arrangement.

Sex offenders who are articulate, of average intelligence, and can afford the employment of their own defense attorney are often able to evade conviction or prosecution or will receive a reduction in the crime they were alleged to have committed.

There is a significant lack of available education and training for those in criminal justice, the courts, prosecutors, and direct law enforcement services regarding perpetrators. To apprehend a sex offender, certain techniques and interviewing skills must be learned. The investigation of a crime scene, how to interview a rape victim, and the importance of properly collecting evidence are often crucial to the prosecution of a sex offender with a paraphilia disturbance.

Many courts, prosecutors, defense attorneys, and law enforcement officers are often unfamiliar with the dynamics and behaviors of paraphilias and will sometimes fail to adequately explore the offender's history. Sex crimes can impact professionals psychologically in a way that produces a certain amount of countertransference. As a result, victims can sometimes still find themselves questioned and scrutinized in a manner not associated with other crimes. This can be traumatizing to the victim and reintroduce psychological wounds encountered by the sexual assault. How many victims of car theft are queried in detail about nonrelated offense issues?

Abel (1989) states that occurrence rates for paraphilias drawn from law enforcement authorities and victim and rape centers is often misrepresented as the result of current reporting patterns. Many victims are still reluctant to report a sexual crime. The number of documented offenses does not reflect the actual number of sexual crimes being committed today. Abel (1989) reports that available criminal statistical information does not actually portray the magnitude of the paraphilia behaviors and related sex-offender population. Inaccurate estimates may be attributed to sexual offenders, as they often commit crimes against victims who are unaware of the offense, such as in inappropriate touching (frottage), and peeping (voyeurism) situations.

The most aggressive sex offenders with repeated offenses receive the most attention by the criminal justice system. The more covert and passive forms of paraphilia receive less attention as the result of the more subtle types of behaviors associated with the crimes.

Prentky and Knight (1993) report that there is a strong hypothesis and some clinical evidence that sexual violence can lead to more acts of aggression against others. Paraphilia acts that cause a sex offender to enter the criminal justice system have often offended sexually on many occasions before being apprehended.

In addition, as with most inappropriate behaviors, once a cycle of aggression and lawbreaking begins, it does not stop until some type of outside intervention occurs. Sex offenders rarely seek out treatment and often only resort to help after being arrested and understanding the possibility of pending incarceration.

PARAPHILIAS TYPES

There are more than forty known types of paraphilias at the present time. However, social and cultural values appear to impact what is or is not sexually appropriate.

According to the American Psychiatric Association (1994), Paraphilias Not Otherwise Specified may include (but are not limited to) telephone scatologia (obscene phone calls), necrophilia (corpses), partialism (exclusive focus on part of a body), zoophilia (animals), coprophilia (feces), klismaphilia (enemas), and urophilia (urine). Paraphilia Not Otherwise Specified is considered more of a residual grouping with sexually aberrant behaviors less frequently observed by clinicians, criminal justice and human service professionals.

Kaplan and Sadock (1998c) report that the category of Paraphilia Not Otherwise Specified includes a varied number of paraphilias that do not qualify for other sexual disorders. Included are hypoxyphilia (hanging, suffocation or strangulation to achieve orgasm), and masturbation (when found to be compulsive, preferred to intercourse), in addition to those listed by the American Psychiatric Association.

There have been no controlled studies on paraphilias, sex offenders, and pornography. Pornography use can be found to be a sexual disturbance, in which an individual is sexually aroused by certain graphic pictures or movies, and experiences some distress if such material is not available. In many cases of sexual assault of adult and child victims, offenders often are found in possession of pornography.

Abel (1989) says rape may meet the criteria in some cases for a paraphilia. Some individuals experience intense, repetitive urges to commit rape at an early age. Such individuals, like others who suffer from a paraphilia, attempt to control their fantasies but at times fail to do so. Guilt will occur after an incident and the urge to sexually assault another victim will decline. However, the urge will build again after a period of time has passed. Many rapists often possess other paraphilias, such as exhibitionism, frottage, pedophilia, sadism and voyeurism.

Approximately 44 percent of paraphilia rapists begin their behavior by way of sexual assault; the majority do not start out with an aggressive form of action. About 26 percent of rapists begin as pedophiles, 9 percent as voyeurs, 8 percent as exhibitionists, 6 percent as frotteurs, 2 percent as fetishists, and the remainder from other less common paraphilia behaviors. The question remains as to whether sufficient research information exists to justify a paraphilia category for rape. It is noted that all major treatment centers for paraphilias have been providing treatment for rapists for a number of years as well (Abel, 1989).

Rapists with a paraphilia component appear to differ from other forms of sexual offenders. For example, a man who receives sexual gratification by sadism (by causing physical harm to a victim or humiliating them in some psychological form) during a sexual assault may be viewed differently than a rapist with a paraphilia. A paraphilia rapist is aroused by fantasies and urges about using force on a resisting victim during a sexual encounter.

Abel (1989) states that a special disorder for rapists with paraphilia features has been considered. The proposed name for this dysfunction was paraphilic coercive disorder. However, this proposal has not yet received support as a recognized disorder. An important concern was the issue of whether rapists would seek to be diagnosed with this disorder in order to avoid punishment. Regardless, the courts and state and federal lawmakers have not been influenced by offenders with other paraphiliac disorders, lessening their accountability. Pedophiles, for instance, who have harmed a child receive sentences that are representative of the crime and physical and psychological trauma suffered by the victim.

Money (1993) has complied a list of the most known paraphilias that are believed to exist at the present time. Several of these paraphilias may be a part of a cluster grouping, overlap, exist solely alone, or may be a reciprocal reaction.

These paraphilias are listed, in part, as follows:

Acrotomophilia. A sexual attraction to persons who possess an amputation. Such paraphilias are erotically stimulated by persons who are missing a leg or arm.

Adolescentilism. Includes individuals who enjoy acting and dressing as adolescents, or having a partner enact such a role. This disorder is also known as hebophilia.

Andromimetophilia. Includes sexual attraction to partners who are transsexual or have had surgery changing their gender.

Apotemnophilia. Occurs when an individual plays the role of an amputee and experiences an erotic response.

Asphyxiophilia. Occurs in individuals who derive sexual pleasure through strangulation, suffocation, or hanging. This disorder is also known hypoxyphilia.

Autagonistophilia. Arousal and orgasm depends upon the individual being observed on stage or being filmed while engaged in a sexual activity.

Autassassinophilia. Sexual excitement is associated with managing the possibility of one's own death.

Autonepiophilia. Sexual arousal is achieved by dressing as an infant and being treated as a baby by a partner or having a companion act out the behavior. This disorder is also referred to as infantilism.

Biastophilia. Erotic stimulation and sexual excitement occurs when a nonconsenting partner is attacked and is sexually assaulted and/or raped. Fear, surprise, and shock are often features associated with this dysfunction. Violence may be threatened or used.

Chrematistophilia. An individual is sexually excited by the act of being charged, forced to pay, or robbed by a partner for sexual services.

Chronophilia. An individual is sexually attracted to a different age group. Pedophiles are an example.

Coprophilia. Sexual activity involves feces being smeared upon the body or ingested.

Exhibitionism. Individuals derive sexual pleasure by exposing their genitals in order to evoke surprise, dismay, shock, and panic from the victim.

Fetishism. An individual obtains erotic pleasure by the use of an inanimate object or article during sexual activity.

Formicophilia. Arousal and orgasm are dependent upon the sensations produced by small creatures such as snails, frogs, ants, and other insects that creep and crawl about the genitalia and perineal areas.

Frotteurism. An individual obtains sexual pleasure by touching or rubbing others, usually a stranger, particularly with the genital area.

Gerontophilia. A clinical disturbance in which the sexual partner must be older, usually at a parent or grandparent age level.

Hybristophilia. Individuals are sexually attracted to a partner who has committed a crime, is reckless and dangerous, may be going, has been, or is in prison.

Hyphephilia. Individuals are sexually excited by the touching or rubbing of skin, hair, leather, fur, and fabric, especially if worn near the breasts or genital areas of the body.

Kleptophilia. Sexual excitement occurs when a persons steals or shoplifts from others.

Klismaphilia. Sexual pleasure is obtained by having an enema administered by a partner.

Masochism. Sexual arousal is dependent upon situations in which one is abused, tortured, punished, disciplined, humiliated, or required to obey and act as a servant. This disorder was named after Leopold Sacher-Masoch, 1836-1895, an Austrian author and practicing masochist.

Mixoscopia. Sexual arousal is obtained by watching others engage in sexual intercourse.

Mysophilia. Arousal occurs from self-degradation. The individual will smell, chew, or use sweaty or soiled clothing or articles of menstrual hygiene for sexual excitement.

Narratophilia. One is sexually aroused by hearing or using words or stories that are pornographic or obscene in content.

Necrophilia. A person is aroused or stimulated in order to achieve orgasm by having some form of sexual activity with a corpse or pretending a partner is dead.

Nepiophilia. Involves sexual activity with an infant child.

Olfactophilia. An individual is sexually aroused by a body odor from a consenting or nonconsenting partner.

Pedophilia. An adult is sexually attracted to a child or preadolescent youth. The individual may experience recurrent fantasies, have urges to engage in or will participate in some form of sexual activity with a child.

Pictophilia. Involves the viewing of pictures, magazines, movies, or videotapes that are considered pornographic and obscene.

Sadism. An individual is dependent upon imposing physical abuse, torture, punishment, or emotional humiliation with a consenting or nonconsenting partner for sexual excitement.

Somnophilia. Sexual pleasure is achieved by awaking a sleeping stranger in an erotic manner, including through oral sex, but does not include force or violence.

Stigmatophilia. Arousal and orgasm are dependent upon having a partner who has been tattooed, scarred, or pierced with bars or rings, particularly in the genital area.

Symphorophilia. Sexual pleasure and gratification is found by arranging, stage-managing, or orchestrating a possible or actual accident or disaster, then watching it happen, such as a traffic collision of several vehicles.

Telephone scatophilia. Sexual pleasure occurs in persons who make or listen to someone make obscene telephone calls.

Transvestism. An individual cross-dresses to obtain sexual arousal and orgasm. Usually males are found to possess this disorder wearing female attire. Masturbation, fantasy, and rituals occur, which may include a partner.

Troilism. An individual depends upon observing a partner engaging in sexual relations with another. The arrangement requires that the partner coordinate the event, in part, by hiring the third party, inviting them to have sex, or being loaned or traded.

Urophilia. Sexual activity includes being urinated upon and/or swallowing urine for the attainment of arousal and orgasm.

Voyeurism. Arousal and orgasm of the voyeur depends upon the risk of being found while watching another disrobe or engage in sexual intercourse.

Zoophilia. A person engages in sexual activity with an animal.

Chapter 7

Rape As a Clinical
and Criminal Disturbance

Rape may be defined as a form of aggression against another; it is an act of violence expressed by forced sex, without passion or caring. Such sexual behavior is used on the victim to display anger, control, domination, hostility, and power. Victims are often coerced, forced, or manipulated in some manner to engage in sexual activity.

On occasion, such assaults can be experimental, opportunistic, preferential, sadistic, or situational in occurrence by the offender. Victims who are unable to render informed consent as the result of being mentally incompetent, or who are minors may be considered victims of rape.

The American Psychiatric Association (2000) does not classify rape as a mental disorder at the present time. The *Diagnostic and Statistical Manual,* Fourth Edition Text Revision, does list two types of sexual abuse that may be considered a focus of clinical attention. These are identified as sexual abuse of child, and sexual abuse of adult. Several task forces have been assembled over the years; they have been unable to resolve the issue as to whether rape is a clinical disturbance or a criminal offense or both, or what special conditions should be factors. As a result, rape remains a controversial issue in criminal justice, human service, and mental health circles. Some researchers believe that a portion of rapists have diagnostic features similar to other paraphilias. It is the inability to make a valid diagnosis with some reliability that continues to impair those within the mental health community from actually defining rape as a clinical disorder. The American Psychiatric Association (1999) reports that a category tentatively titled paraphilic coercive disorder has been examined. Individuals with this disorder would need to experience intense, repetitive urges to commit an act of rape six months in duration and who had either acted on these urges or experienced a form of distress related to the problem. Also, it was noted that some specialists now believe there is enough scientific evidence for the creation of a rape disorder; others have reservations. However, there is wide agreement that the number of individuals qualifying for such a clinical disturbance is small. Noteworthy is the fact that some rapists would attempt to use a clinical disorder to avoid being held accountable for their actions.

RAPE AS A CLINICAL DISTURBANCE

Sadock (1995) reports that rape involves sexual intercourse with a nonconsenting female. The victim of the sexual assault is forced, coerced, or manipulated in some fashion to engage in sexual relations, or is considered underage, or is mentally incompetent to make such a decision. Rape can also occur when the persons are married or are of the same sex.

Indeed, rape may be seen as a dynamic action of men who cannot express themselves in a more socially appropriate manner. Sexual assault may be considered displaced aggression by the male. Anger, aggression, conflict, and fear are often associated with rape. Anxiety and problems with intimacy may be found. Sometimes, forced fellatio and/or anal penetration may occur during a sexual assault incident. These behaviors are deemed acts of sodomy. Sadock (1995) states the criteria for rape should include the following elements:

1. Rape is a sexual activity that is forced and is against the consent of the victim, or the individual lacks the capacity to agree.
2. Slight penile penetration of the victim's outer vulva may qualify for the act of rape.
3. A full or complete erection, with ejaculation by the penis, is not required for the crime of rape.

Groth (1990) suggests that the psychodynamics of rape are complex. In every rape, both aggression and sexuality are themes of the assault. Three patterns can be found in rape:

1. The anger rape, with sex expressed as an aggressive action
2. The power rape, with sex displayed by domination
3. The sadistic rape, in which harm to someone is sexualized in an erotic form (later detail in chapter)

Rape, as a dynamic action, is a representation of sexual behavior that is influenced by status, hostility, control, and dominance. Victims are the vehicles in which such inappropriate behaviors are expressed. The trauma and long-term psychological damage to a victim are not of issue for offenders.

Groth (1990) believes that all nonconsenting sexual encounters are assaultive as an interaction. Therefore, the defining characteristics of rape are the forced assault of another, the victim's perceived fear of harm, and the concern for their physical safety. Sexual assault is a psychological dysfunction that may be either temporary and transient or chronic and repetitive.

Although laws differ from state to state, the legal definition of rape, in broad terms, implies that some form of sexual intercourse occurred against the will of the victim. The specific defining element of rape is lack of consent.

Groth (1990) says mental health professionals have been slow to respond to rape as a possible sexual disorder. Only paraphilia acts are currently considered sexually deviant and are recognized as a clinical disturbance at present. The more passive and unconventional disorders such as fetishism and transvestism have been researched more thoroughly and found to be meet the criteria for a clinical disturbance. As the result, a large proportion of sexually inappropriate behaviors, including rape, are left to the criminal justice system for resolution.

Groth (1990) has noted that the clinical community's reluctance to examine rape as a psychosexual disorder, in effect, places the public and future potential victims at risk. Most rape victims are adult women and children.

Abel (1989) has reported that rape may meet the criteria for a paraphilia, in certain cases. These individuals experience rape fantasy, have repetitive urges to commit sexual assault, and are unable to fully control their behavior. Money (1993) says that some rapists are clinically disordered with a paraphilia distress. Afflicted individuals are only aroused by a victim's fear and associated reaction to a sexual assault.

However, it has been noted that the criminal justice system may be impaired if a clinical diagnosis of rape is offered. Yet more aggressive sexual disorders such as pedophilia already exist and punishment appears to be occurring when merited. In fact, many future victims may be spared harm if a diagnosis was created. Already many rape typologies have been created in an effort to assist those professionals in criminal justice, human service, and mental health in their work with sex offenders. Therefore, it now appears to be feasible that a clinical diagnosis be offered, which may be identified as sexual assault disorder. Such a new proposed sexual disorder would have the following diagnostic criteria:

1. A history of sexual assault behaviors against others that has occurred for an extended period of time.
2. Clinical features include fantasies about sexual harm.
3. Sexual assault urges are difficult to control or manage.
4. Victims of assault are forced, coerced, or manipulated to engage in sexual relations.
5. Consent is of question. The victim is an unwilling adult or child, or is mentally incompetent.
6. Clinical distress is found prior to an assault or if the perpetrator is unable to carry out an assault
7. There is a series of sexual assaults, more than two in which forced, coerced, or manipulated sexual activity occurs.
8. The individual can exhibit anger, control issues, and domination during the assault. Harm, physical force, threats, vulgar language, or the use of a weapon may occur.
9. Sexual arousal will occur prior to, during, or after the assault with events reviewed during masturbatory fantasy episodes.
10. There is depersonalization, a lack of remorse or victim empathy during the incident. Denial, minimization, and rationalization features are exhibited.
11. Full erection in males or complete sexual arousal in females is not necessary for the sexual assault behavior to occur.
12. Vaginal or penile activity, in some fashion, is reported, Fellatio, cunnilingus, or anal activity may be a part of the incident.
13. Other paraphilia behaviors may be found to occur prior to, during, or after the sexual aggression.
14. The assault can be experimental, opportunistic, planned, preferential, sadistic, or situational in occurrence.
15. Family, job, or social functioning is impaired by the sexual aggression.

CHILD MOLESTATION TYPOLOGIES
AND TAXONOMIES

Several rape and child molestation profile outlines have emerged in research. Such profiles may be referred to as typologies or taxonomies. *Typology* refers to a group sharing common features. *Taxonomy* refers to a scientific classification. These typologies and taxonomies are used to define characteristics of sexual offending in a manner useful to those in the field in criminal justice, human service, and mental health professions, as well as those in academia and in research settings. Other reference groups for child victim assault are not listed as a particular typology or taxonomy category, but are used to identify specific sexual misconduct. There are many excellent assessment categories. To provide some reference for the reader, several of these profiles have been included for review.

Groth (1990) states that child molestation is a form of sexual activity in which the offender will hug, kiss, fondle, masturbate, suck, and touch the child victim in some inappropriate manner. Penetration does not occur. Developmentally, such individuals are, in many cases, at the same sexual maturation level as the child victim. Pedophilia is a disorder that can be found in both child molesters and rapists.

Groth's Patterns of Pedophilic Behavior

One of the first classifications on child molesters was developed by Groth (1978). Two groups were identified, which are listed as follows:

Fixated Offender

This offender is sexually attracted to children exclusively. The onset usually begins in adolescence and involves a compulsive type of mood. The offending is planned and is premeditated. Males are usually the primary target for such victimization. However, female victims are also targeted. The emphasis for this type of offender is in sexually stimulating the child and eliciting an erotic response. Such individuals are developmentally immature.

Regressed Offender

This offender has a sexual orientation that is primarily toward adults, with a sexual attraction to children during a temporary lapse. This type of offender has pedophilic interests that have emerged during adulthood. A precipitating stress usually is a contributing factor to the offense. Sexual incidents may be episodic, with the first offense as an impulsive reaction without premeditation. This offender sexually acts out to replace a conflicting adult age-specific peer. The child is used as a temporary substitution. The emphasis is sexual interaction, with the child being elevated to adult status. Alcohol is often used during such incidents.

Lanning's Situational and Preferential Child Molester Typology

Lanning (1992), in an updated analysis combining past research, outlines, primarily for law enforcement officers, a typology of child exploitation. This can also be of help to other disciplines (Lanning, 1992; Hazelwood et al., 1992; Knight and Prentky, 1990; National Center for Missing and Exploited Children, 1990; Lanning and Hazelwood, 1988; De Young, 1988; Abel et al., 1988; Abel et al., 1987; American Psychiatric Association, 1987; Hartman et al., 1984; Dietz, 1983; Groth et al., 1982; Groth, 1978).

Lanning (1992) reports that two separate categories of child offenders exist. These are listed as situational and preferential offenders.

The Situational Child Molester

Such offenders may experience one or more sexual encounters with a child or develop an extended relationship. Usually, only a limited number of victims are reported. Other victims may include the elderly, sick, or disabled. These offenders may be experiencing a particular psychosocial event that promotes their sexual aggression. There are four subgroups in this category, which include: regressed offenders; morally indiscriminate offenders; sexually indiscriminate offenders; and inadequate offenders.

Regressed offender. This type of offender will display sexual misconduct when under such stress as marital or job conflict. Others will offend after a drinking or drug use episode. A child may be selected to act as an alternative partner. Victim availability is important. Incest is often found. Such offenders may or may not use child pornography.

Morally indiscriminate offender. These offenders abuse as a lifestyle pattern. Sexual abuse is an enactment of their global view of life. Often a personality disorder is found. Such offenders may lie, cheat, and manipulate others. Few will demonstrate victim empathy or remorse for their actions. Spouse abuse is sometimes found. They can be involved in nonsexual criminal activity, molest without motivation, use force, and will lure victims with gifts. Violent or nonviolent methods to obtain a victim will occur. Some victims are strangers but incestuous relationships are also reported. Pornography and adult magazines can be found. Offenses are impulsive and reckless.

Sexually indiscriminate offender. Such offenders are sexual experimenters. Many will possess a paraphilic disturbance or features of a sexual addiction. These individuals are constantly in search of a new sexual experience and can be involved in affairs or spouse swapping. Others will have contact with prostitutes. They tend to be law abiding. Many are of a higher socioeconomic background. Most will collect pornography. Child sexual abuse occurs during the search for new experiences. Multiple victims can sometimes be found

Inadequate offender. Offenders may include those with a mental illness, mental retardation, a personality disorder, or some form of dementia. Other features include depression, self-isolating behaviors, impaired social skills, and poor personal hygiene. Victims may be either acquaintances or strangers. Such offenders tend to have multiple victims. Victim availability is important. Parks, playgrounds, and schools are areas used by such offenders to find and later assault children. Such individuals can appear childlike, harmless, or gentle in interaction. Some will live at home with elderly parents and are viewed by the community as social outcasts. Most are involved only in child molestation, but some have been involved in the death of a child.

Lanning (1992) reports that almost any child molester is capable of violence or even murder. However, the Federal Bureau of Investigation has found that those situational molesters most likely to be involved in the death of a child are either morally indiscriminate or inadequate offenders.

Preferential Child Molester

The preferential child molester possesses many features found in pedophilia-disordered individuals. Such persons report sexual fantasies, urges, and erotic imagery involving child victims. Many have a large number of victims. Child victims harmed by this offender group are largely boys. There are three subgroups: seduction offenders, introverted offenders, and sadistic offenders.

Seduction offender. This offender seduces children both emotionally and physically. Such offenders will engage in the grooming of victims. They will court a child in a romantic manner. Attention, affection, and gifts are used to lower the guard of a child. Victims are often from single-parent or dysfunctional home environments. Seduction offenders select children who are emotionally or physically neglected. Such offenders may engage in a number of concurrent relationships. Victim disclosure is highest during the termination stage. Threats of harm or physical violence to the victim may be used to protect the identity of the offender.

Introverted offender. Such offenders experience problems maintaining a relationship with an adult partner. Some may display courtship and intimacy deficits or general social skills problems. Victim selection will include preadolescent children or strangers. Exhibitionism behaviors and obscene telephone calls may be used by these offenders. Other paraphiliac behaviors may be found. Some offenders will develop a superficial relationship with a woman who has children in order to abuse them. Some will use child prostitutes. Erotic imagery, fantasy of children, and masturbation with child pornography is usually found.

Sadistic offender. Sadism, paraphiliac disturbances, and personality disorders are found in such offenders. Such perpetrators will use force to obtain access to a potential victim. Others will use lures such as gifts. Sexual arousal is based on the physical and psychological pain of a victim. These individuals lack victim empathy or remorse for their actions. Victims are viewed as objects for their sexual gratification and need. Behavioral traits include depersonalization. The sadistic child offender is the most likely of this subtype to kill a child. This sex offender is considered to be rare.

Knight and Prentky Typology of Child Molestation

This typology of sexual offending may be used for child molesters. Categories are determined by degree of fixation and amount of contact with the victim. Other sections are determined by offender types, which are divided into six behavioral types: interpersonal, narcissism, exploitation, muted sadism, nonsadistic aggression, and sadism. There are twenty-four cells to this evaluation scale.

RAPE TYPOLOGIES AND TAXONOMIES

Several typologies and taxonomies have developed in regard to the sex offender who rapes or sexually assaults an adult. These typologies and taxonomies are listed as follows.

Groth, Burgess, and Holmstrom (1977) Typology

Power Rape

Such rapists seek a form of power and control over their victims. Intimidation, physical force, weapons, or threat of bodily harm are included. The intention of this sexual assault is to have intercourse. Some victims are kidnaped, tied up, or made to feel helpless without a way to escape. Such offenders have experienced gender confusion or feelings of sexual inadequacy and are seeking reassurance. Assaults are usually preplanned. Behavior is anxiety driven, compulsive, fantasy oriented, and repetitive. There is no actual intention to harm the victim. Two subgroups of this type of sexual offender are described as follows.

Power-assertive rapist. This type of offender regards the rape as an expression of his masculinity, control, and dominance over the victim. The actual rape is a reflection, in part, of the individual's feelings of inadequacy, identity, and self-esteem. Such offenders will have distorted judgment, believing they possess a right to take a woman for sexual purposes.

Power-reassurance rapist. Such rapists will offend in an effort to counter thoughts about sexual problems or feelings. The intent is to place a female in a situation that is controlled, in which she will feel helpless without an opportunity to escape, and cannot resist expressed interest.

Anger Rapist

The behaviors may include anger, rage, contempt, and hatred for the victim. Offenses can include physical harm, beatings, sexual assault, degradation, or the use of excessive force. Anger rapists may use a more sadistic attack that will include tearing clothing off a victim, using profane and abusive language, and hitting the victim. Sexual assault is related to the rapist's rage at perceived rejections in life. Offenders will display little regard for the female as a person and have a history of conflict with women. Little sexual satisfaction is found. Two subgroups of this type of offender are said to exist.

The anger-retaliatory rapist. This type of offender commits sexual assault and rape to express anger, rage, and hostility toward women. Motivation includes revenge, degradation, and humiliation.

The anger-excitement rapist. This type of rapist finds erotic sexual pleasure in the suffering of others. Behavior is sadistic and intended to bring physical and psychological harm to the victim.

Hazelwood Rape Model

Hazelwood (1995) expanded upon the Groth, Burgess, and Holmstrom rape typology model as follows.

1. *Power-reassurance:* This type of offender possesses many of the common features of a sexually disordered person. There are feelings of inadequacy concerning sexual performance. Sexual dysfunction may be a problem. Issues regarding masculinity and sexual orientation are sometimes present. These offenders usually do not intend to harm their victims. Force is limited and is used only to gain submission. Most assaults occur during the evening or night. Attacks are preplanned. Victims are selected in advance and are of similar age to the offender. An apology may be offered regarding the assault. Strangers are the most

likely targets of such an attack. Clothing is often removed to incorporate a fantasy of willingness.

2. *Power-assertive:* Such offenders will use rape as an expression of their need to control and dominate a woman. A moderate level of force is used during the attack. There is no concern for the emotional state of the victim. Offenders tend to select female victims of similar age to themselves. The location of the rape is selected for isolation. Clothing may be torn or ripped as a part of the fantasy ensuring virility. Sexual acts may be repeated. To impair reporting, victims are sometimes left nude without transportation.

3. *Anger-retaliatory:* These offenders use rape as an expression of their anger toward women. The anger is openly displayed during the attack. Assaults may be impulsive and unplanned. Excessive force is used to overwhelm the victim quickly and to gain control of the situation. Victims may be the same age or older. Other victims may be selected to represent unresolved feelings of hostility with another female. Victim availability is a factor. Physical beatings may be a part of the assault. Clothing may be torn or ripped off the victim. Profanity is sometimes used. The offender will experience a sense of calmness following the assault.

4. *Anger-excitement:* Features of sadism are found in these rapists. Such persons obtain sexual pleasure by harming others. Arousal is dependent upon the physical and emotional suffering of the victim. Attacks are preplanned. Victims are usually strangers. The fear experienced by the victim is sexually exciting to the offender. Bondage and demeaning sexual acts are characteristic in such assaults. Victims are often physically harmed in some manner or tortured. The offender may record a part of the sexual assault. No victim empathy or remorse is expressed. This type of rapist is rare.

5. *Opportunistic:* This type of rape occurs while an offender is in the process of committing another crime, such as breaking and entering a home. Such an offender may discover a woman alone and then choose to sexually assault her. The motivation is sexual.

6. *Gang rape:* This type of offense occurs where two or more individuals are involved in the sexual assault of a victim. Usually such offenses have a leader; in cases where there are three or more offenders, one of the rapists may appear somewhat protective of the victim.

Hazelwood (1995) recommends that professionals use caution when using these groups for assessment purposes.

Barbaree and Marshall:
The Role of Male Sexual Arousal in Rape

Barbaree and Marshall (1991) reviewed sexual arousal in men during rape. Two separate groupings were identified, each with its own subtypes.

The Response Control Model

1. *Ability to suppress arousal:* Sexually aggressive males may differ from nonaggressive males by their inability to withhold feelings of arousal.
2. *Response Compatibility:* Rapists can demonstrate both hostile aggression and sexual arousal at the same time versus the reaction of a nonrapist.

The Stimulus Control Model

1. *The cue response:* Rapists show a stronger arousal to certain stimulus cues than nonrapists.
2. *Inhibition model:* Rapists may be less inhibited to stimuli than nonrapists.
3. *Disinhibition of arousal to rape stimuli:* Various factors may impact a rapist, triggering an arousal. Offenders use alcohol, have anger toward women, blame the victim, have a tendency to excuse himself for sexually assaultive behavior, are often exposed to pornography, and have a distorted belief system.
4. *Emotional state augmentation:* The rapist's behavior may vacillate including mood and increased or decreased arousal during the assault.

The MCT: 3 Taxonomy of Rape
by Knight and Prentky (1990)

This taxonomy is used for rape and is of similar design to the child molestation model. However, several differences exist for this model for rape, according to the authors. There are nine categories of rapists:

opportunistic with high social competence; opportunistic with low social competence; pervasively angry; sexual sadistic, overt; sexual sadistic, muted; sexual non-sadistic, high social competence; non-sadistic, low social competence; vindictive, low social competence; vindictive, moderate social competence.

RAPE AS A CRIMINAL DISTURBANCE

Rape as a criminal disturbance occurs on a regular basis within the United States, and is a universal phenomenon in all countries. Groth (1990) states that rape is a legal definition and not a diagnostic term. Rape is a disturbance that severely impacts the victim in both a psychological and physical way. Such a crime is significantly different from other crimes of violence, such as physical assault.

In the United States, only one in six rapes is reported to law enforcement. A rapist will average 7.2 offenses or acts; with the average number of victims totaling 7.0 persons. About 14 percent of women are raped by their spouses. In 1994, in the United States, one rape or sexual assault was reported for every 270 females in the general population. Rape is believed to be increasing four times faster than any other crime (Greenfeld, 1997; Poulos and Greenfield, 1994; Salhotz et al., 1990; Abel et al., 1987).

As a criminal act, Nadelson, Notman, and Carmen (1986) cite rape with the following characteristics:

> Rape has been defined as the act of taking anything by force. Most statutes in the United States define rape as carnal knowledge of a person against the will of the person. Two elements are necessary to constitute the crime: (1) sexual intercourse, and (2) failure to seek or obtain the consent of the victim. Neither complete penetration of the vagina by the penis nor emission of seminal fluid is necessary. Most rapes include force or violence applied to the victim in order to accomplish the act, but acquiescence can be obtained by verbal threat or other circumstances indicating lack of consent. (p. 339)

There are three major elements to a rape complaint during court trial. They are as follows:

1. *The identification of the accused.* The defense shall attempt to prove the defendant is not the offender. The victim has placed blame upon the wrong person.
2. *Penetration did or did not occur.* Medical evidence is crucial on this point. Both the prosecutor and defense attorney will argue the merits of this allegation.
3. *Consent.* That intercourse was granted by the woman to occur on a voluntary basis. Both the prosecutor and defense shall challenge and question witnesses in reference to this issue (Nadelson, Notman, and Carmen, 1986).

Crime Classification Manual (CCM)

The *Crime Classification Manual: A Standard System for Investigating and Classifying Violent Crimes* was published in 1992 by Douglas and colleagues. The manual was created to assist criminal justice and law enforcement officers in the assessment, arrest, and prosecution of violent offenders. Rape and sexual assault are included.

Douglas and colleagues (1992) note that assault includes offenses in which victims are forced, coerced, or manipulated into engaging in sexual activity. Violence may or may not occur. The definition or type of rape and sexual assault may vary by state; there are no universal definitions at the present time nationwide or globally. (This form of crime identification directly impacts statistical data.)

This manual may serve as a helpful guide for those not only in criminal justice, but also for others in human service and mental health. An index coding is used. Some of the CCM listings for rape and sexual assault are as follows.

300. Criminal Enterprise Rape

This type of sexual assault involves coercion, abuse, and assault for possessions, property, or profit:

301. Felony Rape

This type of sexual assault occurs during the act of a felony crime, such as robbery or breaking and entering.

301.01. Primary Felony Rape. This type of rape occurs during the commission of a nonsexual crime. The victim happens to be at the scene of the incident. Victims are usually adult females and are employed or residing at the place of the offense.

301.02. Secondary Felony Rape. The intent of the crime is rape, with a second criminal event occurring, such as robbery. The victim is usually an adult female.

310. Personal Cause Sexual Assault

This type of sexual assault occurs as a result of some type of psychological motive on the part of the offender. Material gain is not the motive.

311. Nuisance Offenses

The offense occurs as the result of the offender's plan for a sexual encounter. A feature of this type of offense is that no physical contact occurs between the offender and the designated victim. There are four subgroups.

311.01. Isolated/Opportunistic Offense. An individual makes a telephone call that turns out to be a wrong number and will curse. Another possible situation may be a person who urinates in a local park after drinking and is observed by a passerby.

311.02. Preferential Offense. This type of individual possesses a psychiatric disorder and sexual gratification is intended. Offenses may involve peeping and indecent exposure.

311.03. Transition Offense. This type of offender is usually young. Such offenders may be only exploring their sexuality and no additional incidents will occur. Peeping is typical.

311.04. Preliminary Offense. This type of sex offender may possess a fetish. During a house robbery, underwear is taken.

312. Domestic Sexual Assault

This type of sexual assault occurs among family members or those who share a dwelling. The incident may be spontaneous or situational. There are two subgroups.

312.01. Adult Domestic Sexual Assault. This type of sexual assault may occur between spouses or individuals involved in a live-in arrangement. Marital sexual assault is an example.

312.02. Child Domestic Sexual Abuse. This type of sexual assault is committed against a child by an adult within a domestic setting. Incest situations involving a child are an example.

313. Entitlement Rape

The victim is forced by the offender into some type of sexual activity. Issues of power and control are associated with this form of sexual assault. Excessive force or sadistic behaviors may be used. Victims may include adults, adolescents, and children. Police should be alert to:

1. Major injuries
2. Reported force by slapping, punching, or kicking
3. Acts of mutilation, burning, stabbing, vaginal or anal damage, insertion of a foreign object
4. Use of humiliation tactics, demeaning remarks, use of feces or urine, forcing of a male to observe incident, or evidence of forced fellatio and/or sodomy

313.01. Social Acquaintance Rape. A prior relationship between the offender and the victim has existed. A personal encounter precludes the assault, as a date, meeting with a friend. There are three subgroups: Adult 313.01.01; Adolescent 313.01.02; Child 313.01.03.

313.02. Subordinate Rape. There is a relationship between the victim and offender. One individual has authority over another. Situations may include student and teacher, police officer and citizen, physician and patient. There are three subgroups: Adult 313.02.01; Adolescent 313.02.02; Child 313.02.03.

313.03. Power-Reassurance Rape. (Please refer to earlier information in chapter.) There are three subgroups which are as follows: Adult 313.03.01; Adolescent 313.03.02; Child 313.03.03.

313.04. Exploitative Rape. An opportunistic sexual assault, involves force which is limited to need, and the offender often does not know the victim. Victims may be adult, adolescent, or child. Acts are often impulsive with little planning. Substance abuse is common among such offenders. Subgroups are: Adult 313.04.01; Adolescent 313.04.02; Child 313.04.03.

314. Anger Rape

(Please refer to earlier chapter information.) Subgroups may include: Gender 314.01; Age 314.02; 314.02.01 Elderly victim; 314.02.02 Child victim; Racial 314.03; Global 314.04. Anger issues are related to this type of assault.

315. Sadistic Rape

(Please refer to current and other chapter information). Subgroups include: Adult 315.01; Adolescent 315.02; Child 315.03. Sadism behavior is exhibited by this offender.

316. Child/Adolescent Pornography

This individual is defined as a collector. Such persons gather, collect, save, maintain, and value pornography that involves children and adolescents depicted in various states of dress, nudity, and sexual activity. Subgroups are listed as follows.

316.01. Closet Collector. The closet collector possesses an interest in child and adolescent pornography. However, such persons will keep their interest a secret.

316.02. Isolated Collector. Such individuals may qualify to meet the clinical criteria for pedophilia. These offenders collect pornography but also engage in sexual activity with children, usually one victim at a time. Victims may include family or neighborhood children.

316.03. Cottage Collector. This type of sexual offender is a pedophile who sexually uses children by way of pornography. Profit is not the central driving force for such individuals. The sharing of child and adolescent pornography with other collectors is a significant factor for such persons. Cottage collectors may work alone or in a group. Their belief system is impaired, and they are of the opinion that children are not victimized.

317. Historical Child/Adolescent Sex Rings

Children and adolescents are used by such groups to make private or commercial photographs, movies, and videos. Such materials are explicit and involve children and adolescents in sexual behaviors or activities.

317.01. Solo Child Sex Ring. An adult will head such a ring, usually a male, who uses victims for illegal sexual behaviors. Victims usually know one another or are aware of one another's existence. The children are encouraged to provide sexual services in exchange for food, shelter, money, or emotional or social support.

317.02. Transitional Child Sex Ring. This type of child sex ring involves more than one offender with multiple victims. The offenders are known to one another and in many cases share the victims. Usually, victims in transitional child sex rings are preadolescent. Children are used and groomed for prostitution. Children are initiated into this type of child sex ring usually by the following means:

1. By pedophiles who have lost interest in a particular child
2. As incest victims who have fled their homes as a runaway
3. From dysfunctional homes with little parental supervision or interest
4. Abducted and missing children

In sex rings, police investigators are encouraged to look for the following evidence:

1. Usually, the offenders will keep most of their personal pornography of victims in their own homes.
2. Finding various cameras, videos, and tapes may be a lead that some type of victimization has occurred.
3. Crime scenes may include the offender's residence, a vehicle, a designated meeting place, or hotel and motels that are considered low risks.
4. Victim marking, including vaginal and anal scarring, bruises, abrasions, skin tears, with possible sexually transmitted diseases.
5. Victims are often fearful; harm or threats have occurred.

317.03. Syndicated Child Sex Ring. A syndicated child sex ring is a structured group organization that is supervised by one or more leaders. The purpose of such a group is for the recruitment of children, the making of pornography, delivery of sexual services, and keeping customers. Such rings include multiple victims.

318. Multidimensional Sex Rings

This type of ring may be the most difficult and complex for law enforcement officers to investigate. Such rings appear to have four components in common:

1. Multiple young victims
2. Multiple offenders
3. Fear as the controlling factor
4. Bizarre and/or ritualistic-like behaviors

318.01. Adult Survivor Sex Ring. During therapy, it is learned that a patient was once sexually abused and was involved in a group practicing some type of sexual abuse. Reporting victims are usually adults and female.

318.02. Day Care Sex Rings. Sexual abuse has been reported involving day care centers. Victims are multiple in number. Offenders may also be multiple in number. Such cases, when found, involve children of preschool age. Fear and bizarre behaviors with rituals are often associated with this type of sexual offending.

318.03. Family/Isolated Neighborhood Sex Rings. In family and isolated neighborhood sex rings, children are usually the reported victims. There may be multiple offenders. Crime scene locations may include apartments, remote communities, and isolated rural settings.

318.04. Custody/Visitation Dispute Sex Rings. This type of report occurs during a custody dispute when one parent or other person is alleged to have sexually abused the child.

319. Abduction Rape

An abduction rape occurs if victims are forced against their will from a location and are sexually assaulted. An abduction occurs if a person is coerced, threatened, forced, held in detention, moved by vehicle, and/or is ransomed. Subgroups are: Adult 319.01; Adolescent 319.02; Child 319.03.

330. Group Cause Sexual Assault

This type of sexual assault occurs when there are three or more offenders. Group dynamics may be a factor in this type of rape.

331. Formal Gang Sexual Assault

A gang is defined as an organized group of individuals. Such gangs will share a mutual goal, mission, or reason for existence. Subgroups are: Single victim 331.01; Multiple victims 331.02.

332. Informal Gang Sexual Assault

This type of gang is loosely structured, without specific goals or a reason for existence. Such gangs may have formed rather quickly. Subcategories are Single victim 332.01; Multiple victims 332.02.

390. Sexual Assault Not Classified Elsewhere. This category is used for sexual assault incidents that are not found in other sections.

Chapter 8

Sex Offender Characteristics

Today, sex offenders are found to cross all diagnostic and demographic groupings. Such individuals may be family members, neighbors, or acquaintances, rather than strangers to the victims. Age, race, gender, employment status, income, religious affiliation, sexual preference, and criminal history may not always serve as a possible variable in assessing sexual deviancy.

Nonetheless, Whitaker and Wodarski (1989) correctly point out that the general consensus of the mental health community is that sex offenders do not form a homogeneous group; they are a combined heterogenous population of several groups of persons, each of whom represents some type of abnormal sexual behavior which is harmful to another person.

Clinically, this assessment is attractive, but the premise sometimes impairs and often confuses professionals in criminal justice, human service, and health care in assessment, intervention, and treatment program modality development. Sexual disorders, like any clinical problem such as substance abuse or a thought disorder, possess many subgroups or specific problem features.

Today, research is beginning to identify certain behaviors that can be directly correlated with a particular sexual disturbance. As with most problems, when sexual disorders are examined closely in a scientific context, they tend to lose a certain amount of their mystery. More material is expected to surface as further study occurs with sex offenders. Evidence supports that certain basic characteristics or behaviors may be found in sex offenders as a group. These generalizations appear worthy of examination and review.

SEX OFFENDERS VIOLATE LAW

First, sex offenders share one very important characteristic: they have committed a sexual act that violates law. Sexual offending is a criminal action that interferes with the rights of another. The victim of the offense was found to be unwilling or was incapable due to age or mental capacity to provide consent at the time of the event.

Offenders are usually first identified by the type of sexual crimes they have committed. Crime classifications, depending upon the offense, may range from severe forms of sexual assault to more covert and nonphysical behaviors.

Sexual incidents involving children, forcible rape, or exhibitionistic acts are examples of actions that well exceed accepted forms of appropriate sexual conduct and are considered violations of law. Some offenders who commit highly visible crimes are quickly arrested; others avoid apprehension for years. The more covert may avoid disclosure indefinitely. Most sex offenders have committed multiple crimes prior to their first arrest.

Knopp (1984) emphasizes that the criminal justice system occupies a significant role in who is determined to have committed a sexual crime and how they are processed through the system. This method can differ dramatically in law from state to state as to who is arrested, prosecuted, incarcerated, and/or is referred to treatment services. Social and cultural attitudes can influence a society's tolerance level for certain types of sexual behaviors and whether they are considered a criminal offense. An example of this mixed message is reflected by the age of consent to marry. Certain states permit minors to marry, while other states restrict marriages with an age limitation and consider consensual sexual relations between a minor and an adult to be unlawful.

Sex Offenders As a Visible and Growing Population

Sex offenders are a visible and growing population. As noted in Chapter 2, according to Greenfeld (1997), about 234,000 sex offenders are in some type of correctional care. These figures do not account for offenders who have been released from prison, those who are on probation or parole, or those who have escaped prosecution. Using a conservative measurement, during the next decade the criminal justice system can expect to provide services for more than 2 million sex offenders. Also, the sex offender population is growing at a rapid rate within the penal system. This population group alone has grown in state prisons by 330 percent since 1980. Such a rapid increase in itself may not present concern. However, given the fact that each one of these offenders has probably harmed on multiple occasions presents significant issues for community safety and the protection of future victims.

THE SEX OFFENDER PSYCHOLOGICAL PROFILE

Sex Offenders Are Different

O'Connell, Leberg, and Donaldson (1990) report that sex offenders are different from other types of psychotherapy patients. Most persons who enter therapy do so to resolve a problem or conflict that is impairing them in some manner. Such individuals are motivated to receive treatment services. However, most sex offenders do not seek help on a voluntary basis; instead they enter therapy as the result of an external stimulus, such as the decree of the court or probation officer, the fear of incarceration, or the opportunity for parole. It is extremely rare for a sex offender to reveal their deviancy on their own without outside pressures. Many sex offenders do not see themselves as being a danger to others. They often report during interviews that they had no plan to harm children and that it just happened. Sex offenders will attempt to hide behind the trappings of their family, job, and position within the local community. Some offenders distort reality to the extent that they themselves begin to believe that the offense did not occur.

Sex Offenders Possess Multiple Paraphilias

Research has found that most sex offenders possess multiple paraphiliac behaviors. This information is helpful for the mental health professional who has been asked to complete an evaluation of an offender.

As discussed in Chapter 6, Abel and colleagues (1988) found that only 10.1 percent of paraphilia-disordered individuals had one diagnosis; most were afflicted by two or more paraphilias.

Many sexual offenders can possess a passive-like disorder, such as a fetish, that does not directly lead to a situation of assault. However, this same individual may also suffer from pedophilia and will sexually molest children. Such an individual, for example, may use children's underwear, taken during a prior offense, as a part of a fantasy and masturbation process. However, the pedophile's urge to reoffend will grow as the fantasy diminishes. Another victim is then selected and seduced in some fashion by the offender. To enrich the continuation of the fantasy process, the new victim's underwear is taken by the offender.

Sex Offenders and Onset

The majority of reported paraphilia disturbances are said to have started during childhood or adolescence. Reportedly more than 50 percent of all paraphilias, regardless of diagnostic category, began before age eighteen (Abel, 1989).

A significant incident—psychosocial stressor—may have occurred during the offender's childhood. This event may have been extremely traumatic for the offender, who may have been sexually abused as a child. Less severe examples may include an accidental encounter with a couple engaged in sexual intercourse, inappropriate sexual boundaries between parents, or an erotic experience that is sexually deviant, such as finding a magazine that displays women in a degrading and abusive manner.

The fantasies and behaviors associated with paraphilias may have their beginnings in childhood, but they become more defined and elaborate during adolescence and early adulthood. The reenactment of fantasies will become even more advanced in adulthood and may last over the course of an individual's lifetime (American Psychiatric Association, 1994).

Sex Offenders As Victims

Research continues to reveal that offenders have experienced sexual trauma in some form during their formative years. In early studies, Groth (1990) noted that approximately one-third of rapists and child molesters had experienced some type of sexual trauma as a child. However, it was suspected that this number was rather conservative. In a more recent survey, Greenberg, Bradford, and Curry

(1993) found that more than 40 percent of pedophiles and hebephiles had been victims of childhood sexual abuse.

Most practicing clinicians have long suspected a connection between childhood sexual abuse and sex offending. The offender's crimes may be viewed as a form of reenactment of their own sexual abuse. However, there continues to be some disagreement of the magnitude of this problem among researchers. The validity of offenders presenting accurate or misleading information is of concern. A part of this research struggle may represent, in part, the conflict about sex offenders in society. The percentage of those offenders who were sexually abused is expected to continue to be a subject of debate.

Education and Employment

Many sex offenders are well educated and gainfully employed. In one study of 561 sex offenders, approximately 26 percent had graduated from high school, 21.1 percent had attended one year of college, 12.2 percent had graduated from college, and 7.6 percent had finished graduate school. Also, this same study found that 64.6 percent were fully employed or attending school. Only 9.3 percent were temporarily unemployed; 11.1 percent were unemployed more than one month (Abel et al., 1987).

Such findings are contrary to the stereotypes that have emerged regarding sex offenders. The image of a sex offender who is unemployed, has little education, and is socially impaired appears to be unfounded by clinical study results.

Sex Offenders and Relationships

Professionals should be careful about making hasty assessments involving sex offenders and relationships. A number of offenders are either married or involved in a serious relationship with an adult companion. This information challenges former stereotypes of sex offenders who once were imagined to be rather disheveled and inadequate persons who were unable to form relationships with an adult partner. A sex offender with a paraphilia disturbance may present as a paradox.

During a survey in 1987, (please refer to Chapter 6), approximately 50 percent of all sex offenders interviewed were found to be married or involved in a significant relationship (Abel et al., 1987). All sexual offenses were represented in this study of offenders, including such clinical disturbances as exhibitionism, fetishism, frotteurism, pedophilia, sexual masochism, sexual sadism, transvestic fetishism, voyeurism, other paraphilias, and those with a history of rape.

In addition, persons with a paraphilia disorder can also perform sexually in a nonparaphiliac manner. It was once assumed if an offender suffered from a particular sexual disorder, he or she was unable to engage in more acceptable forms of sexual activity. Most individuals can perform sexually without the use of paraphilia acts or related behaviors (Abel, 1989).

Victim Empathy

Sex offenders are emotionally distant individuals who are unable to relate with others on an intimate basis. Most offenders display a lack of concern or empathy for their victims.

Groth (1990) reports that the rapist's most prominent defect is the absence of any close, emotionally intimate relationships with another person. Such impaired individuals show little capacity for warmth, trust, compassion, or empathy. Relationships among sex offenders are usually found to be without mutuality, reciprocity, or a sense of sharing.

Hildebran and Pithers (1989) note that sex offenders tend to display resistance even to developing victim empathy. Two factors are found to be significant to this phenomenon. First, the sex offenders are reluctant to stop fantasies that have been a source of pleasure for a number of years. Second, offenders may be seen as emotionally underdeveloped persons.

O'Connell, Leberg, and Donaldson (1990) report that it is rare to find a sex offender who initially displays empathy for his or her victim. Most therapists consider victim empathy a key element in the treatment process of sex offenders. Individuals who are unable to develop empathy remain at risk to reoffend. However, the prospect of developing empathy can also trigger fear, humiliation, and shame in many sex offenders, which are similar feelings that the offenders created in their victims. Learning empathy, therefore, can be a rather frightening or difficult experience for an offender.

SEX OFFENDERS AND THEIR CRIMES

Truthfulness and Honesty

Sex offenders often experience difficulty being truthful. This is one of the most common characteristics or behaviors found in offenders. Most criminal justice, human service, and mental health professionals cite this as a typical behavior found among sex offenders.

O'Connell, Leberg, and Donaldson (1990) report that sexual offenders usually are not willing to reveal information about their deviant actions. Such individuals have developed a set of defense mechanisms with which they will hide the truth and have become extremely adept at concealing information. It is rare for sexual offenders to report their sexual abuse of others voluntarily. Naturally, many fear their actions will lead to involvement with the criminal justice system. Offenders fear intervention, prosecution, and incarceration; others express social, familial, and occupational concerns.

Equally important during the treatment process is the need for an offender to be honest about his behavior. A program of treatment is dependent upon offenders developing the ability to be honest with themselves and others. Many sex offenders have spent years lying to and misleading others. As a result, such individuals are also dishonest with themselves. Some will display this behavior by lying about an incident that could result in a reoffending situation.

Truthfulness and issues of honesty can be an ongoing problem for a sex offender even after he or she has admitted to the offense. Reality checks should be made on a fairly regular basis. An initial evaluation is important.

Acknowledgment and Responsibility

Almost all sex offenders will display a reluctance to acknowledge that an act of sexual abuse occurred. This should not be confused with the above category of truthfulness.

O'Connell, Leberg, and Donaldson (1990) report that the offenders' reluctance to acknowledge the offense is a defense mechanism used to avoid admitting that a criminal sexual act did occur. Offenders are typically resistant to acknowledging the full nature and extent of the deviant behavior. However, treatment can begin only when the sex offender is willing to acknowledge that a sexual offense occurred. Treatment must then focus on helping offenders acknowledge that: (1) the problem is related to their behavior, (2) it has caused the victim harm, and (3) they gave permission to themselves to offend.

Offenders who are unwilling to acknowledge their behavior cannot be treated successfully. As with most disorders, the patient must first accept the illness in order to begin to recover. A patient who denies a clinical disturbance possesses a poor prognosis for recovery. Accepting responsibility for behavior is an important element when working with sex offenders. The offender may acknowledge the sexual event but qualify his or her behavior by blaming the victim. An example would be offenders who complain that their abuse was produced by the provocative clothing worn by a child—excuses made in an effort to rationalize their deviancy.

Denial, Minimization, and Rationalization

Denial, minimization, and rationalization are three behaviors that a therapist should be alert to when treating a sex offender. These behaviors are part of the defense mechanism system and should be viewed separately from the section on acknowledgment.

However, like acknowledgment, sex offenders who deny their offenses are not likely to benefit from therapy. Treatment cannot be of value for such offenders. An offender must admit to the offense in order to benefit from treatment services (O'Connell, Leberg, and Donaldson, 1990).

An offender who minimizes or gives only token acknowledgment of the crimes will be difficult to treat. Offenders who on occasion justify, excuse, or rationalize their behavior can be used to an advantage in a treatment setting. Such offenders are admitting, in a limited manner, that a sexual offense did occur. However, such behavior, if not resolved, will impair the treatment and the offender will remain at risk to reoffend.

Offenders who deny that a sex offense has occurred are at risk to reoffend if permitted to remain in the community. A more controlled environment may be more appropriate for such offenders. Incarceration should also be a consideration.

Defense Reactions

Lanning (1992) notes that pedophiles will display several predictable behaviors when confronted about an abuse case. These reactions include denial; minimization; justification; fabrication; mental illness; sympathy; attack; guilty, but not guilty; after conviction; and suicide. They are (in part) as follows:

1. *Denial:* Typically, a sex offender first denies the allegation and may appear astonished, confused, shocked, or even angry about the report. Family, friends, co-workers, or others may be used to avoid arrest.
2. *Minimization:* An offender may attempt to rationalize or minimize the assault when the evidence against him or her rules out denial. The type of crime and number of offenses may be distorted.
3. *Justification:* Child offenders will develop a rationalization system and believe that their behavior is misunderstood and that they are moral, caring persons.
4. *Fabrication:* Some offenders invent stories to explain their behavior in an effort to hide the sexual abuse. Fabrication may include such reports as conducting a scientific study on children or teaching a child about sex.
5. *Mental illness:* A child molester may report a mental illness if other attempts to avoid arrest fail. (Lanning cites a disclaimer regarding a cautionary statement about the use of diagnostic categories. *The Diagnostic and Statistical Manual of Mental Disorders, Fourth Edition Text Revision,* by the American Psychiatric Association [2000], may serve as a reference.)
6. *Sympathy:* Offenders using this defense technique will display regret while noting their familial, civic, and community achievements and their own unrelated personal problems.

7. *Attack:* The offender may develop a defense plan that includes a personal attack as an offense. A pedophile, for instance, may harass, threaten, or even bribe victims and witnesses, while attacking the reputations of the case professionals.

8. *Guilty, but not guilty:* A plea bargain agreement is offered by the pedophile and defense counsel to avoid trial. The court may order a sentence, although the offender maintains innocence. This may vary from state to state. Such an arrangement can impact sentencing, treatment, and community safety. (An Alford plea permits an offender to plead guilty without making an admission to the crime; "Nolo contrendene" permits a plea of "guilty, but not guilty" to avoid civil action.)

9. *After conviction:* New information may be offered by a child offender (as another form of reaction) to law enforcement officers after a conviction regarding other molesters and crimes involving children. A polygraph test may be appropriate.

10. *Suicide:* A serious reaction in certain cases involving middle-class offenders is the risk of suicide attempt at any time after the arrest or court hearing.

OTHER BEHAVIORAL CHARACTERISTICS

A number of other behavioral characteristics in sex offenders are noted by the clinical and research community. These are listed as follows:

1. Sex offenders usually possess a very rich fantasy life. Masturbation is usually reported as a part of the offender's sexual activity. Nearly all sexual offenders in treatment report being sexually aroused by fantasies of their current or past deviant activities, which they reenact during masturbation (Abel, 1989).

2. Sex offenders evolve or graduate in their style of sexual aggression. Paraphiliac behavior is found to be pleasurable and is likely to be repeated if no consequence occurs (Abel, 1989).

3. Sex offenders who possess a history of substance abuse are more likely to offend when using alcohol or drugs. More than

40 percent of rapists have substance abuse problems (Groth, 1990).

4. Typically, sex offenders derive some pleasure from their sexual deviancy. Many have developed impaired forms of sexual expression that are a part of their lifestyle and commit acts of abuse because it makes them feel good (O'Connell, Leberg, and Donaldson, 1990).

5. Adult and child offenders display a lack of insight and judgment. Often they are unable to understand the full harm and consequence of their sexual aggression (Groth, 1990).

6. Approximately 56 percent of all rapists in one survey were found to have some type of personality disorder (Groth, 1990).

7. Rapists sometimes display problems with impulse control and a distorted belief system as well as a need for instant self-gratification (Groth, 1990).

8. Sex offenders, including rapists, often view persons as objects, which is a form of depersonalization (Groth, 1990).

9. Sex offenders (paraphiliacs) are usually male (Abel, 1989); women sex offenders are an increasing clinical population (Mayer, 1992).

10. Rapists often display a pattern of reckless behavior as their deviancy progresses. Many fail to consider the consequences of their actions and will act many times without thinking (Groth, 1990).

11. Sex offenders possess histories of disordered family systems. In general, the more dysfunctional the childhood experience, the more severe or problematic the paraphilia (Meyer, 1995).

12. Sex offenders who experience a reduction in their testosterone levels can display improved behaviors with less acting out (Meyer, 1995).

A SEXUAL OFFENSE CHAIN

A sexual offense chain displays common behaviors exhibited by offenders in periods before, during, and after an offense. Such information is helpful when working with a sex offender. A number of excellent diagrams have evolved through the years outlining possible sexual abuse cycles or scenarios. One of the most recent models and useful diagrams to be released is by Eccles and Marshall (1999). Based upon the relapse prevention and cognitive behavioral diagrams, an offense chain for sexual offenders is summarized as follows:

1. There is an offense-free mood state.
2. An event occurs in some form, and several possible incidents happen, such as seeing oneself as a victim.
3. There is a feeling of entitlement or right to sexual pleasure; the individual starts to regress.
4. Positive thoughts about offending are found.
5. High-risk behaviors and deviant fantasies begin.
6. Cognitive distorted thinking is reported (e.g., a woman deserves to be raped, a child is sexually provocative).
7. The individual makes victim contact and enters a cognitively distorted mood state.
8. He or she sexually offends a victim.
9. The offender engages in qualification and rationalization of the crime.

Chapter 9

Theory and Treatment

Many theories discuss what may have caused a paraphiliac disturbance to develop in an individual. Aberrant sexual behavior is a complicated developmental process and is unique to each person. Behavioral, biological, familial, environmental, and social influences all may be considered factors

Criminal justice, human services, and mental health professionals are willing to offer intervention services, but remain unsure as to what is in the best interests of the community, victim, and offender. This confusion is further muddled by unclear intervention guidelines. Should persons with a paraphiliac disorder be treated, punished, or both? Law, in the United States, has historically held wrongdoers accountable. However, unless society is prepared to incarcerate all those who have committed a sexual crime on an indefinite basis, treatment programs appear to be merited. Such a philosophy demonstrates a planned effort to limit future victims while helping those who offend to change.

Reid (1997) suggests that it may be practical to distinguish those paraphilias which do not intrude upon the wishes of others, as in fetishism, from those which intrude but are nonviolent, as in exhibitionism, and from those which are both intrusive and aggressive to others, as in pedophilia.

Patients who exhibit sexual aggression, such as in child molestation and rape, may often possess other problem disorders of impulse control or antisocial behavior. Clinically, certain persons may never be receptive to treatment services, while others are open to assistance. Research has started to emerge in the areas of biological, neurological, and organic influences. Some other areas of study include behavioral and psychosocial factors. This chapter is about theory, what influences sexual aggression, and available models of treatment.

THEORY AND SEXUAL ASSAULT

Schwartz (1995c) notes that a dynamic action occurs in sexual assault. Two elements are key components for abuse, as well as for any criminal act. The first is motive; the second is a releaser, which allows the motive to bypass accepted cultural, personal, and societal laws and be expressed in an improper manner. Such a hypothesis can be helpful when working with sex offenders and providing treatment services. Motivation can include a distorted system of beliefs, values, thoughts, feelings, and behaviors. Such a system then sets the stage for the offender, who eventually decides to act out his or her sexual issues, regardless of the consequence; he or she then violates the rights of others and the law.

A number of theories have evolved in recent years. Currently, there are almost 1,600 specialized programs based upon a particular theoretical perspective. Theories can be found in addictions, anthropological, cognitive-behavioral, evolutionary, ego psychological, Jungian, neurosis, political, psychoanalytical, relational, relapse preventional, and societal studies, as well as in many other areas.

Schwartz (1995c) has summarized several of these theories. Some of these are as follows.

Addictions Theories

Sexual addiction theories have ties with substance abuse and the addictive process. Sexual addiction is described as a dysfunction in which the individual exhibits reckless, out-of-control, self-destructive behavior, with disregard to consequence and inability to stop the inappropriate action. There is an ongoing desire and promise to limit the behavior, such as with alcoholics or drug abusers, but the individual is compulsive and driven to continue to have sexual encounters. There can be a marked mood change, preoccupation with obtaining sex, and social, occupational, and familial impairment. Both men and women may suffer from this problem, although the majority of sexual addicts are male.

Anthropological Theories

Each culture has defined behaviors that are sexually appropriate or deviant. In the United States, laws vary even by state as to what may constitute a sexual offense. For instance, laws pertaining to adultery, fornication, indecent liberties with a minor, incest, marriage to a minor, sexual battery, sodomy, sex between relatives, and rape may differ widely by state. There is no known sexual behavior that has not been endorsed by some society or culture in time. Prostitution, allowed in parts of Nevada, is illegal elsewhere in the United States. Nonetheless, many European countries lawfully permit prostitution within certain restricted areas. Also, European countries covertly endorse extramarital relationships for men as long as they are discreet in their affairs. In Australia and the New Hebrides islands, certain tribes approve of homosexual relations between adults and male children. In New Guinea, ceremonies involving homosexual conduct as well as marriage to preadolescent brides is permitted. The Caroline Islands natives are reported to permit senile men to enlarge the genitals of prepubescent females to enhance sexual performance. In several Middle Eastern and Indian cultures, a man may have more than one wife. Tibetan culture allows multiple husbands. Certain religious groups have approved of more than one mate.

Behavioral Theories

Behavior theories are concerned with problems and how those inappropriate actions can be resolved with specific defined goals of help. Sexual deviation is a learned behavior, according to theorists. An example may be a certain sexual interaction for an individual. If the behavior is deviant in action, it can then be reenacted during future sexually related events. Masturbation and fantasy can be a part of the reenactment. Eventually, if the deviant acts are repeated on a regular basis, a paraphilia is likely to emerge, according to behavioral theory. Sexual activity becomes distorted as the deviancy continues and more inappropriate forms of sexual activity occur. Deviation may be the result of classical conditioning. Trauma may be the result of sexual activity being displayed in a repetitious form. Psychological and related problem behavior can be related to sexual assault or molestation during childhood. Covert seduction by a parent or close acquaintance can impact the sexual development process. Operant conditioning may contribute to the learning of sexually inappropriate behavior, such as in a child who is sexually abused on a repeated basis and is brought to climax; this behavior can being imprinted upon the psyche. As a result, operant conditioning may contribute to the learning of sexually inappropriate behaviors. Modeling can also influence sexual behavior. A child raised in an incestuous environment may later display such behavior in a similar manner.

Biological Theories

Recent research has started to closely examine the significance of biological, neurological, and organic factors influencing deviant behavior. Sexual aggression may be related, in part, to head injury, obsessive-compulsive factors, problems of mental illness, organic problems, seizure disorder, testosterone level, and other biological factors. Trauma may also be found to be a contributing factor in changing the brain in a manner that can influence sexual acting out. Offenders who were sexually abused as children is one example. Some have experienced symptoms of post traumatic stress disorders. PTSD has been largely overlooked as a factor influencing sexual aggression in sex offenders. The trauma impacts the deviant thought process and fantasy system. Fantasies stored in the visual cortex can become vivid and sexually arousing. Also, the temporal lobes, limbic system, and hippocampus may contribute to the fantasy system for offenders. A high testosterone level in males may produce aggression. Persons with a family history of sexual deviancy may be more at risk to offend, but it is presently unknown if this is a learned or genetic trait.

Cognitive-Behavioral Theories

Cognitive-behavioral theories are involved in working with people on a here-and-now basis. Such theories promote the identification of specific problems and how to resolve them within a short period. The treatment is directive and focused upon finding a solution to enhance the quality of life. These theories emphasize how a patient may use negative thoughts on a recurring basis to impact mood and depression. Sex offenders often display a history of negative self-perpetuating thoughts that influence behavior. A distorted way of viewing life will develop, which includes justification or minimization. Some offenders will develop a sense of entitlement and will rationalize their actions. Cognitive-behavioral treatment promotes therapists to examine the sex offender's impaired thought process, define the problem, and identify specific goals for resolution. This approach encourages the identification of the presenting problem, exploration of the offender's thought process, definition of goals, and resolution.

Ego Psychology Theories

Ego psychology theories emphasize a person's ability to resolve problems and develop appropriate strengths to cope with social realities. Sex offenders have failed to achieve the normal stages of development: their ego system is fractured. A cognitive distortion of beliefs is present and, as a result, sexual misconceptions may appear. The superego does not provide the ego with a proper values and moral system. As a result, the id emerges and promotes primitive urges to surface. Sexual perversions are permitted to develop because the superego fails to offer guidance and direction to the ego. Offenders with paraphiliac behaviors will permit themselves to act in an impulsive manner. To violate another sexually is approved by their faulty ego system. Sex offenders often display reckless and dangerous sexual behavior. Ego psychology theorists emphasize the lack of control in such individuals who fail to evaluate the consequences of their actions or the impact that sexual aggression will have on victims.

Evolutionary Theories

Evolutionary theories, which are related to other perspectives, are rather controversial in approach—defining sexual aggression as a form of reflex and instinctual urge to procreate. Rape, for example, may be viewed as a sexual act to pass on the genes of a species. Therefore, males will seek out available opportunities to have sexual intercourse with females. These theories are considered obsolete by feminists and are inappropriate when assessing a child molester. Humans, by these theories, are considered members of the animal kingdom and may retain certain biological programs of behavior. Evolutionary theory has impacted other models from addictions to societal treatment approaches.

Family Theories

Research has examined the role of the family and sexual deviance. Theorists note that the physical and psychological trauma for a child growing up within an incestuous home will certainly impact sexual development. Some difference of theory exists as to whether the sexual deviancy may be viewed only within the context of the immediate family or the family of origin structure. In addition, there is a difference of opinion as to whether the inappropriate sexual behavior should be viewed in terms of the pathology of the individual who offends or in terms of a sexually dysfunctional family system. An illustration may be a child who sexually abuses a sibling. The question is: Do we consider the pathology to be within that person or is he or she the product of a dysfunctional family? Family therapy views one member's actions as an extension of the whole system.

Jungian Theories

The goal of Jungian theory is to help one find an acceptable lifestyle that enhances creativity. The apex for this theory is individuation, in which a person is able to develop their own special identity through growth in life. Such development will permit the individual to change. The unconscious process is important in this theory. Archetypes representing universal symbols, such as the mother and father, are of significance. A form of conflict may emerge during the development process if one is presented with an experience that challenges the archetypes expectations. Incest by a seductive parent with a child destroys or impairs the sacred role of the mother or father. Incest is taboo in most cultures and impacts the growth of the child and his or her sexual development. Incest may lead to deviant behavior in the child, including sexual aggression and paraphilias. In this theory, *phallos,* a masculine symbol of the penis, will commit acts of sexual assault and destruction without *eros,* the feminine features representative of love and integrity. Therefore, an offender can display sexual aggression without remorse. In this theory, the individual will remain unaware of his or her incompleteness and impaired ability to secure an appropriate love relationship. Without treatment, offenses may occur.

Neurosis Theories

Although *neurosis* is an outdated term in traditional psychoanalytic work, the theory is still of significance to those learning about sex offenders. *Neurosis* is a term used to define features of anxiety, excessive fear, nervousness, irritability, and other similar problem behaviors. A perversion or deviant act provides some possible relief of distress to a sex offender. Notwithstanding, the action still produces conflict in the individual. Sexually deviant acts may be seen as a part of the neurotic process related to personality disturbance. As a result, although the need for gratification may be fulfilled by a man who exposes his genitals, conflict and feelings of inferiority and insecurity continue to exist. A pedophile may offend, but his deviancy and impaired ego structure will continue to cause perpetuating feelings of inadequacy.

Psychoanalytic Theories

A paraphiliac may be viewed as an individual who has failed to achieve the developmental process of maturation within psychoanalytical theories. As a result, a certain level of anxiety evolves and a sexual perversion develops, providing an outlet for sexual and aggressive behaviors, thoughts, and feelings. Basically, this anxiety is transformed to the fear of castration. Boys discover they are different from girls and are frightened by the possible removal of their penis by the jealous and threatened father. To cope with a seductive mother, certain persons may attempt to preserve their childhood by way of anxiety and phobias. Individuals who have been reared by such mothers may develop certain paraphiliac behaviors to displace their anxiety. For instance, a male who develops transvestism behaviors and enjoys dressing in female attire may be regarded as expressing his unresolved feelings about his mother. Indecent exposure situations and window peeping may be observed as suppressed anxiety about castration, through the display of genitalia. The symbolism of a particular object that is sexualized by a person with a fetish may be viewed as an attempt to calm anxiety by displacing sexual impulses to other items. These theories focus upon the importance of anxiety and how certain perversions develop, thus providing an outlet for sexual aggression, thoughts, and feelings.

Political Theories

The feminist movement has had a strong impact upon sexual behavior. Until the 1970s, many forms of abuse, including child molestation, sexual assault, and rape were recurrently minimized in the

United States. The feminist movement brought forth a new examination of sexual abuse and the extreme trauma that victims experience. In the past, the victim of a rape was often blamed and her past sexual history was permitted to be discussed in court. Adult victims of sexual assault were repeatedly questioned by those within the justice system as to whether the offender had been influenced by provocative behavior or dress. Child molestation was frequently unreported or only minimally investigated. Many child offenders were not prosecuted prior to the feminist movement. Sexual abuse of children was covertly permitted, socializing the female to her role as subordinate to the male. Society in the United States has encouraged men to be aggressive, to act in a dominant manner, to show force, to disregard the refusal of women, and to overpower the female. Women, in the past, were encouraged to be dependent, passive, weak, and fearful.

Relational Theories

Individuals constantly change, impacted by their surroundings. Relational theories emphasize the critical role that relationships hold for individual development and sexual deviance as an interactional manner. Sex offenders are affected by those persons who have influenced them in some manner. A child molester, for example, who was abused sexually as a youth is impacted by such a relationship. An individual who suffers from sexual masochism may have been strongly influenced by sex that involved acts of bondage or humiliation.

Relapse Prevention Theories

Relapse prevention (RP) theories were developed from past forms of addiction treatment. Relapse prevention theories encourage persons who are trying to change their behavior by anticipating possible situations that may produce an offending situation. RP is focused upon educating and supporting the individual in order to maintain a recovery level of nonoffending behavior. Relapse occurs when the individual fails to avoid situations that lead to sexual offenses. Such a theory promotes behavioral change by encouraging individuals to modify old forms of thinking with newcoping skills. Victim empathy is encouraged. Sex offenders frequently depersonalize victims during offending situations and view those they harm as objects rather than people. Relapse prevention encourages appropriate sexual conduct and behavior. Sex offenders are encouraged to examine their behavior and the psychological impact they have had upon their victims. Ofenders are encouraged to identify their target populations and situations that could produce a lapse, or slip, leading to another sexual assault.

Societal Theories

Theorists have studied the morals and values of cultures in regard to sexual conduct. Current laws in the United States reflect the attitudes of the present guidelines pertaining to sexual offenses. However, in every society, the governing power structure defines what is sexually permissible and what is not acceptable. Often law is dictated by a select few who do not always share the same value system of a culture. Religion may be a factor. Abortion is a hotly debated issue in the United States. A woman who is raped and becomes pregnant may or may not encounter support if she chooses to have an abortion. Minors are permitted to marry in many states and in other countries. However, if that same child has consensual relations outside of wedlock with an adult, it may be considered a sexual offense. Certain films, television shows, and pornographic literature promote a distorted and often violent belief that women may actually desire to be sexually assaulted. These confusing messages impact both children and adults.

BASIC TREATMENT PRINCIPLES

Reid (1997) reports that the clinician who works with a paraphiliac disordered patient should have an orientation that is therapeutic in approach rather than punitive in manner. Therapists should be comfortable with their feelings regarding sexuality.

Equally important is the therapist's ability to feel at ease with those deemed as criminals or social outcasts as the result of history. These attributes are important when the patient is exploitative or aggressive, or demonstrates pedophilia behaviors. Certain countertransference issues will arise and will need to be understood and managed in an appropriate fashion.

Several issues may be expected to arise requiring intervention and assistance by a clinician. Patients with a history of sexual offense are prone to have family and marital issues, a variety of legal difficulties, social issues, and job problems. In addition, patients may exhibit problems of addiction, symptoms of anxiety and depression, and periods of extreme guilt and shame, all of which increase the potential for self harm.

SPECIFIC TREATMENT MODELS

Reid (1997) reports that several basic treatment models are currently being utilized in work with paraphilias. It is important for the treating clinician to remember that several of the sexual disorders are similar in nature. For example, although a specific sexual behavior may be displayed in a different manner, the goal of the paraphiliac is to experience a form of sexual excitement. As a result, many sex offenders often exhibit two or more paraphilias. A voyeur may also possess fetish behaviors; a pedophile may display features of exhibitionism.

In addition, it is important to note that for many offenders, sexual aggression is an expression of other psychosocial feelings. Anger and rage, poor self-esteem, depression, and feelings of inadequacy may be problem issues. Sex offenders project stress and frustration in a sexual manner. In addition, sex offenders who had a childhood that was emotionally, physically, or sexually abusive have developmental impairments. As a result, these past traumas, if untreated, may be expressed later in a sexually deviant form. Therefore, the abuse by an offender may not be necessary for sexual or physical pleasure. Some offenders report severe distress, shame, and disgust following an act of sexual aggression.

Reid (1997) reports that several basic forms of therapy modalities are helpful when working with a sex offender. These treatment models are listed as follows:

1. Insight-oriented or psychoanalytic psychotherapy
2. Behavioral or cognitive-behavioral therapies
3. Fading
4. Masturbatory satiation

5. Covert sensitization
6. Biological treatments
7. Family therapy
8. Relapse prevention therapy
9. Surgical treatment

Insight-oriented or psychoanalytic psychotherapy may be used for patients who exhibit some desire for help and possess ego strength and intelligence. These forms of therapy view the patient's behavior as a symptom of internal conflict. Patients appear to respond to such therapy, although no outcome studies document success on a long-term basis. Such therapy is not recommended as the sole approach of work with intrusive and aggressive paraphilias but may serve in an adjunct form.

Behavioral and cognitive-behavioral therapies are said to vary in their effectiveness. Initially, success with these therapies was positive during the first months of treatment, particularly for those patients monitored by the criminal justice system. Some treatment methods have included negative reinforcers, such as electric shock or snapping a rubber band against the patient's skin. In the past twenty years, passive aversion therapy has moved to self-management or skills training.

Fading, masturbatory satiation, and covert sensitization are considered parts of the behavioral or cognitive-behavioral grouping. Fading occurs in fantasies that are gradually changed from deviant to more appropriate thoughts. Masturbatory satiation involves patients learning to masturbate to appropriate fantasy thoughts. Covert sensitization involves switching to a consequence if an inappropriate fantasy occurs.

Biological treatments are reported to display significant clinical promise. Particularly effective are antiandrogenic, serotonergic, and luteinizing hormone-releasing medications. Therapy is recommended in combination with these drugs. Such medications have been found to be excellent in decreasing sexual drive and impacting mood or obsessional features.

Family therapy or involvement in working with a sex offender is important. Family often may play a role in encouraging an offender to acknowledge the offense. As well, family involvement may be an important motivator for the offender during the treatment process.

Relapse prevention is recommended for certain sex offenders. This model promotes a recovery program in which an offender avoids situations that would lead to a relapse or a reoffense.

Surgical castration is the least used method of treatment in work with sex offenders. The removal of the testes is reported to be effective in recidivism behavior of sexual sadists, pedophiles, and rapists.

SEXUAL DISORDERS AND TREATMENT SUGGESTIONS

Typically, a sexual disorder or paraphilia may be found in a sex offender during an assessment. These clinical disturbances are seen as abnormal and deviant. A paraphilia is a sexual condition in which an individual is sometimes dependent upon and aroused by a certain behavior, fantasy, or stimulus in order to achieve sexual excitement. The features for a paraphilia disorder include recurrent, intense sexually arousing and unusual fantasies, sexual urges, or behaviors. (Please refer to Chapter 5.) Reid (1997) has summarized each paraphilia disorder, with suggested models being used by clinicians in treatment. These are listed as follows.

Exhibitionism

Exhibitionists are among the largest groups of paraphiliacs referred for treatment services. Individual, family, or group psychotherapy models are commonly used for this patient population group. Exhibitionists are the most responsive of the paraphilias for individual therapy, although caution should be used. Many exhibitionists are receptive to an insight-oriented or cognitive-behavioral type of psychotherapy. Also, a referral to a psychiatrist for possible medication services may be appropriate, as the result of an anxiety or mood disorder. A number of these patients usually are referred to group services, with individual and family therapies serving as adjunctive form of care. Exhibitionists may present complaints of anxiety, depressed mood, a marked loss in special interests or pleasures, appetite or sleep disturbance, fatigue, poor self-esteem or feelings of worthlessness, problems of concentration, and, on occasion, suicidal ideation or behavior. Often there is a history of marital discord or sexual dysfunction manifested as bouts of male erectile disorder. Treatment that focuses on the distress and desire to expose should be addressed in therapy. Also, other issues related to obsessive behaviors, such as anxiety-producing situations, may merit attention by the clinician. In addition, insight-oriented psychotherapies should address any identified "triggers" that may exist for patients in their occupational, family, or social life. An example may include an exhibitionist who exposes after experiencing anxiety due to conflict. Since exhibitionists usually have a high number of victims, it is important to have a personal relapse plan developed in the event that a lapse occurs.

Fetishism

Sex offenders are rarely referred to treatment for only a fetish disorder. However, during the clinical assessment, a fetish may be revealed by the patient. Some patients do appear for treatment as the result of partner or marital problems, with a fetish being reported as a presenting problem. Family therapy is usually the recommended choice of treatment if no referring court is involved. Usually, the companion experiences feelings of rejection as the result of the partner's fetish interests. A family systems therapy model may be selected as a course of treatment if the symptoms are mild. An educational component should be included. Anxiety and guilt may need to be addressed. Fetish behavior in which no lawbreaking activity has occurred should be treated differently from incidents leading to court involvement. Couples should be encouraged to discuss their feelings about the fetish in an open manner, including how the behavior interferes with sexual relations. Men who have committed crimes involving fetish action may merit additional group therapy services. Individual treatment should address anxiety, distress, guilt, and triggers. In some cases, covert sensitization and masturbatory satiation is used. Little research information is available on fetishism only. Severe cases of fetishistic behavior may also be found in rape situations. The primary course of treatment should be group therapy with individual and family therapy as support.

Frotteurism

Frotteurism involves touching and rubbing against a nonconsenting person for the purpose of sexual arousal. Victims are often found in crowded areas and places in which escape may occur if the behavior is discovered. An offender may touch the victim about the breast, buttocks, genital area, thighs, or other portions of the body. Most paraphiliacs with this disorder do not seek out treatment unless arrested. Individual or group therapy may be an appropriate form of psychotherapy for such offenders. Other forms of treatment may include medication services.

Pedophilia

Pedophiles who enter treatment are usually male, although more females are now being referred for clinical services. Initially, a clinical assessment is recommended for a pedophile that may include an interview, psychological testing, and the possible use on males of a penile plethysmograph. To determine treatment goals, it is important to properly identify particular populations that the offender responds to in a sexual manner. Psychodynamic psychotherapy is currently being used with pedophiles. This therapy approach assumes that the individual possesses an impaired sexual development history and may be immature or fixated regarding a particular victim group. Other pedophiles may regress and offend only as the result of some type of psychosocial stressor. However, the insight-oriented psychotherapies are not well accepted among the clinical community for pedophiles. Relapse prevention and some portions of covert sensitization treatment appear more appropriate for this patient group. A model that is confrontative or direct, rapid, and focused on victim empathy is important. Group or individual therapies can be used to correct the offender's cognitive distortions about victims, children, and women, as well as his or her own sexuality. Family therapy may be used as an adjunctive form of treatment. Psychiatric services and related medication needs should be considered for this patient type.

Sexual Masochism

No current studies exist in literature involving specific models for treatment of sexual masochism. As a result, current clinicians are using individual, family, and group therapies that address anxiety, depression, and other mood disorders. Also, therapies being used may include assertiveness training, enhancement of self-esteem and confidence, and exploration of occupying the role of victim. Certain patients no longer find pleasure in being mistreated and desire help in finding solutions for this disorder. Individual psychotherapy, in combination with pharmacological services, may prove to be helpful to patients. In the event that intensive psychotherapy is considered, the clinician will need to identify and explore causative conflicts and help the patient find less harmful coping skills or defense mechanisms. This form of paraphiliac behavior is deeply entrenched in individuals, with a feeling that their humiliation is sexually gratifying; it usually merits long-term treatment services. Relapse behavior can be expected to occur occasionally.

Sexual Sadism

Patients who express sexual sadism behaviors with a consenting partner may never enter therapy. Offenders who commit acts of sexual aggression against others should be closely evaluated. Sexual sadists who are aggressive, injurious to the victim, and predatory should be considered extremely dangerous. A clinical assessment must be comprehensive. Such patients usually are not appropriate for outpatient treatment services; if they come to the attention of the criminal justice system, usually they are referred to highly structured forensic inpatient psychiatric hospitals or prison settings. Medication treatment services are recommended. Follow-up studies completed during the 1960s and 1970s regarding surgical castration and stereotactic neurosurgery revealed successful results among sexual sadists, pedophiles, and individuals deemed paraphilia rapists.

Transvestic Fetishism

Patients with transvestic fetishism seek treatment only as the result of discovery. Occupational, social, or family conflict may contribute to a referral for treatment services. Others may be referred by the court for help. Clinicians may expect to encounter anxiety, depression, and other mood disorders in this patient group. It is important to reassure patients that transvestism does not imply homosexuality or impotence. This information may be particularly important when working with a couple in treatment. Transvestites should not keep their sexual activities, fantasies, or urges a secret from their partner. Disclosure or description of activities may first need to occur in the company of a therapist. The prognosis for treating transvestism is limited, with reported success from therapy lasting only a short time in most cases. Individual and marital therapy are most often used to treat this disorder.

Voyeurism

Persons who are suffering from a voyeurism disorder rarely seek treatment until social or law enforcement authorities intervene. The prognosis for this disorder is not good; psychotherapy is rarely ever directly helpful for patients. However, some insight-oriented psychotherapy and exploration of sexual urges may be of help for patients in controlling their desires to peek. Medication services have been attempted and some success has been reported. Most offenders who are arrested for voyeurism may best be served by a program that utilizes a relapse prevention model. The risk to reoffend can be lessened, on occasion, through group treatment.

Paraphilia Not Otherwise Specified (NOS)

Persons who present symptoms in this residual category merit a clinical assessment prior to any treatment intervention. Treatment, depending upon the type of disorder, may merit individual, marital, family, or group psychotherapy services. Other patients may respond to a particular medication protocol. Treatment criteria for the offender may be based in part upon the level of intrusive behaviors, and the expectations established by the criminal justice system.

Chapter 10

Individual Therapy

Psychotherapy is usually a part of the treatment protocol, in some fashion, for almost any known behavioral problem or clinical disorder. Surprisingly, only a limited amount of information is available for reference at present for use in treating sex offenders on an individual basis.

Salter (1988) notes that a good treatment program for sex offenders actually may need to be hybrid in form, utilizing a combination of several existing therapies already proven successful. This approach may be useful when choosing a particular individual therapy model for a sex offender.

Generally, sex offenders are much more alert to the nuances of the treatment process than most other patient population groups. Such individuals fantasize a great deal and relate in a sexual manner to many issues. A subject of conversation that is not considered sexual by a treating clinician can be perceived and misinterpreted to represent something entirely different by someone with a paraphilia problem.

Therapists must keep in mind that onset for most paraphilia disorders is reported to occur during adolescence. Sexual development was impacted by some event in the past and a cognitive disturbance occurred. Ego functioning is impaired. Reality testing for a sex offender is distorted; insight and judgment is sometimes very poor regarding forms of acceptable social conduct. This does not mean that an offender cannot benefit from therapy, but that certain limitations may exist.

Offenders are usually manipulative individuals who have learned to seduce others emotionally in order to abuse. Typical sex offenders will lie, deny, minimize, or rationalize their offense. Even skilled clinicians can be mislead by a sex offender. Therapists may desire to carefully assess the clinical needs of a referred offender, including whether individual psychotherapy can be an effective intervention.

A TREATMENT PHILOSOPHY

Salter (1988) recommends that any program created for sex offenders (writing primarily about pedophiles) should have a defined philosophy and/or a model mission outline. Some treatment programs are vague, without specific guidelines. A road map establishing a direction of care, with detailed goals, plans, and objectives, is recommended. A clinical philosophy is summarized as follows.

1. Child molestation is the result of a deviant arousal pattern or the inappropriate transfer of nonsexual problems to sexual aggression.
2. Goals of therapy for offenders may include: to learn methods to manage their deviant arousal and impaired impulse control behavior; the use of plans or obstacles to prevent reoffending; to help the offender to solve problems in a nonsexual manner.
3. Sex offenders must take responsibility for their actions without the use of denial, externalization, manipulation, minimization, or projection. Nonoffending spouses who may have known about the abuse should be held accountable.
4. Child sexual abuse is a treatable problem—corrected by helping the offender to learn ways to avoid reoffending—but therapy should not imply a cure.
5. Family problems may increase the risk of a reoffense and should be addressed.
6. Victims are not responsible for the sexual abuse. Sexual abuse is harmful to the development of a child.
7. A sex offender clinician should be willing to network or provide assistance and support to other professionals.

INDIVIDUAL OR GROUP THERAPY

Maletzky and Steinhauser (1998) report that individual therapy is considered the "gold standard" among treatment services offered to sex offenders. Such an approach allows the development of transference between patient and therapist—an important concept in working effectively with such patients.

Trust between a patient and therapist takes time and cannot be quickly achieved. Many sex offenders are defensive, embarrassed, and resistive; they will attempt to avoid revealing specific sexual behaviors. Individual therapy is seen as being more powerful than group therapy in permitting some offenders to disclose information about their histories. Individual therapy can be useful in working with an offender on cognitive distortions, issues of fantasy, intimacy, and self-esteem, masturbatory reconditioning, and the specific problems of sexual deviancy. Family, social, or job problems may also be discussed.

Kaplan and Sadock (1998c) report that insight-oriented therapies are commonly used to treat persons with a paraphilia disorder on an individual basis. This type of psychotherapy is said to enable a patient to understand the dynamics of their behavior and factors related to the disturbance. Specifically, such treatment models allow patients to examine events prior to a sexual action. Many sex offenders often act on impulse without evaluating the consequences of their behavior. Insight-oriented psychotherapy permits patients to explore their fantasy system, impaired judgment, and beliefs about their sexuality.

Werman (1984) recommends that supportive psychotherapy techniques be considered when treating patients who possesses difficulty managing their impulses or sexual urges. Sexually aggressive acts may be pleasurable to these patients. Fantasy contributes to a ritual, leading sometimes to sexual aggression. The use of identification, transference, and role modeling can be effective treatment tools. One goal of supportive psychotherapy is to strengthen the cognitive functioning level of a patient, whose developmental formation was impaired in childhood. Normal coping mechanisms do not work for some individuals. Structural support is needed to shore up ego dysfunction.

In addition, Pessein and colleagues (1998) report that individual therapy can be used with sex offenders on a time-limited basis. Such an approach is helpful in preparing an offender for group therapy. Using this method of therapy, sessions are concentrated upon such specific issues as childhood victimization or other related problems, such as marital discord. Additional subjects covered during individual work may include behavior therapy in areas of covert sensitization or relaxation training. Offenders may also work on improving interpersonal skills that would aid their progress in a group therapy session.

Actually, individual therapy can be of benefit to both the sex offender and the clinician. Such a therapy model permits the offender to receive treatment and guidance in a therapeutic setting at one's own pace. The therapist is able to learn detailed behaviors, history, and patterns that cannot be obtained in a group setting. Individual therapy allows for more in-depth treatment to be provided to the patient. Almost all sex offenders are found to be receptive to individual treatment services, from the high-functioning, educated, articulate patient to those in adolescence to the mentally ill. The individual treatment format may need to be adjusted to the patient's level of functioning. However, it should not be implied that individual therapy should be the treatment model of choice for all offenders.

Most providers currently use group therapy as the primary model of work with sex offenders. The peer group has a tremendous impact upon the perpetrator and, as a result, most therapists tend to recommend group therapy as the primary model of care in work with offenders. A number of sex offenders are not motivated by the individual treatment process and will deny, distort, or lie about their past behavior. Some will express reluctance when questioned about their misconduct. Others will attempt to blame the victim or misrepresent, project, or rationalize the offense. Many will attempt to seduce the therapist emotionally. Group therapy may be more effective in resolving offender denial and rationalization of the offense. More patients are served by group therapy within a time-limited period—especially if there are agency limitations.

Ideally, a combination of both individual and group therapy models may be of value when working with the sex offender. Each model has particular clinical strengths that may be of help in treating a sex offender. Family therapy can be of great help in work with sex offenders—particularly in incest situations.

Salter (1988) reports that behavioral therapy for sex offenders on an individual basis has been proven to be effective in a number of programs. There are both advantages and disadvantages in using an individual model.

Advantages of individual therapy are listed as follows.

1. The patient receives more time with the therapist.
2. In programs that use both individual and group therapies, one clinician may provide the group therapy component, while a

second therapist may see the patient individually, in an effort to decrease offender manipulation.
3. Treatment assignments can be paced with the patient's ability and measure of success.

Also, in comparing individual therapy to group treatment, the following issues may be noted:

1. A large group of patients that adheres to a designated format is lengthy and time consuming.
2. Group members are not likely to progress at the same rate.
3. An open-ended program requires a group to repeat steps for a new member.
4. Individual clinical issues may conflict with group goals.
5. Different populations are mixed together in a group situation.
6. Resistive patients can impact the dynamics of the group.

Some disadvantages of an individual model may include:

1. It is time consuming.
2. It is more costly to provide.
3. It does not promote universality, interpersonal learning, or corrective behaviors by peers.
4. Both rural and urban programs may experience staff coverage problems or schedule conflicts in providing individual care.
5. Agency constraints may exist as a number of patients may require transport at different times to therapy.

SEXUAL RECOVERY THERAPY

Sexual recovery therapy is a treatment approach that follows Salter's (1988) recommendation that a hybrid version be utilized which combines several proven therapies into one model for work with sex offenders. Since there continues to be a deficit in specific reference techniques in work with sex offenders, sexual recovery therapy (SRT) may be considered by clinicians as an option in providing services to this special population.

SRT may be used in both individual and group therapy situations with sex offenders. In addition, this treatment may be used in inpatient or outpatient settings or in correctional facilities. Some clinical modification, as in all therapies, may be required according to patient need.

SRT is humanistic as a modality and views the sex offender as an individual who has specific problems meriting intervention. Certain psychiatric and psychological malfunctions have occurred for the person. SRT treatment may not be appropriate for all sex offenders. SRT is insight-oriented in approach with behavioral and supportive features. A therapist using SRT must be willing to be direct as well as empathetic when merited. Addiction or relapse issues, cognitive restructuring, and reality methodologies may be incorporated if needed.

A guideline for sexual recovery therapy for individual treatment is as follows.

Referral

Basically, a case involving sexual deviancy begins at the time of referral. This is a difficult time for an offender, who has just been found guilty of a sexual crime. Defense mechanisms are heightened and a number of behaviors may be expressed. SRT is seen as an intervention for certain patients who are receptive to treatment. However, the initial request for assistance by the patient may be somewhat self-serving in order to avoid jail or conflict with the court. Persons awaiting trial may not always be appropriate for SRT until the judicial process has been completed. A supportive therapy-based model of treatment instead may be applied to this type of consumer. Other individuals who present a risk to the community may merit incarceration.

Assessment

The SRT model emphasizes the importance for the offender to acknowledge the crime and accept responsibility for the abuse that occurred. Denial, minimization, and rationalization may be found. Offenders who refuse to acknowledge their misconduct in a designated period are not appropriate candidates. Initial sessions may include up to eight meetings. A clinical interview should be held.

Testing may also be appropriate. An assessment should include history regarding fantasy, deviant sexual behaviors, masturbatory practices, planning, rituals, victim selection, and type of offending. All records, police reports, and victims statements should be reviewed. The therapist should address reporting law requirements of unknown victims.

Engagement

To provide any type of therapy, a clinician must first engage a patient. The therapist will need to be hopeful, encouraging, but concrete. A dialogue may be started between the therapist and patient as to why the offender was referred to treatment. Defense mechanisms by the patient will be displayed but should not be the focus during the engagement process. Offenders who are court ordered may remain guarded and can merit assistance. Why not try therapy? What does the offender have to lose, except time? An example that can be helpful is to tell the patient he or she already has been found guilty and sentenced. Therefore, there is no harm in talking. Such exercises permit some face saving for the patient. Patients are more willing to agree to therapy if they feel they have some control in the decision.

Expression

Importantly, this may be the first opportunity for the offenders to express anger, anxiety, concern, fear, grief, or sadness in regard to their sexual deviancy, and to talk openly about the incident. The offender may have experienced family, social, or occupational problems. Some transference may begin at this stage, although patients will remain somewhat guarded at this point in treatment. Boundary setting and negotiation usually occur during these first sessions. Clinicians need to remember that lying and deceitfulness are behavioral characteristics of sex offenders. Yet a therapist should be careful about appearing judgmental. A willingness to help is appropriate, combined with a direct manner that does not condone sexual aggression.

Acknowledgment

Full admission without qualification will need to occur at this stage for the therapy to advance. Offenders are not allowed to offer a token admission to the crime. Therefore, total acknowledgment is seen as a major turning point and may be considered a clinical mile-post in the treatment process for the offender. Most sex offenders have spent years in denial while fearing discovery. Some patients will report that they only admitted to their crime in court as part of a plea bargain arrangement and are innocent of the offense. Offenders who present this situation may be told that this is fine but they cannot be treated by the program; therapy will need to be terminated. Such pa-tients may be told that if they were suffering from cancer and treat-ment was available, their cooperation and acceptance of the illness would be needed for success. Cancer patients who refuse treatment cannot be offered assistance. This example may facilitate acknowledg-ment. Denial, rationalization, and victim blaming is not acceptable. More details are usually revealed at this stage. Most sex offenders re-lease information about their past history in a "layering" fashion.

Accounting

A cost analysis should be requested. Sex offenders are often dis-mayed when asked to complete a detailed financial summary of the cost of their crime. By using a monetary measurement, the tragic emo-tional toll the crime has cost is exhibited. What is the cost of one sexual assault? What is the value of a family, a marriage, or a child? A house may have been mortgaged or sold to pay attorney fees, court costs, and restitution. Prison or jail should be included in this cost review. A job or wages have been lost. Neighbors, friends, and co-workers avoid contact. Each event or problem should be assigned an amount of money; the cost of offending is high. What is the emotional and psy-chological cost for the victim? Interestingly, a sexual crime is rarely committed for money.

Challenging and Detailing

Sometimes offenders will admit to the sexual offense but are reluc-tant to offer details. Rationalization, repression, or intellectualization may have been a part of the justification process. To promote recovery, a therapist will need to request that the patient describe more details of the offending behavior. This stage of treatment is more advanced in information gathering than the assessment portion component. Therapists can anticipate a variety of defense mechanisms to be exhibited during this portion of treatment. Usually displacement, depersonalization, humor, passive aggression, projection, or suppression may be displayed, along with other behaviors. The offender's sexual deviancy is reviewed. As before, the masturbatory fantasy system, target population, victim selection, type of offense, and crime site locations will need to be discussed. Psychosocial stressors should be examined. These sessions are structured to challenge established defense obstacles created by the offender in order to allow the sexual aggression. This stage of treatment may involve several sessions. Sessions may increase in intensity at this level.

Strengthening and Hope

Many patients possess ego deficits or weaknesses. During this period, further rapport between the clinician and offender will probably develop. As a result, it is important to symbolize the work by noting courage the patient has displayed. To enhance the cognitive rebuilding of the patient, a period of supportive-oriented strengthening will need to occur. The clinician complements the patient for his or her labor. Validation of accomplishment is important to this interaction. This stage may be extremely helpful to the consumer. Hope and encouragement is given. Transference continues to evolve or occur. Self-esteem, a lack of self-confidence, and problems of intimacy are concerns that will need to be addressed.

Developing Empathy

Developing victim empathy and remorse are important elements in the SRT program. Offenders will need to review the emotional and/or physical pain they have produced for others. Victim humiliation, shame, and life problem adjustment should be a part of this stage of work. Offenders are encouraged to formally recognize the abuse. Most abusers have treated their victims as objects for their pleasure. Blaming, depersonalization, minimization, projection, and rationalization are behaviors reported by offenders in an effort to qualify the sexual abuse. Offenders should be asked to call their victims by name, and if they do not know their names, to use a substitute. Male offenders tend to quickly report that they are remorseful for their actions, while female offenders are more willing to explore the physical and psychological aspects of the harm they have inflicted upon someone. Therapists should not accept a token expression of remorse by an offender; instead, they should review in detail how the victim was impacted by the sexual abuse. For example, the offender could be asked to describe the victim twenty years in the future. Assign readings about victims. Will the victim have relationships, marry, or experience companion problems? Will the victim become a drinker, change jobs frequently, and engage in self-destructive behaviors? Describe various victim problems, for certain offenders may believe no real trauma occurred.

Apology and Atonement

Critical to recovery are the elements of apology and atonement for misconduct. During treatment, this issue is often brought up by offenders. Atonement is important for healing. Since most offenders will not meet their victims, request that a letter of apology be completed. The letter should be addressed to the victim but never mailed. Apology by action, letter, or word, is symbolic in enhancing the therapy process. Also, some type of reparation as a form of restitution should be recommended. One example may be the donation of money to a special charitable organization, such as a shelter for abused persons. A token amount of money is not appropriate. In some cases, if approved, the money may be directed to the victim. Such a treatment approach should be carefully evaluated. Atonement also enhances ego development, self-esteem, and victim empathy. Seeking forgiveness, even in an indirect manner, is a powerful step for the offender.

Past Sexual Abuse

Some offenders may have been victims themselves. Many times childhood sexual abuse is reported in treatment. Offenders should be informed that victims are not responsible for the abuse, and inappropriate sexual behavior with a child was harmful to the child's development. Therapists should be alert to possible suicidal thinking, plans, or actions, since childhood sexual abuse reports increase the risk of self-harm. Revelations of child sexual abuse incidents can be emotionally painful for the offender.

Repeat Detailing

Sexual abuse is wrong. The offender has hidden under the cloak of secrecy, denial, and rationalization. Again, repeat detailing of crimes with the offender. Specific details should occur. Offenders are expected to reveal more of their history of sexual deviancy. Clinicians should never assume all information has been reported. Clinicians should ask "Tell me again, why did you harm that victim? What was happening in your life?"

Sexual Education

Social skill development and acceptable forms of conduct are addressed at this stage. Some human sexuality information may be merited. Many offenders often possess misinformation about anatomy. Personal hygiene may be an issue.

Changing Sexual Behavior

Sexual changing is related to the desire to avoid reoffending. As a change in behavior occurs, a new attitude begins to form. A sexual reframing of behavior has started to emerge. Offenders may comment on how their lifestyle has changed. For instance, substance abuse may have been a related issue. Exercise may be may a part of the treatment protocol as a substitute for drinking. Social, occupational, and family problems may be explored. Many offenders possess lifestyle difficulties and develop maladaptive coping behaviors. Now more appropriate behaviors are being exhibited. Repeatedly, it is important to recognize the positive gains that the patient displays. This stage is noted by further ego development, improved self-esteem, and a reluctance to engage in destructive behaviors. Therapists will want to process the changes with the patient. Patients will continue to experience transference.

Sexual Restructuring

Sex offenders often have developed inappropriate responses to reacting to a problem. Here, during the sexual restructuring stage, the offender is encouraged to explore ways to handle stress and conflict in nonsexual ways. The client is questioned and is asked if they want to continue to live a difficult life or change. Warning signs that could lead to a slip, lapse, or reoffending situation are discussed. The offense chain should be explored, as well as ways to avoid relapse. Again, offenders will need to be able to describe their target population, victim selection, style of offending, triggers, deviant masturbatory fantasies, and high-risk situations. Role-playing may be included. Negative thinking, cognitive distortions, issues of self-esteem, problems of intimacy, and sexual offending behaviors are explored. Insight and judgment problems may be found. Journal keeping or the use of a tape recorder may be requested in an effort to monitor patients during the restructuring phase. Stimulus satiation and covert desensitization may be used.

Sexual Recovery and Insight

Insight occurs when patients develop an understanding of why they engage in certain behaviors. The initial stages of treatment have now occurred with the sex offender. This stage of SRT may last for an extended period of time. Essentially, this may be considered the middle stage for the SRT model. This portion of treatment is directed at exploring behavior, childhood history, psychosocial stressors, lifestyle, and how sexual offending has impacted the offender. Issues may include anger, anxiety, control, depression, loneliness, problems of intimacy, and self-esteem. The sexual misconduct is examined. Patients are encouraged to reflect upon their behavior and examine issues that prompted their sexual aggression. Some measure of insight is expected to occur in phases as recovery evolves.

Personal Safety Plan

Offenders are requested to review plans and goals for the future. A written personal safety plan is recommended. This plan may include the following: the offense chain; rituals; planning; victim selection; target population; types of crimes; postoffending behavior; high-risk situations; ways to avoid slips, lapses, and reoffending situations; available support persons; list of persons to call in the event of a potential relapse; ways to stop deviant fantasy; a mission statement to remain honest, truthful, and offense free; consequences of a reoffense.

Preparation for Termination

The final stages of individual therapy for a sex offender involve the issues of termination. Sex offenders have a history of abandonment issues. Many have been reared in chaotic, emotionally, physically, or sexually abusive homes. A therapist may be the first person that the offender has been able to interact with in a positive nonsexual manner. Therefore, termination should be carefully planned for a sex offender. A sex offender should never be terminated quickly. Termination should be a gradual process with sessions occurring less frequently over time. As the treatment process draws to a conclusion, the progress of the offender may be reviewed. Sex offenders usually continue to reveal additional information throughout the treatment process that may impact the direction of therapy. Risk factors will need to be monitored.

Review for Termination

The patient is now ready to be released from treatment. Once again, support and encouragement are given to the patient. The client's progress is reviewed, and his or her work is complimented. Again, all risk factors should be addressed. No sex offenders should be informed that they could not relapse. Community safety issues should be considered by the therapist.

Termination

Individual therapy sessions now appear no longer to be merited. Offenders are encouraged to continue to work through their recovery program with the assistance of their personal relapse prevention plan. Some patients may desire to end individual therapy but may express an interest in remaining in an aftercare program as a safeguard. No offender should ever be denied the continuation of treatment services if requested. Appropriate support groups may be a part of the aftercare plan. Booster sessions should be offered if an offender desires to resume treatment.

Chapter 11

Family Therapy

Family therapy may be used in providing treatment services to sex offenders. Currently, family therapy is used by some clinicians as one intervention option with individuals who have committed acts of sexual abuse. In other circumstances, such a psychotherapy may serve as a secondary therapy to support individual and group work.

Minuchin and Fishman (1981) report that the family is a natural group that has evolved certain patterns of interaction. Such patterns are a part of the structure of a family; they govern the function of individuals within the family system.

Sex offenders are often found to be from families that were chaotic or dysfunctional. Violence may have been a part of the family dynamics that included physical, emotional, and sexual abuse. Many report problems with boundaries and determining which behaviors are deemed acceptable or unacceptable by family or societal standards.

Minuchin and Fishman (1981) define family therapy as an effort by a clinician to help a family experience reality as the individual members experience it. The therapist will learn the interactions that form the structure and shape of a family and the way that individual members think and behave. The worker becomes, thus, an agent for change, providing interventions and positive actions.

This chapter is about family therapy and how several different models may be employed with sex offenders. Some specific clinical techniques shall be provided for working with families who possess sexually abusive, inappropriate, or permissive behaviors.

FAMILY THERAPY TECHNIQUES

To begin, family therapy is a process in which a therapist works with a related group of persons in the realignment of the structure of their system. A certain amount of spontaneity is a part of the family systems model of therapy. Therapists must be able to interact with a family in a fluid manner, in which any interaction that occurs does not deter treatment services. Interventions may sometimes be unplanned. Behavioral patterns have become distorted in a sexually abusive family system. A therapist may provide a reordering in hierarchies for the family to be restructured.

This model of therapy includes the use of an identified patient as the alleged symptom bearer of a dysfunctional family system. Actually, the conflict may be the result of other family transactions in a sexually abusive system. The process will involve changing previously held interactions to forms that are more appropriate without abuse.

Although Minuchin and Fishman (1981) did not specifically write about any one group, these techniques of therapy may be applicable when working with sex offenders and their families. Summarized are several concepts in family therapy developed by Minuchin and Fishman (1981). They include the following: joining, planning, change, reframing, enactment, focus, intensity, restructuring, boundaries, unbalancing, complementarity, realities, and constructions. These stages, with references to sex offenders and their families, are described as follows.

Joining

The therapist must be able to start the mechanisms that drive the family system to preserve homeostasis. To achieve this goal a therapist joins in a partnership with the family in a common goal for change. A level of rapport is developed. A sexually abusive family unit may be found to be chaotic; its boundary systems are difficult to determine at a glance. Certain members may appear to be extremely enmeshed within a system, in which individuals are overly involved with one another; whereas other members of a sexually impaired family system may be disengaged and individuals operate separately without the support of others within the family structure. A therapist must not appear judgmental in order to join such a family.

Planning

Family therapists must first develop a hypothesis of how a possible family system operates. Planning treatment follows, as a clinical intervention evolves, to develop a road map to provide services. The sex offender may appear to be a passive member within a family system. Another member may appear to be overly involved in the operational structure of a family unit. Conflict may exist between an offender and his wife. The victim, a daughter, molested by the husband, may present separate problems and may be acting out. Therefore, a hypothesis is part of the planning process, as therapy is structured to help the family.

Change

All families will need to be challenged in some manner if sexually inappropriate behaviors are to be resolved. Change must occur for a family to function in a less destructive manner. Sexually abusive families come to therapy because normal coping mechanisms of interaction have failed and members are in crisis. The identified patient may be the sex offender or the victim, if the case involves incest in a family. The system is a complex unit and, if underfunctioning, the members may be displaying inappropriate behaviors. The job of the therapist is to undermine the existing homeostasis while creating a change.

Reframing

Reframing is essential to the family therapy process. One of the first problems in working with a sexually abusive family system is to determine what this family's reality is. The reality of a particular family may differ vastly, according to the history or life experiences of the members. Behaviors may have become dysfunctional or distorted, with unauthorized permission or colluded permission to sexually abuse those inside or outside of a family. Therapy starts when there is an agreement that the behavior must be modified through reframing to become more socially acceptable.

Enactment

The art of enactment requires a therapist to permit family members to interact with one another in a transactional manner. Family members should be encouraged to talk with one another while the therapist observes from a distance. The therapist will need to disengage from the family system at this point and watch as members talk among themselves about a particular subject or problem. A therapist may encourage the offender to talk with his wife about a particular family problem. During the course of the family's interaction certain information is revealed, providing insight about family interaction. Later, a clinician may make verbal observations about how certain exchanges of behavior occur between family members. Clinicians should be spontaneous and interactive after observations have occurred. A sense of urgency may need to be produced by a therapist for certain sexually abusive families.

Focus

Family therapy requires a clinician to focus on a portion of interaction that is significant for change. The clinician will select and organize data that have meaning for a family. Although a large amount of information has been presented to the therapist, it is important that only the most relevant data be used for a theme for work. A session may occur in which the interaction between an offender and a particular member becomes the focus of therapy. The offender has displayed deviant behavior toward a family member. This behavior becomes the focus and is the selection of the theme, which has meaning for the family.

Intensity

Family therapy includes intensity as a treatment approach in work with families for change. Sexually abusive families may differ in what communication they tolerate among members. Often simple interactions involving one family member and another are enough to create conflict. Whereas in other situations a high level of intensity is required to reveal emotion. Intensity is a difficult process for a family. It can also be rather unsettling for the therapist at times. A clinician should monitor strong interactions closely, but will need to be careful in order not to intervene before certain emotions are displayed, exhibited, or expressed. Some level of intensity must occur for a family to change in a structural form. Usually, the family must "hear" the message. Sexually abusive families do not modify behavior without crises.

Restructuring

Restructuring is a process in which the family is reorganized by a change in their interactions. Sexually permissive families require restructuring. Certain destructive behaviors must be discontinued. The therapist must intervene to encourage change. An example would include the covert seduction of a teenage female by a grandfather. Her parents would be requested to establish limits for the grandfather. As a result, a change in this family occurs and new boundaries are established. The parents are empowered to protect their daughter. The restructuring of a family must involve the premise that it is in their best interest to make changes. Families need to be flexible for growth. Traditions that are not particularly destructive or harmful to the family process are continued or maintained.

Boundaries

Boundary development is an important part of family therapy treatment. Often it is helpful to observe the way that a particular family will sit in session. Effective techniques can be used with sexually abusive families by observing, commenting, restructuring, while encouraging more acceptable behaviors. Boundary making may be viewed as successful when a particular interaction is accomplished in a positive manner. Most sexually permissive families require changes in their interaction. Certain members of the family system may be encouraged to become more involved. A passive mother may be asked to be more active and verbal in the protection of her children. She may inform the offender that it is no longer appropriate for him or her to bathe the children. Boundary changes may be demonstrated verbally, nonverbally, through interaction, or by structure. A change in boundaries for a sexually abusive family should occur when inappropriate behaviors are found to exist.

Unbalancing

Therapists who use boundary setting are attempting to change a family subsystem pattern of interaction and distance. Whereas in unbalancing, the goal is to change the hierarchical relationship of a subsystem. A therapist will work to challenge and change behaviors, rather than accept the arrangement that exists. Thus, an unbalancing of the system will occur. In working with sexually abusive families, clinicians may align themselves with one family member, while deleting the power of another. Family members may be confused at times by this technique, since they expect a therapist to display an objective opinion and behavior during treatment. In sexually permissive families, the therapist may need to join with a particular individual in an effort to unbalance the hierarchical structure. For example, the therapist may join in coalition with the mother in an effort to unbalance a relationship in which the offender was permitted covert approval to sexually abuse a child. Unbalancing a family system may produce positive changes when individual family members are able to experiment with new roles and functions in an interpersonal manner. Such changes may produce a new frame of reference or reality for family members.

Complementarity

In family therapy, the complementarity process includes helping members to see their belonging is larger than one individual. Similar to unbalancing, this process encourages the family to examine the whole hierarchy. Each person impacts the other. As a result, in the complementarity process, therapeutic goals are to help members realize that more than one person in the family is the problem; to ensure that no one individual has control of the system; and to ensure that each family member's actions are a part of the whole sum. Sexually permissive families tend to focus on one person and do not evaluate how individual members may have contributed covertly to an incestuous situation. A mother was aware that her acting-out adolescent daughter was being abused by her husband, but feared confrontation could lead to divorce. The acting-out daughter may be singled out as the identified patient, while other family members continue to remain separate from the problem. In working with sex offenders and their families, it is important that members are encouraged to see that deviant behavior impacts the family system.

Realities

A sexually abusive family entering therapy has a distorted sense of reality in many cases; it has a limited perception of what is actually true. The family has lost a larger worldview of appropriate forms of behavior. Sometimes, the family system is rigid and controlling of other members. As a result, the therapist may need to repair and restore the basic level of functioning of the family. Sexual abuse in a family creates confusion. A belief system that is misleading becomes a part of the family's reality. As a result, a therapist will need to construct, challenge, and change members, building an arrangement that is workable and accepted by the family.

Constructions

A family has developed a reality that is, to them, the maintenance of their belief behaviors. Sexually abusive families have chosen a preferred program that is destructive and harmful. Clinicians will begin by changing the rigidity of the system. A new method of interaction is constructed through therapy, which is more sexually appropriate. It is important to monitor and be aware of family language and how members interpret what is acceptable and not acceptable forms of behavior. The therapist, in constructing the family's new reality, is encouraging a different worldview of what is normal and what is now unacceptable. Deviancy that was permitted or endorsed is no longer accepted in the interactional system.

THERAPY OF ADULT SEX OFFENDERS

Madanes, Keim, and Smelser (1995) have developed a series of steps for therapy of adult sex offenders. Such a structured model of family therapy is useful in working with sex offenders. Each stage is organized and planned. The goal of this model of therapy is to carry out one step, then graduate to the next level. On occasion, several steps can be accomplished in one therapy session. In other situations, therapy may, at times, move very slowly but the goals remain clear for both patient and clinician. This form of therapy that is presented involves treatment with adults who have committed incest or have sexually abused other family members. The therapy program that is outlined by Madanes, Keim, and Smelser (1995) is focused upon work with the offender who is a father. The steps of this model follow.

Step 1: Exposing the Offense

Initially, it is recommended that the offender be removed from the home. The court should forbid all contact between the offender and the victim. The clinician begins treatment by meeting the offender alone, then gradually bringing in other members of the family as treatment progresses. In some cases, the victim may not desire to meet with the offender, requiring separate sessions before family therapy proceeds. It will be important for the therapist to convince the victim that nothing will be asked of him or her except for presence in the session for a few minutes. Victims are informed that they do not have to talk to the offender or even look at him. All that is requested is that they listen to and hear what the offender may have to say. The first step, therefore, is to obtain a clear and specific picture of the abuse.

Step 2: Confronting Why It Was Wrong

Step two involves the therapist being direct—confronting the father about his behavior and why it was wrong. The level of confrontation will depend on the father's level of denial. The father will need to accept responsibility for his actions and fully understand how he harmed this child in order for therapy to progress. The offender should be monitored during this stage of treatment for possible suicide attempts. A patient may believe that the sexual abuse did not interfere with the child's normal development. As a result, the clinician may need to ask the offender why sexual abuse is wrong. How does sexual behavior with an adult impact a child's development?

Step 3: Explaining Spiritual Pain

A sexual attack may be viewed as an assault against the very spirit of an individual. A psychological or spiritual pain is experienced by a victim of sexual abuse. The assault was committed by someone that the child trusted, loved, and was dependent upon. Developmental growth is sometimes impaired by sexual abuse. Possible problems should be explored in detail with the offender.

Step 4: Revealing Other Victims and Victimizers

Step four includes the offender identifying all those that he has sexually abused over the course of his lifetime. During this session, the offender may reveal that he was sexually abused himself. However, the clinician must inform the offender that victimization is no excuse for sexual assault against another. Specifically, the offender should know that sexual abuse is extremely harmful to another individual. Offenders may reveal during this stage of therapy that other victims in the family may exist.

Step 5: Acknowledging the Spiritual Pain of the Offender

In therapy, it is important for the clinician to acknowledge the psychological or spiritual pain that the offender himself has experienced. Some grieving and recognition of emotional pain is important to the offender's treatment process. Many offenders who have been sexually abused themselves may voice recognition of their own childhood sexual abuse. Also, offenders may be experiencing social, occupational, and family problems as a result of their sexual behavior.

Step 6: Recognizing the Mother's Pain

The therapist, at this stage, should acknowledge the emotional pain that the mother of the victim is going through. To promote recovery for a family, a clinician may tell the mother of the victim that the sexual assault on her child was also an attack on her, because this was someone that she loved and whom she wanted to protect. The mother was also victimized by the sexual abuse.

Step 7: Apologizing on the Knees

During this portion of therapy, the clinician shall ask the offender to get on the floor on his knees in front of the victim and express an apology to the child. The offender will be expected to display sorrow, remorse, and repentance for what he has done to the child, as well as assume full responsibility for his actions. The offender must not blame the victim and will promise the child that he will never do this again. The family and the therapist should be expected to judge whether the offender is sincere during this process. All family members should be present during the apology session. The act of apology is symbolic and expressive of the humiliation that the victim experienced.

Step 8: Asking for the Mother's Apology

The therapist must also ask the mother of the victim to get on her knees and apologize to the child. She will be expected to express sorrow, remorse, and repentance for not protecting her child from the sexual abuse of the father. This step is viewed to be almost as important as the father's apology. It is clinically important for the mother to apologize for failing to protect her child. Also, the apology by the mother is considered significant because children are fearful of the abuser, particularly when it is the father. The child is usually threatened or sworn to secrecy. The apology assists in the restoration process of healing the relationship between the mother and child.

Step 9: Discussing Consequences of Future Crimes

It is important that the clinician review with the adults of the family the consequences should the father molest any child again. All members of the extended family may be involved in this discussion. The primary goal is to make clear to the sexual offender that no additional doubt or suspicion of sexual abuse may occur; if there is reason to believe that an additional incident has occurred, he will be expelled from the family. At this stage in the treatment process, the family will be encouraged to place as much pressure upon the offender as possible to prohibit or restrict the possibility of a reoffense occurring.

Step 10: Finding a Protector

A special protector for the victim, someone who is considered to be responsible, trusted, and caring within the extended family system may be selected. Usually, it is not appropriate for the mother to be selected initially, as a result of her failure to protect the child. Once a protector is selected, he or she is invited to therapy sessions and is informed of the special requirements of a protector's duties. The protector will be much like a guardian, monitoring the child and alert to signs that abuse has occurred or is about to begin again. Signs of sexual abuse are reviewed with the designated protector.

Step 11: Deciding on Reparation

The family has reviewed the sex offending status of the father and has decided that the father may make reparation to the child. Such an act should require some sacrifice on the part of the offender. Reparation symbolically represents the offender's issue of overcoming his own emotional pain and the child's need to heal and recover from the sexual abuse. Examples may be that the father would open a special savings account in the name of the victim or that he must deposit a designated amount of money every month to the child's college education fund. The reparation should not be a token experiment, but something that is meaningful and requires considerable effort for the offender.

Step 12: Focusing on Sexuality

A relapse treatment program must be developed with the offender. The offender will need to develop insight in regard to his sexual offending behavior. The therapist will encourage the offender to develop a relapse plan in which he will not act upon inappropriate sexual impulses or urges in the future. In the event that inappropriate sexual fantasies occur, a plan of action is to be developed in which the offender would leave the scene and make contact with the therapist. Also, it is helpful that a part of the plan includes the offender informing a family member of the possibility of a reoffense occurring.

Step 13: Finding a New Metaphor

Sexual abuse is the result of an individual's inability to express problems in a nonsexual manner. As a result, it is important for the therapist to inquire if the offender is himself a victim of childhood sexual abuse. A goal of the therapy process is not only to stop deviant sexual behavior but also to end all forms of violence within the family system. Offenders will need to learn to express problem behavior in nonsexual forms rather than in sexual acting-out behaviors. The clinician, by use of a metaphor, enables the offender to develop insight in regards to violence and how it impacts others. Clinically, it is important at this point for the offender to understand that sexual violence is a harmful act and that such behavior has brought physical and psychological pain to another. These sessions will need to be intense emotionally—highly charged with the reframing of the meaning of violence and the offender's lifestyle being reviewed.

Step 14: Presenting Suicide

Sex offenders may be considered at a high risk for suicide or committing some form of harm on themselves. Clinicians need to give offenders hope and show optimism that with work they can change, the victims can heal, and the family members can move on to a better lifestyle. It is clinically important for the therapist to show respect to the offender; he should be told that his life does have meaning and quality. Suicide prevention strategies should be a part of treatment.

Step 15: Finding Meaning in Life

Reparation and healing should be included as goals for the offender. Hopefully, as the recovery process continues and new meaning is found in life, there is a reduction in the potentiality for suicidal behavior. However, it is important for the offender to recognize that only he can heal himself, and that reparation is necessary for healing to occur. Shame and pain are sometimes natural consequences of inappropriate behaviors. However, if an individual is willing to partake in reparation in treatment, there can be meaning to one's life again, which gives rise to optimism.

Step 16: Developing Empathy and Compassion

The biological mother of the offender may be invited to participate in this stage of therapy. Other important mother figures to the offender may be appointed in the event that the natural mother is no longer available. This person had a significant influence upon the offender's life. During sessions, such a mother figure will discuss openly her own suffering and difficulties so that feelings are revealed. Empathy and compassion are encouraged during this treatment stage. Harm, sexual abuse, and feelings for his children will be explored. Love and protection, as the offender himself needed when he was a child, will also be reviewed. In this manner, the clinician will work toward preventing additional reoffending behavior from occurring.

Step 17: Fighting Loneliness

Sex offenders are often socially ostracized by the community. It is helpful for the clinician to intervene and assist the offender in developing a supportive social network. Such a social network may include friends, relatives, and members of the community who have not separated from the offender. The offender will gain hope by interacting with a social support system. Loneliness will no longer be as destructive to him, thus diminishing his desire to act upon his sexual urges.

Step 18: Restoration of Love

This process should occur before the termination of therapy. In an effort to restore some love for the offender, whether from his wife, his mother, or siblings, it is important that restoration of love occur at this point in treatment. In the event that the patient has separated from or divorced his wife, hope should be given to the offender that he will find another companion as he continues to work through a recovery program and stabilize.

Step 19: Restoring the Offender As Protector

Again, before therapy ends, the therapist must bring the father back to his role as designated family protector. It should be emphasized that this is a role that he should always have displayed and exhibited without inappropriate behaviors occurring. The clinician may emphasize to the family that the father will always provide financial support whether he continues to reside in the home or not. The father, as protector, can be encouraged in sessions to speak to the victim and other children and advise them on issues of concern in their lives. However, it should be noted that the father will never again be the exclusive or primary guardian of the victim and other children, although he will be expected and encouraged to develop a protective relationship with the children and family.

Step 20: Learning to Forgive Oneself

Offenders often suffer from thoughts of the harm that they have committed against others. These thoughts often never leave them and, as a result, offenders often experience problems in forgiving themselves. Clinicians must say that it is important to remember the past so that additional incidents do not occur. It is also important to separate: The offender should never forget what he did to his victim, yet the memory should not impact other issues regarding his life, allowing him to advance in recovery. Clinicians should be encouraged to ask the father how often he thinks it is important to recall what deviant sexual acts he committed and how they impacted his victim. Ruminating thoughts are often characteristic of offenders who report that, if they progressed in therapy, they think about the abuse they committed against the victim on a regular basis. The clinician may inform the offender that each time he remembers the abuse, he should do a good deed in an effort to symbolically display a positive nonsexual act, replacing past inappropriate behaviors. This method enables the offender to restore his self-image.

MULTIPLE SYSTEMS MODEL

Trepper and Barrett (1989) report that incestuous abuse is both a psychosocial stressor and the result of psychosocial stress. Few family problems cause as much physical and psychological harm as child sexual abuse. The multiple systems model is recommended as a form of therapy that integrates a number of treatment modalities into one form of psychotherapy.

Specifically, this form of treatment encourages the clinician to look at the relationship among various external family and integral systems rather than focusing upon only one group. As a result, this model not only encompasses the whole family, but also is used with individuals including the offending father, the parents' families of origin, and even friends, peers, colleagues, and extended family members. This clinical approach endorses the premise that the therapist must not treat just one system, such as only the offender, but instead must provide intervention services for all systems that have been found to contribute to the sexual abuse of the identified victim.

The multiple systems model is found to be clinically useful in providing an assessment of sex offenders and related treatment planning issues. Furthermore, the multiple systems model promotes the clinical assumption that there is not only one cause of incestuous sexual abuse. Rather, the hypothesis is that all families are endowed with a degree of vulnerability based upon environmental, family, individual, and family of origin factors. As a result, these designated factors may be expressed in a sexual manner in the case of incest if a precipitating event occurs and the family's coping skills are impaired.

The multiple systems model has a number of advantages in working with sex offenders and their families.

1. It increases clinical utility in providing a thorough assessment of the offender.
2. It encourages the clinician to consider a wide variety of variables allowing for more informational data for assessment.
3. It promotes treatment when it is merited, rather than where it is assumed to be an appropriate intervention (some sex offenders may merit individual therapy as a result of sexual fantasies and urges, while others may not require such treatment services).
4. It is symbolic in meaning to a family in terms of assessing the chaos and destructive behavior of sexual abuse, permitting individuals to fully understand and appreciate the complexity of incestuous behaviors.
5. It may be used by a variety of clinical disciplines and is flexible as a treatment modality.

The multiple systems model is divided into three stages of therapy. Trepper and Barrett (1989) outline the multiple systems model as follows.

Stage 1: Creating a Context for Change

The first stage of therapy in the multiple systems model is estimated to take from four to six months. Stage one therapy attempts to: (1) create the context that change is possible; (2) acknowledge that change is difficult and setbacks may occur; (3) introduce flexibility into the family system, permitting change; (4) respect and care for all persons as individuals, although the clinician does not approve of incestuous sexual abuse.

Stage 2: Challenging Behaviors, Expanding Alternatives

The second stage is the longest of the three treatment groups, lasting approximately one year. Individual and/or family members may have contact with the clinician approximately two times per week. During stage two therapy, the clinician takes dysfunctional behavior patterns, belief systems, and interactional behaviors and designs interventions to provide interruptions for them. The therapist offers alternatives for inappropriate actions or behaviors. These interventions are designed specifically to reduce the family's vulnerability for a relapse, which would allow incestuous behavior to occur. In treatment, family therapy sessions may address the dysfunctional repetitive interactions that have produced or led to incestuous abuse. Marital sessions may serve to help couples establish boundaries for the marriage and to make decisions about the future of the relationship. Individual sessions for the offender may help explore feelings of victimization, the misuse and abuse of power and control, sexual feelings, behaviors, problems, and self-esteem. Group therapy for the offender, wife, and victim is used to expand and intensify the issues found during family sessions.

Step 3: Consolidation

Stage three is referred to as consolidation because the family, at this point, is expected to integrate all the changes that have occurred during the course of treatment. Their own style and personality is then expected to be displayed in a more appropriate fashion, with psychosocial stressor events being expressed in a nonsexual manner. During stage three treatment, family members usually provide the therapist with information about their families and inform the clinician of what action was taken. Little direct therapeutic intervention occurs during this stage of therapy as compared to stages one and two of this model. Stage three interventions are displayed by therapeutic rituals and enactments. The purpose is to reinforce the changes that the family has made and their ability to resolve problems in a nonsexual or destructive manner. This is accomplished both in individual and family sessions.

Chapter 12

Group Therapy

Group therapy is used widely among clinicians treating sex offenders. A primary goal is to stop sexually abusive behaviors. Such treatment may be offered on an inpatient or outpatient basis or in a correctional setting. Individual and family therapy services may serve as important collateral options.

Basically, group therapy may be defined as a form of psychotherapy conducted with two or more individuals in a clinical setting with a therapist. The actual therapy model may vary according to the needs of a particular patient population group. In general, group therapy for sex offenders is found to be a practical, efficient, and an economical method of rendering services to a number of persons with similar treatment needs.

This chapter reviews the group therapy process, while offering some techniques used with sex offenders. In addition, some general group treatment principles incorporated today by many sex offender treatment providers are discussed.

A BRIEF HISTORY
OF SEX OFFENDER GROUP THERAPY

Group therapy started to achieve influence again in the clinical community after World War I and World War II (Allen, 1996, 1990a,1990b; Ettin, 1989; Mullan and Rosenbaum, 1978). During the 1920s and 1940s in the United States, a large number of veterans returned from combat requiring psychiatric treatment services. The sheer volume of those needing care required therapists to offer help by placing patients in groups. Group therapy can be traced to Ancient Greece.

As with other therapeutic approaches in counseling, group therapy has evolved over the years as a rather eclectic approach of treatment; such a therapy is very effective and works well with patients. There have been many outcome studies in which both short-term and long-term changes have been documented to have occurred in patients. A group process directly impacts the patient and his ego system, creating an opportunity for a corrective emotional experience to occur. Compliance, identification and internalization are a part of the change (Allen, 1996; Opalic, 1989; Pattison, 1967; Bloch and Crouch, 1985; Yalom, 1985; Corsini and Rosenberg, 1955; Yalom et al., 1967; Mann, 1966; Kelman, 1963).

Outcome Measurement Results

Clinicians are reporting success with sex offenders who enter treatment for group psychotherapy services. Unfortunately, only a limited amount of research has been completed on sex offenders who are involved in treatment programs. Research has demonstrated thus far, in most cases, that sex offenders do indeed respond to treatment much like any other patient group. The problem of recidivism plagues sex offender treatment and group therapy. Some sex offenders do relapse. As the result, there has been a tendency to speculate that sex offenders are not responsive to available clinical services, including group therapy. In the past, this same type of hypothesis was once popularized in mental health circles about substance abuse.

One of the first inpatient programs for sex offenders was started at Atascadero State Hospital in California during the mid-1950s. This program was known as the "Emotional Security Program" and patients participated in group therapy sessions. Both rapists and pedophiles were said to be a part of this treatment program. Self-governing committees were permitted to offer therapeutic decisions about the program. Sexual psychopath laws were in vogue at the time. Later, at Western State Hospital in Washington, a program was developed for offenders. These groups were operated by members without a therapist present. Therapists did review videotapes of the session or written notes completed by an attending member. This form of group treatment became known as structured self-help. Some problems were reported as members experienced interpersonal conflicts or issues.

Philadelphia General Hospital was the first facility to develop an outpatient group for sex offenders. Most offenders treated through this program were exhibitionists and were on probation or parole. The groups encouraged social conformity, control of impulses and urges, and assistance with problems of social isolation. A follow-up study was completed on the Philadelphia program which compared ninety-two offenders who participated in the group therapy project with seventy-five persons provided only general supervision. A recidivism rate of only 1 percent was found for the patients treated in the groups, versus a 5 percent relapse rate for others. In addition, of the general supervision group, 27 percent committed crimes other than sex offenses, compared to 3 percent of the group therapy patients. However, a later study reported a problem in which those same patients did worse than persons only on probation. A reason for such a different outcome was never determined (Schwartz, 1995b; J.J. Peters Institute, 1980; Peters and Roether, 1972; Peters and Sadoff, 1971; Peters et al., 1968; Schultz, 1965).

Early research recidivism data about the Atascadero program revealed that the highest risk of relapse for rapists occurred within the first year of release. Pedophiles who relapsed did so with the greatest frequency two or three years after discharge (Pithers and Cumming, 1989; Sturgeon and Taylor, 1980).

Specialized group counseling or psychotherapy has been used in the past to treat paraphilias. These groups may be considered specialized as they are composed only of persons with sex-related problems. Paraphiliacs usually are reluctant to discuss their deviancy when placed in a group of individuals that do not possess a history of sexual offending (Berlin, Malin, and Thomas, 1995; Berlin, Hunt, and Malin, 1991).

In an outcome study, Berlin, Hunt, and Malin (1991) followed more than 600 sexually disordered patients who had been involved in treatment. All had received specialized group therapy services as a part of their treatment program. In addition, some of the patients had also received antiandrogenic medication. During a five-year follow-up survey, the recidivism rate was less than 8 percent.

In another study, Pithers and Cumming (1989) surveyed outcome recidivism rates among patients of the Vermont Treatment Program for Sexual Aggressors. This Vermont program uses a relapse prevention treatment model in working with sex offenders. Group therapy is a component of this model. Significant empirical information was found among those patients involved in a follow-up sample. Twenty rapists were followed for a period of six years, of which three (15 percent) were reported to have committed an additional sexual assault. In comparison, 147 pedophiles were followed, with four (3 percent) reoffending. According to survey results, of the four relapses by pedophiles, two occurred within five months of the start of the survey, while a third one took place three weeks after the offender discontinued contact with the outpatient therapy network.

SOME BASIC ELEMENTS FOR SEX OFFENDER GROUP THERAPY

Kaplan and Sadock (1998c) report that group therapy is of use as a treatment intervention for sex offenders. A sex offenders-only group, led by a therapist, is able to offer direction and support, while confronting denial, minimization, and rationalization. Appropriate forms of social interaction, sex education, various relapse prevention strategies, stress management, and victim empathy may be addressed in such groups.

Yalom (1985) suggests that actual therapeutic change is an enormously complex process. Several elements are found to be significant to the group therapy process and are universal for any patient group, including sex offenders. Yalom's clinical factors, with reference to sex offenders, follow.

1. *The instillation of hope:* Sex offenders often ask if they can change. Many enter treatment depressed or in despair, with a sense of hopelessness. Therefore, clinicians need to offer hope qualified by the importance of working in a program of recovery.
2. *Universality:* Sex offenders will report social desolation, rejection by family and peers, and the community. Group offers commonality with others in similar circumstances.
3. *Imparting of information:* A part of the treatment process should include information on sexual deviancy and ways to improve upon nonoffending behaviors.

4. *Altruism:* Sex offenders in a group often derive great benefit by lending support to one another. Self-esteem is often improved in offenders who are of help to other group members.

5. *The corrective recapitulation of the primary family group:* Adult offenders have experienced dysfunctional homes during childhood. Sometimes, past family dynamics can be revisited in an effort to stop further sexual acting out.

6. *Development of socializing techniques:* Sex offenders display impaired social skills and intimacy deficits. Group interaction, guidance, and role-play promote acceptable behaviors.

7. *Imitative behavior:* Therapists serve as role models for patients. Behavior will be imitated as the transference process occurs during treatment. Members are influenced by peers.

8. *Interpersonal learning:* Change may occur in therapy through interpersonal relationships with peers, the corrective emotional experience, and the group as a social microcosm. Insight about deviancy and a merited modification in behavior may occur.

9. *Group cohesiveness:* As with most patients, offenders possess a need for a safe place to express their feelings. However, these needs should never validate or qualify an offender's sexual deviancy. In general, evidence suggests that cohesive groups promote self-disclosure, group attendance, participation, and influence-ability of members for a positive therapeutic outcome.

10. *Catharsis:* A cognitive change is related to catharsis and behavior. A member of a group has acquired new information or personal insight for catharsis to occur. Sex offenders usually enter treatment with a variety of misinformed beliefs and values. Group therapy permits sex offenders to examine their deviant actions. Insight to a catharsis may transpire.

11. *Existential factors:* The dynamic focus is upon the basic human concerns of life, death, isolation, freedom, and meaning. Sexual aggression is an extreme form of inappropriate expression of unmet developmental needs. Childhood problem histories, difficulty with intimacy, life without meaning, poor self-esteem, and social isolation are common problems for sex offenders.

Kaplan and Sadock (1998a) report that each patient approaches group therapy in a different manner. Patients learn that others share similar problems. Sex offenders, for example, will use typical maladaptive behaviors, defense mechanisms, and inappropriate ways of relating to others during group. The group process for sex offenders allows individuals to become more introspective about their deviancy and current level of functioning. By entering a group, sex offenders must suspend their previous ways of coping to gain acceptance.

Several therapeutic factors for the group treatment process may be considered. Examples involving sex offenders are listed by Kaplan and Sadock. They are as follows:

1. *Reality testing:* A group permits patients to test their sense of reality. Offenders often enter group with many problems, including a distorted belief system about sexual behavior.
2. *Transference:* Sex offenders, by transference, can model a therapist and imitate behaviors exhibited by a leader. Reenactments that are planned with caution with the leader serving as the parent, the offender as the child, may occur.
3. *Identification:* Patients will identify with the clinician or other patients. Leaders need to monitor the influence that a one member may have upon others. Role-playing can be used.
4. *Interaction:* Group pressure will play an important role in a group member's behavior. Other members can have a very positive impact upon their peers. Pressure to conform is a useful therapeutic tool in a treatment group for sex offenders.
5. *Other therapeutic factors:* These may include acceptance, consensual validation, contagion, empathy, insight, inspiration, interpretation, and ventilation.

STARTING A SEX OFFENDER TREATMENT GROUP

Sex offender groups are formed like any other group. A therapist or agency will note that a particular patient population merits treatment and then will set out to provide appropriate clinical services. Many experienced sex offender providers may lead a group without a coleader. However, this usually is not recommended for a beginner who desires to work with sex offenders.

To start a sex offender group—whether the therapist is a beginner or experienced clinician—can be a rather daunting or even intimidating undertaking. Traditionally, sex offenders will withhold information, lie, or offer a misrepresentation of their sexual aggression. Anxiety, court-ordered attendance, fear of discovery, secrets, and shame are some of the issues presented. Any group will shut down if betrayal is suspected. Yet the principles and goals of a sex offender group cannot be compromised. Reoffending must be reported. Duty-to-warn issues are present for community protection. Also, location, referrals, space, and time are factors to consider when starting a group.

Friedman (1983) recommends that beginners select a cotherapist carefully. A mismatch of cotherapists, even those with skilled group work experience, can lead to conflict when working with patients, including sex offenders. Ideally, it is best to pick a friend or known colleague with a personality and clinical style that is in concert with one's own treatment beliefs. Sex offenders are very intuitive individuals who are sensitive to the nuances of conflict and will pick up on any differences that may exist between therapists. Commonality will help during emotional interactions of patients. Good communication skills between therapists are vital.

The site location of a sex offender group is an important component. Due to safety issues, level of risk, and possible acting-out behavior, many clinicians are using sites that are located at the local court, correctional settings, human service department, probation and parole office, or other similar agencies. Sex offender groups should not be conducted in isolated areas with no support staff. Outpatient programs in private practice or public sector should have available support staff. Other groups are held in more confidential, discreet, or private surroundings.

Clinicians will need to monitor both the content and process of a sex offender treatment group. This approach, also, is different from other kinds of psychotherapy group models in which process is considered more important than the content. Due to the nature of the subject content, a leader must remain alert not only to the dynamics of the group process but also to what is actually being verbalized by members in the session. A rapist may be voicing issues that would lead him to reoffend. An exhibitionist may be describing behaviors of fantasy prior to an incident.

Most therapists recommend a mix for a sex offender group. Sex offenders are not considered a heterogenous patient population group. However, certain sexually disordered groups tend to be more passive than others. As a result, a number of mental health professionals regularly include both rapists and pedophiles in the same treatment group. Rapists usually possess more emotional energy and are more interactive. Pedophiles tend to be more quiet and passive in group sessions.

Sessions vary in length; some groups meet for one hour, while other sessions exceed two hours. Most therapists find that one and one-half hours is an acceptable amount of time for a sex offender group. Some groups meet weekly or bimonthly. Other sex offender groups meet several times per week. Special groups, for maintenance purposes, may meet only monthly.

Marshall, Anderson, and Fernandez (1999), in a cognitive behavioral treatment approach, note that Kear-Colwell and Pollack (1997) are of the opinion that, in therapy, an extremely aggressive, authoritarian, or confrontational manner for sex offenders can produce only limited or negative benefits. This style is negative in format, lacks genuine empathy, causes patients to feel vulnerable and powerless, and impacts self-esteem. Strong-willed offenders will become resistive, argumentative, or disruptive. Other clients may only readjust their style of manipulative behavior in order to offer token acceptance of the therapist's demands. Some clients are removed if they fail to conform to the designated format. Garland and Dougher (1991) are of the opinion that clinicians who are confrontational do so to act out their own needs, rather than to address the clinical problems of their patients.

The purpose of a therapy group is to promote change in behavior. To achieve this goal, an emotionally charged atmosphere must be created that stimulates interpersonal interaction between group members. Therefore, an important task of a group leader is to establish and maintain clinical conditions that will permit these intense interactions to occur on a regular basis, leading to intimate self-disclosure (Friedman, 1983).

To promote self-disclosure by a patient requires the therapist to first reduce feelings of anxiety while facilitating the interaction of the group. Conditions for self-disclosure, in general, occur after patients experience an atmosphere of some mutual trust, which include feelings of support, confidence that the self-disclosure will be heard respectfully, listened to with empathy, and responded to honestly.

However, a therapist also can expect periods in which a direct manner is effective with a patient. The clinical expectations for a member in group may need to be raised; denial, distortion, minimization, or rationalization cannot be permitted. Such behavior will hamper the progress of other members and the risk to reoffend increases if such behavior is present. Outpatient group leaders must also address public safety issues.

GROUP THERAPY MODELS

Group therapy models vary according to the treatment needs of a particular patient population. Sex offenders as a patient group require certain clinical issues to be addressed during the treatment process. This section reviews several group therapy programs or models of treatment that have been used for sex offenders. Such models can be used in a correctional setting and with inpatient or outpatient programs, with some modification. Many excellent programs exist, but these are too numerous to review. Several different models were selected to offer the reader a cross-section of available programs.

One group therapy model, outlined by Salter (1988), is used in Washington State. Outpatient treatment groups can contain between twelve and sixteen members, meeting weekly for two-hour sessions. Groups can be held evenings to avoid conflict with members' work. Tardiness and absences should be treated seriously by group leaders; termination from the program could result.

Groups should be heterogeneous, and include exhibitionists, rapists, pedophiles, and other sexually deviant individuals. Homogeneous groups, such as a group only for child molesters or pedophiles, may be impractical for most rural areas.

Group members are to begin each session with a "layout." A full layout will include the member's name and statement that he or she is a sex offender. In addition, members are expected to recite all offenses, triggers that prompt offending, and a review of deviant impulses in the past week and how they were handled. Also, the layout includes the number of times the individual masturbated and whether fantasies were appropriate or inappropriate. Finally, the member is expected to report on current sexual activity, and what he or she would like discussed on the agenda for the evening. A complete layout can be rather time consuming. Leaders are urged to keep the group moving by encouraging members to speed up, if merited, or even to stop the process if stalling is suspected. A modified or partial version of layout may be applicable. The full version is useful when a new member enters the group.

Peer group leaders are used in this treatment model. Nominations for a new peer leader are accepted for each evening group. Two nominations are expected. The peer nominees are then expected to describe what they would do if elected that week. A discussion is then held, followed by a vote. New members are considered as candidates for the treatment group. On the first evening, members stand and tell the new candidate what sexual offenses they have committed. After this process is completed, the group is then free to question the candidate about his or her sexual offense history. Some minimizing and denying is expected, but it is confronted; the new candidate is given a period to work on the expectations for the treatment group. The new candidate is not reviewed for membership until all requirements for membership are completed, which takes several months.

To be considered for membership, the candidate must learn the rules and regulations of the treatment group. New candidates must take responsibility for their sexual offenses and talk about past crimes. Also, offenders are expected to describe their masturbatory fantasies. In addition, candidates must learn to be helpful to other group members and do their homework assignments. The entire group is expected to vote on membership of the new candidate, but staff may overrule a decision of the group. All candidates must be accepted into the group by unanimous vote. Reunification with family cannot occur until after the candidate is admitted to the group.

Vermont Treatment Program for Sexual Aggressors

Pithers, Martin, and Cumming (1989) reviewed the Vermont Treatment Program for Sexual Aggressors, created in 1982. This was one of the first programs to use relapse prevention for sex offenders. The Vermont residential program component relies heavily upon group therapy due to treatment efficiency and efficacy. Individual, marital, and family therapies are used when merited. Therapy groups are reported to focus on the following areas:

1. *Victim empathy:* Sex offenders tend to view their victims as objects for pleasure—nonpersonal beings who are faceless. Offenders are encouraged to see the full damage of their abuse.
2. *Personal victimization:* Some offenders themselves have been victims of sexual abuse. Groups include an opportunity for these offenders to discuss the effects of their childhood sexual abuse.
3. *Emotional recognition:* Sex offenders report problems of identifying mood states and appropriate action and reaction. Offenders who have identity issues concerning their masculinity project their confusion through anger in order to suppress their fears. Such a group recognizes the relationship between thoughts and actions.
4. *Anger management:* Groups help offenders express their anger and feelings in an appropriate, nonsexual manner.
5. *Communication skills:* Sex offenders often experience problems communicating their thoughts and feelings. Groups are used to assist offenders in developing improved interpersonal relationships skills and intimacy issues.
6. *Knowledge of sex:* Treatment groups work on basic issues of human sexuality. Many sex offenders lack accurate information about sexual anatomy and related functioning. Sexual beliefs and misconceptions are explored in these groups.
7. *Cognitive distortions:* Sexual offenders report many thinking errors leading to acts of sexual aggression. An example may include a pedophile who believes that an early sexual experience for children is of help to them.
8. *Behavior therapy for sexual arousal disorders:* Sexual arousal to inappropriate behaviors, such as rape or child molestation, related to fantasy and actual offense is explored. Behavioral therapies used may include covert sensitization, masturbatory or verbal satiation, orgasmic reconditioning, and olfactory aversion.
9. *Relapse prevention:* Offenders work in a relapse prevention program to avoid situations that could lead to a relapse or reoffense.
10. *Transition:* Members leaving residential treatment and returning to an outpatient setting are involved in group work that assists patients in the transition back to the community.

11. *Problem-solving techniques:* Offenders are encouraged to consider high-risk situations that might lead to an offending situation. Problem-solving strategy sessions are used in group to discuss coping reactions in an effort to avoid relapse.

Relapse Prevention

Several forms of group psychotherapy for sex offenders are now available for clinical use. One such form of group therapy that has gained interest is relapse prevention (RP). Relapse prevention, which comprises group therapy elements, is a self-management program designed to teach individuals ways in which they may avoid reoffending. Relapse prevention is a program that combines both behavioral and cognitive interventions. Laws (1999), a clinician, theorist, and advocate of RP, reports the model that has advanced the treatment of sex offenders. He notes that a national or international modified model is now merited.

The specific components of relapse prevention are outlined by Abel and colleagues (1992) and Pithers and colleagues (1983). RP was first developed as a prevention strategy for addictive behaviors and was later modified for sex offenders. The RP model notes a relapse will follow a sequence in behaviors. These are listed as follows:

1. The sex offender, upon completion of a treatment program, will first feel confident, but this can lead to the development of a false sense of security
2. Apparently irrelevant decisions occur leading to problem situations
3. High-risk situations, which place the offender at risk to reoffend
4. Failure of an adaptive coping response to a difficult situation
5. Lapse, which may include deviant sexual fantasies
6. The abstinence violation effect, with feelings of failure or a need for gratification
7. Relapse occurs

Treatment includes:

1. Identification of offense precursor situations
2. Stimulus control, by being able to remove oneself from problem areas

3. Avoidance strategies that evoke lapse
4. The programming coping responses to difficult event
5. Escape planning to physically leave an area of risk
6. Coping with sexual urges that occur impairing recovery

Pithers, Martin, and Cumming (1989) report that sex offenders must demonstrate consistent and enduring behavioral changes before release. Several objectives must be met prior to discharge from the program, which are as follows:

1. The sex offender must describe his or her personal high-risk situations.
2. Offenders must verbalize coping strategies for each high-risk situation.
3. The offender must be able to anticipate new risk situations and have ways to effectively cope without reoffending.
4. An offender is expected to express appropriate forms of verbalizing anger rather then resorting to sexual aggression.
5. An offender must demonstrate his or her understanding that individuals have a right to possess their own sex roles in society, with the provision that they are not illegal.
6. The offender must demonstrate decreased arousal to stimuli that, in the past, would cause a sexual offense.

Vermont sex offenders referred to outpatient treatment groups agree to comply with the following:

1. Assume full responsibility for sexual misconduct.
2. Apologize to his or her victim and acknowledge responsibility without qualification.
3. Sign a waiver of confidentiality for admission.
4. Attend all sessions and pay for cost of treatment.
5. Do not disclose information about other clients to anyone outside the group.
6. Interact on an active basis in treatment and demonstrate regular progress.
7. Complete all assignments, such as writing of life story, victim-empathy readings, and related homework.
8. Encourage family members to participate in the treatment program.

9. Do not possess or use pornography.
10. Consent to plethysmographic testing.
11. Report any contact with members outside the group.
12. Follow any additional requirements established in the treatment group that have been identified as high-risk situations.

Sexual Recovery Therapy Model

The sexual recovery therapy (SRT) model may be modified as a group therapy, for sex offenders. The SRT model is outlined in detail in Chapter 10. Basically, this approach is seen as motivational without a confrontational component. A structured format can be used but adjusted as needed. Treatment at times may be direct, but the SRT model promotes a humanistic approach. However, there may be times when a leader may desire to increase the intensity of sessions in an effort to promote change. The therapy is insight oriented and behavioral in format, with supportive features. Addiction, cognitive restructuring, and relapse prevention modalities may be included in the model, when deemed appropriate. Guidelines for the SRT model are as follows:

Referral. Treatment begins at the time of the referral.

Assessment. A clinical assessment and related testing should occur. Offenders may begin the program and attend up to eight sessions before formal admission to the group is approved. Criteria for admission is based upon acknowledgment, behavior, level of denial, desire for treatment, and group interaction.

Engagement. A patient will need to be engaged by the group leader as a part of the therapy. Some rapport will need to occur. Senior members are expected to help new candidates working into the program.

Expression. This is a time for patients to express feelings about their losses. Anger, grief, and sadness may be displayed and can be therapeutic.

Acknowledgment. Full admission of the sexual abuse must occur at this stage without qualification. This is viewed as a clinical turning point for the offender.

Accounting. A cost analysis is requested. How much have their sexual offenses cost? This can be an insightful exercise.

Challenging and detailing. To promote recovery, a therapist may increase intensity, raise anxiety, and challenge the offender's defense mechanisms at this stage. Detailing of the crimes and victims is expected. Group members will be expected to describe their target population, victim selection, style of offending, triggers, cognitive distortions, masturbatory fantasies, and offense chain.

Strengthening and hope. Hope and encouragement are given to the group members. Validation of the work done thus far is recognized. Issues of self-esteem and intimacy are influenced.

Developing empathy. Offenders often see their victims as objects and minimize the harm they have caused. Victim empathy should be a part of treatment, which impacts remorse. Group members are asked to describe how their victims are affected by the sexual abuse.

Apology and atonement. Apology and atonement is a critical component in the treatment process. Such actions are considered symbolic and healing. Some type of reparation should occur.

Past sexual abuse. Many offenders are themselves victims of past sexual abuse incidents. Suicidal behavior should be monitored when such information is reported. Such revelations can promote recovery, empathy, and nonoffending behavior.

Repeat detailing. Sex offenders often release information in a "layering format." Again, leaders should ask group members to review their histories of offending, all past deviant behavior, victim selection, style of attack, fantasy, masturbation, offense chain, and triggers.

Sexual education. Group members discuss social skills, sexual issues, and acceptable forms of behavior. Basic human sexuality information may be reviewed.

Changing sexual behavior. Changing sexual behavior is a key element in an effort to avoid reoffending. This reframing is strongly influenced by a new lifestyle that is free of sexual deviancy. Again, the patient's accomplishments are noted. Such sessions encourage ego development and improved self-esteem. There is now reluctance to engage in sexual aggression. Groups will discuss these new learned behaviors.

Restructuring sexual behavior. During the restructuring phase, the patient is encouraged to examine ways in which problems are resolved in a nonsexual manner. Psychosocial stressors that lead to sexual aggression are discussed. This is a cognitive approach that permits patients to articulate ways to avoid reoffending. Fantasy and masturbatory practices are discussed. Stimulus satiation and covert desensitization may be used.

Sexual recovery and insight. No offending is reported. Sexual deviancy and related behaviors have ceased. Insight has begun to occur. This is considered the middle stage of treatment in the SRT model.

Sessions include discussion of childhood history, psychosocial stressors, lifestyle problems, and the impact of sexual offenses. Issues of anger, anxiety, control, depression, loneliness, intimacy, and self-esteem are addressed in group. Recovery is seen as an evolving process.

Personal safety plan. A safety plan for each patient is encouraged. Their offense chain, psychosocial stressors, victim selection, type of offending, high-risk situations, coping skills, and ways to avoid offending should be included in this plan.

Preparation for termination. Patients begin the preparation for release from the program.

Review for termination. Support and encouragement is given to the patient. His or her progress is reviewed.

Termination. The patient is released from the program. An aftercare program should be part of any termination plan.

Cognitive Behavioral Treatment of Sex Offenders

A therapist using a cognitive behavioral treatment approach with sex offenders may be directive and will focus on the patient's presenting problem. This treatment approach is promotes a "here and now" format, with specific designated goals. Marshall, Anderson, and Fernandez (1999) recommend the use of cognitive behavioral therapy with sex offenders using a group model. The treatment program is based in Canada, and is used in correctional facilities serving sex offenders. Emphasis is placed on improving self-esteem; changing cognitive distortions; denial and minimization; victim empathy; social skill functioning; problems of intimacy; sexual preferences; aversion therapy; covert sensitization; and masturbatory reconditioning. A revised offense chain is used as a part of a relapse prevention plan for patients in the treatment program (Eccles and Marshall, 1999).

Some Other Group Models and Suggestions

Ingersoll and Patton (1990) outline a group therapy model for incarcerated offenders. This model is structured and can be confrontational in manner if merited. However, members are to be treate`d with respect. Denial, rationalization, and minimization are addressed. Several basic components are important in this treatment modality, which are summarized as follows:

1. Complete a history review of potential candidates.
2. Perform a clinical assessment of candidates selected for the program.
3. An initial group meeting is held; rules, time, and location of the group are reviewed.
4. Encourage the acceptance of personal responsibility for sexual aggression.
5. Members who experience a reaction in regard to assuming responsibility for their actions are helped.
6. Reeducation and sensitization—assisting offenders in reevaluating their distorted thinking, learning to permit feelings and emotions to occur—take place, as well as finding ways to cope with these new behaviors.
7. Termination occurs last, with a few sessions spent on finding alternative ways of coping with problems that arise in life without reoffending.

Prendergast (1991) has suggested some group "musts" that should occur during the group therapy process with sex offenders. These are summarized as follows:

1. Direct but do not interfere; the therapist maintains control without dominating group interaction, permitting members to talk, vent feelings, and share information.
2. Keep the focus on the session or topic, but allow a member to change subjects when they become too emotional, painful, or threatening.
3. Do not take sides or become judgmental; therapists should not be too quick to intervene when a group member is being confronted in a session. Sex offenders are more willing to listen to peers than professionals.
4. Never give answers; ask indirect questions. It is more important for the patient to find the answer than for the therapist to offer the solution.
5. As with any insight-oriented therapy, group treatment with sex offenders requires members to struggle and experience periods in which they feel anxious and frightened and want a quick fix to a situation.

Some errors committed by therapists in group work with sex offenders listed by Prendergast (1991) include:

1. Starting the group in an adversarial manner
2. Showing a lack of empathy or interest
3. Making threats to group members—e.g., if they fail to follow an assignment, they will be referred to their probation officer
4. Possessing a lack of clinical skills regarding group treatment and sex offenders
5. Badgering a group member in a manner that exceeds clinical value
6. Using too much interpretation and members fail to understand the message
7. Failing to be alert to a patient's readiness to acknowledge his or her offense or attempting to force an admission too soon
8. Taking control of a group too soon when a problem occurs, therefore dismissing the members' ability to resolve problems for themselves
9. Becoming too defensive during an encounter in the group
10. Playing the victim if the group does not follow his or her plans
11. Alienating members by making excessive demands, using too much control, or forcing topics that are not significant to the group
12. Talking too much, thereby inhibiting group interaction

Chapter 13

Special Populations

This chapter reviews certain groups of sex offenders that exist today without a specific clinical sexual classification. These special population groups are defined by age, behavior, gender, other contributing mental disorders, or sexual misconduct. Treating such groups presents special challenges for therapists.

Therapy or intervention can be restricted by laws or cultural assumptions that impair professionals. Schwartz (1995c) notes that the definition of a sex offender is largely determined by the society mores of the times. In the United States, for an example, each state uses different guidelines as to what is sexually offensive. Rape, pedophilia, indecent exposure, adultery, sodomy, oral sex with an adult, or marriage to a minor can each be treated differently by different prevailing state laws. Federal statutes add to the confusion with separate legal standards. Globally, the definition of sexual deviancy is even more diverse in determining what is appropriate, depending upon the presiding culture.

ADOLESCENT SEX OFFENDERS

Sexual acts of aggression by juveniles have been dismissed in the past by system providers. Several factors have contributed to the underreporting of adolescent sex offenders. These factors may include the following:

1. Reluctance to report youthful offenders because of their age
2. Concern, fear, and shame for the victim
3. Families minimize or deny abuse

4. Sexual aggression in youth not always formally recognized by mental health and juvenile justice
5. A deficit in the knowledge base of human service providers
6. Sex offenders not seeking treatment themselves
7. Plea bargaining within the justice system; a sexual assault often changed to a nonsexual offense (Knopp, 1982)

Definition and Statistical Information

Perry and Orchard (1992) define the adolescent sex offender as an individual between the ages of twelve and eighteen years who engages in sexual behavior that is unlawful or socially inappropriate. Both male and female adolescent sex offenders commit acts of aggression. Sexual relations can be either consensual or nonconsensual, but are considered lawbreaking since a minor cannot provide informed consent for sexual relations.

The average adolescent male sex offender, during a lifetime, can abuse approximately 380 victims. Studies have found that as many as 50 percent of all adult offenders started in adolescence (Perry and Orchard, 1992; Abel, 1984). Some offenders first start their abuse prior to preadolescence, beginning as early as eight or nine years of age (Perry and Orchard, 1992; Groth, Longo, and McFaden, 1982; Johnson and Berry, 1989).

Approximately 91 to 93 percent of adolescent offenders are male. Most have contact or are living with both parents at the time of the offense. Few have prior convictions, but the reported offense does not often represent their first sexual assault. The offender may have a history of victimization. Many have experienced physical abuse, witnessed domestic violence, or lived in a home that included inappropriate sexual behaviors. One in three offenders has been convicted in the past of a nonsexual delinquent offense. The population group most likely to be sexually abused is preadolescent children between seven and eight years of age, usually female. The victim, in most cases, is not related to the offender. The sexual abuse is unsolicited and involves genital touching and/or sexual penetration in approximately 60 percent of the reported cases. Coercion or force may be reported (Ryan, 1997).

Clinical Features

Generally, in addition to age, the adolescent sex offender may be distinguished by the following elements (Perry and Orchard, 1992; Bera, 1989; O'Brien and Bera, 1986; Bera,1985):

1. Offenses tend to be planned, usually not impulsive, acts; the assault primarily is not sexually motivated but is an expression of aggression and control.
2. Clinical features may include anxiety, antisocial attention-seeking behavior, denial, immaturity, interactional difficulties with the opposite sex, low self-esteem, loneliness, masturbatory fantasies as prelude to an abusive act, manipulation, problems in communication, progression in sexual offenses, projection, school problems, sexual identity issues, social development impairment, suppression of feelings, and rationalization; also, the victim is usually younger than the offender.
3. The offenses are a reflection of need for recognition, approval, and power.
4. Offenders have mothers who display impaired nurturing characteristics and fathers who are distant with only limited contact.

Seven typologies have been identified:

1. *The naive experimenter:* Eleven to fourteen years of age, limited sexual offending history, sexually naive, involved only in one or two offenses, victims are younger, no force
2. *Undersocialized child exploiter:* Abuse can be chronic, manipulative, motivated by a need for intimacy and self-importance
3. *Pseudosocialized child exploiter:* Good social skills, limited acting-out history, presents as self-confident, may also be a victim, sexual aggression has been going on for an extended period, motivated for sexual pleasure through exploitation, rationalization, little remorse
4. *Sexual aggressive youth:* A product of an abusive and chaotic family system, history of antisocial acts, poor impulse control, substance abuse, sexual assault involves force, motivated to have power and domination, to express anger, humiliate the victim

5. *Sexual compulsive youth:* Family system emotionally repressed and rigidly enmeshed, abuse repetitive and compulsive, offenses usually involve voyeurism and exhibitionistic acts, motivated by anxiety
6. *Disturbed impulsive youth:* Likely to have a clinical disorder, severe family dysfunction, substance abuse, learning problems, offenses tend to be impulsive, impaired reality testing
7. *Group influenced youth:* A young teenager, no prior antisocial history, influenced by peer group in a sexual assault

Treating Adolescent Offenders

A number of programs are now available for the adolescent sex offender. These programs may be found on an inpatient, outpatient, or residential basis. Most clinicians use models of therapy that are family or group based in approach. Individual therapy is not recommended as a primary modality. Most therapies used today reflect a behavioral, cognitive-behavioral, family systems, or relapse prevention approach model.

Several authors (Madanes, Keim, and Smelser, 1995; Perry and Orchard, 1992, 1989; Pithers et al., 1988; Breer, 1987; Bengis, 1986; Smith, 1985; Creeden and Sandford, 1984; Knopp, 1982) have made contributions to the treatment of adolescent sex offenders. Their work is outlined as follows:

Assessment

The assessment format for adolescent sex offenders is similar to the evaluation process for adult abusers. The protocol recommended is as follows: information obtained prior to interview; clinical interview of the adolescent sex offender; psychological testing; interview with parents; reinterview offender; process all assessment data; report to referral source.

Program Treatment Components

Several basic treatment components should be incorporated in a program for adolescent sex offenders. These may include the following:

1. An emphasis on the need to assume responsibility for the offense
2. A focus on victim empathy and remorse
3. Identification of the offense pattern and development of strategies to avoid reoffending
4. Sexual education programs and classes in anger management
5. Personal competency work to enhance communication skills, social and relationship development, stress management, and related issues, such as dating

Individual Therapy

Individual therapy can be used with adolescent sex offenders in combination with other forms of treatment. Psychotherapy should be focused on helping the offender with issues related to sexual aggression and other nonoffending behaviors, such as a problem at home. Sessions permit a therapist to give feedback to the offender regarding his or her progress in group. Supportive psychotherapy methods can be used.

Family Therapy

Family therapy can be of help in treating both adult and juvenile sex offenders. A family systems model approach can be used. The steps are as follows: exposing the offense; confrontation; revealing victims; acknowledging the emotional pain; recognizing the mother; offender apologizes on his or her knees; consequences of reoffending are discussed; finding a protector in the family; reparation; issues of sexuality; sexual aggression as a metaphor; prevention of suicide; finding meaning; empathy and compassion is discussed; feelings of loneliness are reviewed; restoration of love; the offender becoming the protector of the family; forgiveness.

Group Treatment

The primary objective of a treatment group is to help the adolescent avoid a reoffending situation. An adolescent sex offender group may possess the following guidelines:

1. Group members are expected to honor confidentiality and keep information contained to sessions.

2. An offender who reveals a new sexual offense will be reported.
3. Offenders must talk about their offense.
4. Offenders must use the first names of the victims.
5. Rationalization is not accepted, nor is inferring the victim was receptive, provocative, or that it just happened.
6. No vulgar or sexist language is permitted.
7. Group members must not interrupt one another and must permit others to talk in sessions.
8. Members are required to participate in group discussions.
9. Members must be on time for group sessions.
10. Homework assignments are expected to be completed in a timely manner.
11. Group members should not be judgmental of others.
12. Absences must be excused.
13. Members are responsible for getting to group (if outpatient).
14. No eating is allowed in group.

Inpatient and Outpatient Group Therapy

Group therapy is one recommended model of treatment for adolescent sex offenders in both inpatient or outpatient settings. Such therapy groups are distinguished by several factors and are listed as follows:

1. This form of therapy can serve a number of patients at once.
2. Such a model uses the peer group to support appropriate behavior.
3. A group is able to address social isolation, shame, secret keeping, communication problems, and other behaviors in a positive manner utilizing peer nurturing.
4. Group treatment is more powerful than individual treatment.

Relapse Prevention Model

A relapse prevention model, in a modified form, can be used in an adolescent offender program, which is outlined as follows:

1. Identify offense patterns and styles of coping, including early antecedents and specific determinants, apparently irrelevant decisions, high-risk situations, inadequate coping.

2. Use a cognitive-behavioral approach to focus on developing coping skills that prevent reoffending behavior.
3. The offender develops an awareness of warning signs that indicate he or she may be regressing, including work on understanding lapse, the abstinence violation effect of tuning out, and relapse.
4. The development of a long-term relapse prevention plan.

Treatment Recommendations

Clinicians often struggle with whether to treat the patient on an inpatient, outpatient, or residential basis. An adolescent offender should be receptive to treatment, admit to the crime, accept responsibility, display remorse and victim empathy, offer a detailed history of the crimes, be truthful, not possess a chronic and sustained history of violent assaults, have a flexible ego, which can be influenced by therapy, have a supportive family, be involved in a program that occupies free time, and have a community network system involving other agencies to be considered for outpatient treatment. An adolescent offender who has a violent assault history, multiple victims, limited remorse, escalated in frequency of offenses, is antisocial, possesses a delinquent history, has received prior outpatient treatment services, and has no family support is more suited for a residential program.

ANTISOCIAL PERSONALITY DISORDER OFFENDERS

Sex offenders with antisocial personality disorder (ASPD) represent a large proportion of individuals referred for services offered by the criminal justice, human service, or mental health systems at the present time. This disturbance may be the single most common clinical link found that is shared among sex offenders as a group. Incredibly, however, research thus far has been limited.

Available data indicate that approximately 29 percent of all men charged with rape alone had antisocial personality disturbances (Knopp, 1984; Abel, Rouleau, and Cunningham-Rathner, 1986). This equates to a population of nearly one-third of all rapists exhibiting some form of an ASPD disorder. Another interesting study (Berger et al., 1999) has found that ASPD can be found in approximately 42.2 percent of individuals with sadistic personality disorder. The American Psychiatric Association (1994) estimates that ASPD may be found in 3 percent of all males, and 1 percent of all females in community samples; but in clinical settings the prevalence estimates are higher, from 3 percent to as high as 30 percent. Prevalence rate samplings are even higher in correctional, forensic, and substance abuse environments.

ASPD patients, like sex offenders, historically are resistant to treatment services. Denial, minimization, and rationalization are common characteristics found in both groupings. ASPD, as defined by the American Psychiatric Association (1994), includes such features as: lawbreaking; deceitfulness or lies; impulsiveness; displays irritability and aggression; shows reckless behavior; is irresponsible; shows a lack of remorse; shows indifference; rationalizes.

Ruegg, Haynes, and Frances (1996) report that the first decision in working with any ASPD patient is deciding whether to offer treatment. Therapists considering therapy for ASPD sex offenders may consider a specific protocol. In general, factors for therapy with an ASPD patient may include:

1. The presence of an Axis I disorder, which is often treatable
2. Motivation as the result of lifestyle dissatisfaction and a desire to change
3. An external outside force, such as a court or prison situation
4. A past history of positive relationships indicating a capacity to form alliances
5. Behavior that is impulsive and is followed by some regret or remorse
6. A desire to live outside of prison

Treatment

Sex offenders with an ASPD disturbance can present as being very articulate, engaging, or interesting individuals. However, many are also manipulative, resistant to treatment, and will lie at any opportunity. As a result, it is important for the therapist to quickly establish expectations for these patients. The following guidelines are recommended for treatment:

1. Patients should be court ordered for outpatient treatment or on probation or parole.
2. Inpatient or correctional facilities can use other forms of clinical support to ensure compliance, such as the use of privileges.

3. A clinical assessment should be completed prior to treatment.
4. Offenders who enter treatment should be able to acknowledge their offense, identify their victim and target population, accept responsibility for their actions, and express some degree of remorse within eight sessions or be terminated.
5. Psychotherapy should address thinking errors, deviant arousal patterns, and values and behaviors.
6. A treatment contract should be completed with each patient, noting that honesty and truthfulness will be expected.
7. No reoffending or other criminal action will be allowed.
8. No alcohol or drug use will be permitted.
9. Engaging the ASPD sex offender is essential to the treatment.
10. Encourage transference.
11. Therapy with the ASPD sex offender should be specific, concrete, and reality based.
12. An educational component should be used.
13. Use humor when appropriate; levity and laughter can be effective, as many ASPD offenders are egocentric.
14. Set boundaries early in therapy.
15. Be realistic, fair, and direct during difficult topics.
16. Require self-study and special readings.
17. Encourage journal keeping.
18. Long-term psychotherapy is recommended.
19. Individual therapy may serve as an adjunct model.
20. Group therapy should be the primary model of treatment.
21. Be alert to emotional seduction and those who manipulate others in therapy.
22. Peer pressure is effective in work with ASPD sex offenders.
23. Build a group slowly, permitting members to evolve with a shared sense of a basic foundation.
24. Modeling should occur by the therapist.

FEMALE SEX OFFENDERS

Criminal justice, human service, and mental health professionals have started to acknowledge the existence of female offenders as a special population group. In the past, female perpetrators went under-reported, hampering intervention services by system providers. In one report of victims, 5 percent of girls and 20 percent of boys had been sexually abused in some form by women (Mayer, 1992; Finkelhor and Williams, 1988).

Factors influencing the low reporting of female offenders include the following: females may conceal sexually deviant actions through socially appropriate behaviors; female offenders who commit incest are reported less than those who violate others in a sexual manner outside of the family; and boys sexually abused by adult women are reluctant to report an offense (Mayer, 1992). Also, Mayer (1992) reports that societal standards differ for men and women. Males are socialized to express aggression and to sexualize their feelings of rage and impotence. Females are perceived as vulnerable individuals who are incapable of harming others. It is thought that women could not sexualize relationships, eroticize anger, or associate power and control with sexual needs. Culturally, females are stereotyped as physically and psychologically incapable of committing acts of sexual abuse. This double standard has carried over to female sex offenders.

Some Clinical Features

Current data indicate that women as sex offenders are increasing as a clinical population. A large number of offenses involve same-sex molestation situations. Sexual assaults with adult partners sometimes occur with female molesters and may have included coercion by the companion. There are both similarities and differences between female and male sex offenders. Such factors may include how defense mechanisms are displayed, power and control issues, victims as objects, and histories of sexual victimization during childhood (Mayer, 1992).

Male and female offenders share a common clinical theme in their role of power over a victim. This dynamic is significant in the sexual abuse. Women as well as men are influenced by the psychological and or physical hold they may possess over a victim. The use of control and manipulation are themes that are found in female offenders. Female offenders may be more likely to have a history of sexual abuse or other significant trauma than men. Males are more likely to treat their victims as an object, rather than as a person, than a female offender. Women are much more likely to have a shared relationship with the victim. Anger, if present, is expressed in a different form in female offenders when compared to males. Sadism is extremely rare. Female offenders tend to internalize their anger, as compared to male offenders, who externalize emotions. Defense mechanisms for female offenders may also include devaluation of self, displacement, dissociation, isolation, repression, and undoing.

Female Offender Types

Matthews (1998) notes three types of female offenders: (1) a teacher-lover, who becomes involved with a minor male; (2) the predisposed, a victim also, who acts out her molestation with children; (3) the male-coerced, who sexually abuses children with a male companion, either in or out of the home.

The teacher-lover female offender becomes involved in a relationship with a child as the result of a combination of interactions that eventually leads to a sexual relationship. These encounters usually are not forcible; the victim usually becomes supportive of the relationship. This type of offender may have power over the victim, and hold a position of authority in some form. Victims tend to be acquaintances, male, and are preadolescent or adolescent. The initial incident may not be planned, but later actions are organized and scheduled.

The predisposed offender may display paraphilia interests. Many of these female offenders have a history of victimization themselves. The offending may be seen as a reenactment of their sexual abuse. The target population may be the offender's own children. A number of these victims may be female, and can be preadolescent or adolescent in age. This type of offense is usually preceded by fantasy acting out. Most incidents are planned to some degree and follow a sexual abuse cycle pattern. Force is sometimes reported if the victim is reluctant to comply.

Male-coerced female offenders are involved in a relationship with an adult, either a husband or companion. Substance abuse may be involved during the sexual assault. These female offenders are encouraged by the companion to engage in sexual relations with a child. Usually, the adult male will observe the offense or engage during a part of the sexual assault. Target victims may be female or male, are preadolescent or adolescent, and can be a family member, acquaintance, or even a stranger. The initial offense can be unplanned by the offender, who has been manipulated by the companion. Additional offenses can be planned or scheduled, with some resistance or reluctance on the part of the female offender. Force and coercion may be used by the adult male companion on the female offender.

Treatment

Matthews (1998) reports that the first stage in providing treatment services for the female offender requires the clinician to see the patient as both a perpetrator and victim. Both roles are interrelated. To treat only the perpetrator, one fails to acknowledge the humanity of the offender. To treat only the victim issues negates the harm the offender has done to another person. Genuine empathy for the offender's victim cannot be expressed until the patient is able to understand their own emotional pain and destructive behavior. Female offenders have a history of suppressing their feelings. They have forgotten how to articulate their emotions in an appropriate way. Therefore, the natural progress in treatment is to empower the offender in voicing her own emotional pain, which, in turn, acts as a turning point in her recovery process. It is recommended that the patient meet the following therapeutic goals: acknowledge the sexual abuse; accept responsibility; define individual emotional and behavioral factors; address issues of self, and their specific offending type; work on victim empathy; develop exit criteria; develop a prevention and aftercare treatment plan.

Therapy Goals

The therapy goals of treatment should be directly related to the type of offending typology that has been identified. A generic form of psychotherapy for all female offenders is not considered suitable.

Matthews (1998) suggests that in working with the teacher-lover offender the most important goal is to have female offenders recognize the harm they did to another individual. Initially, such offenders report that they are angry because they have been held accountable for their actions while their victims are excused from prosecution.

Some female offenders believe that the victim is equally to blame in this type of sexual relationship. Clinicians should help the perpetrators understand how their position of power impacted the sexual abuse of the victim. Also, it is important to help the offender understand that as an adult she was responsible for establishing boundaries. It is also beneficial to educate this type of offender in the developmental stages of a child or adolescent, the problems of role confusion, and sexual identity.

The predisposed patient presents as the most clinically challenging of the three female offender typologies. These individuals have very few coping skills. Their ego functioning is often impaired. The id may contribute to problems of impulse control and sexual acting out. The superego displays many misconceptions regarding appropriate behaviors. Such patients can be provocative and permissive in their interactions with others. This patient is most likely a victim of childhood sexual abuse herself. The family is disengaged, chaotic, and nonsupportive.

A primary goal will be to help this offender build back her self-confidence. Self-esteem must be elevated in order for the patient to realize that people care for one another. An adult need for validation must be met by other adults rather than by children. An important goal for clinicians with such patients is addressing childhood issues. These offenders may both love and hate their parents, desire but fear an adult partner. They can cling at times, and reject during other periods. Such offenders have difficulty trusting. Paraphiliac behavior will also be represented; offenders will need to explore their fantasy system, masturbatory practices, deviant behaviors, and cycle of offending.

The male-coerced female offender may have first started offending with the assistance or coercion of a male partner. As a result, a primary treatment goal for such patients is to decease their issues of dependency. Self-esteem is important in the recovery process for this type of offender. Such patients should be helped in psychotherapy to become more independent. These offenders need to learn that they can function without a male partner. Assertiveness training or proper job search skills may be helpful.

The male-coerced offender usually has been involved in an abusive relationship that has eventually led to the sexual abuse of a child. This type of offender fears abandonment and will do almost anything to keep the relationship intact with her husband or companion. Initially, the companion will introduce the female to alternate forms of sexual misconduct, which may include affairs or group sex. Later, the sexual behavior becomes more bizarre, then a child is introduced and is sexually assaulted.

Individual, Family, and Group Treatment Suggestions

The treatment format for a female sex offender should be given serious consideration before psychotherapy is introduced. Individual, family, and group formats are all considered usable formats of therapy for female offenders.

Group therapy is the preferred treatment model for female offenders. However, due to the limited number of female offenders referred for treatment, many clinicians have no option but to offer individual or family therapy services. Clinicians should never consider placing a female offender in a group with male offenders. This treatment is inappropriate and can place both the female offender and the group at risk. The dynamics of a female offender are too different for any benefit to be derived in a male group. Also, many female offenders are victims of sexual abuse; placement in a male group could be clinically harmful.

Matthews (1998) reports success with an individual and women-only group therapy approach, and notes male and female offenders are different. For instance, women rarely use others as accomplices in offending situations. Also, women use force, violence, or threats much less often in their sexual offending than males. Men start abusing earlier than female offenders, with many males starting in adolescence. In therapy, men tend to forgive themselves much quicker than women do. Women will develop empathy for victims earlier in psychotherapy then men and will remain ashamed of their behavior for an extended period. Women tend to self-report abuse more often than men; those who do so are more likely complete a program of therapy.

One Treatment Model

Mayer (1992) outlined one suggested model of therapy for female molesters. This treatment protocol is both behavioral and supportive in approach. Supportive components are as follows:

1. Obtain disclosure by acceptance and trust building with the therapist.
2. Reduce or relieve stress by reassurance, validation, and development of improved insight.
3. Decrease isolation through group therapy.
4. Interrupt blocking by encouraging ventilation.
5. Listen, role-play, write unmailed letters.
6. Improve self-esteem through group therapy.

Behavioral-environmental components are listed as follows:

1. Redirect behavior that is more socially acceptable.
2. Clarify beliefs about victimization, the cycle of abuse, and arousal patterns.
3. Enhance depressive mood states and anxiety problems by helping the offender develop a larger behavioral and emotional support system.
4. Offer relaxation and stress management techniques.
5. Increase emotional support through group therapy.
6. Suggest alternate behaviors for problems that would lead to offending.
7. Provide educational or medical referrals to other agencies.

Chapter 14

Other Special Populations

Sexual deviancy encompasses a broad spectrum of behaviors. Due to the enormity of sexual dysfunction found in societies, some behaviors or groups are not always easily identified by system providers. This chapter reviews other special population groups that have appeared in recent years to merit services.

In addition, this section continues to explore reported treatment programs in the United States and in other countries for sex offenders in general and those in more diverse population groups. For example, the treatment success for sex offenders was documented by Weiss (1999) in the Czech Republic who found a recidivism rate of 17.1 percent of 953 patients in a study of sex offenders involved in a course of therapies. The program was started in 1976 and included both inpatient and outpatient services. Goals of the program included: adjustment of behavior, information acquisition, change in defense mechanisms, development of insight, strengthening in cognitive control, attitude and value change, sexual adaptation, and social reintegration. Clinical goals were achieved by assessment and diagnosis, specialization departments, psychotherapy that used individual and group therapy in psychodynamic and cognitive-behavioral forms, social interventions, pharmacotherapy, and the penile plethysmograph.

SCHIZOPHRENIA AND PSYCHOTIC DISORDERS

Numerous studies have been completed on schizophrenia. However, research and available literature about patients with schizophrenia and psychotic disorders who have committed sexual offenses have been sparse. There has been little investigation conducted, to date, on this patient population group. As a result, available treatment information is limited.

Phillips and colleagues (1999) note in one study of patients that approximately 21 percent of individuals with a diagnosis of schizophrenia were found to be dangerous, meriting inpatient hospitalization. All participants in this group were male and had exhibited antisocial sexual behavior. Reportedly, fewer than one-half of this population had been convicted of a sexual crime. In nearly all of these cases, sexual violence was found to have first postdated illness onset by an average period of five years. Also, at the time of their present hospitalization, all patients were found to be displaying psychotic symptoms at the time of the sexual misconduct.

Chan, Lim, and Ong (1997) completed a study on sexual "modesty" offenders remanded to a state mental hospital. "Modesty" offending was said to include touching, grabbing, kissing, or fondling incidents. This Singapore survey found that the majority of offenders hospitalized for this frottage behavior were schizophrenic or mentally retarded. Nearly 45.3 percent were schizophrenic. Most of the offenses were committed during the day. Only 15.4 percent of those hospitalized had a prior history of sexual offending. Most were competent at the time of the offense.

Phillips and colleagues (1999) report that mentally ill patients who commit acts of sexual aggression merit individual and group treatment services. Such therapy may involve problems of sexual misconduct and other related behaviors. Areas of treatment may be focused upon anger management, interpersonal relationships, and social skills.

Currently, there is a lack of programs available for dually diagnosed sex offenders offered in the clinical community. Persons with schizophrenia can display aggression, anxiety, anger, confusion, delusions, hallucinations, paranoia, and impaired insight and judgment skills, poor reality testing, self-isolating behaviors, and inappropriate forms of sexual misconduct. The clinical community has been slow to respond to the treatment needs of sex offenders who are mentally ill. Also, there is a lack of skilled clinicians who are willing or able to work with this population. Regardless, community safety remains a chief concern.

Many successful programs have been established for schizophrenia in which a supportive therapy model approach is used. Such a program would also appear to be appropriate of dually diagnosed sex offenders. As a result, the following clinical guidelines may be considered:

1. Individual and group therapy models may be used.
2. A supportive psychotherapy model is recommended.
3. An insight-oriented psychotherapy is not recommended.
4. Denial is not accepted, but a confrontational approach should not be used.
5. Anxiety may produce a psychiatric relapse.
6. Encourage the patients to acknowledge their offenses in a helpful manner.
7. Promote honesty and responsibility for behavior.
8. Patients who are reluctant to acknowledge their offenses should not be terminated.
9. Therapy should remain in the "here and now" stage.
10. Revelations of childhood sexual abuse should be evaluated by the therapist.
11. Patients should be encouraged to discuss their crimes and offer some details about their offense history.
12. Self-disclosure can be difficult for the schizophrenic patient.
13. Remorse and victim empathy may be reviewed, but schizophrenic patients are often unable to display meaningful insight as a result of their illness.
14. Therapy should always be hopeful, supporting existing ego defenses.
15. Therapists should remain watchful of both content and process, for possible reoffending behavior may be revealed.
16. Expect limitations in patients.
17. Treatment should be simple, concrete, and include an educational component.
18. Encourage patients to identify types of crimes, target population, methods of victim selection, fantasy, and cycle of offending.
19. Partial or full remission is required for such therapy.
20. Patients need to acknowledge their mental illness and features of their disorder.
21. Medication should be discussed.
22. Treatment should be long term.
23. Treatment services should never be denied, unless clinical harm is suspected.

Interestingly, more information is available for the treatment of the mentally retarded sex offender than the dually diagnosed mentally ill offender. Clinicians may find useful reference information for the treatment of dually diagnosed patients by reviewing literature on the mentally retarded sex offender.

THE MENTALLY RETARDED SEX OFFENDER

Mild or moderate mentally retarded sex offenders are the most likely candidates to be considered for therapy. The severe or profound mentally retarded individual usually is not an appropriate candidate for specialized sex offender treatment services due to cognitive limitations.

Kaplan and Sadock (1998b), in general, recommend the following treatment formats for the mentally retarded: education for the child; behavior, cognitive, and psychodynamic therapies; family education; social intervention; and pharmacological intervention. Most therapists providing sex offender treatment will rely upon a combination of therapeutic techniques—proven successful with nonoffending mentally retarded individuals.

However, there are three items that distinguish the intellectually disabled sex offender that are important in providing appropriate treatment services (Cumming and Buell, 1997; Haaven, Little, and Petre-Miller, 1990). They are listed as follows:

1. Confrontation of denial is not found to be helpful; a more incremental disclosure approach is recommended, with testing data used to promote acknowledgment.
2. These patients experience more problems in caring for themselves, living skills are a greater obstacle, and such individuals can become dependent on staff involved in their treatment.
3. Self-esteem is an issue that impacts the therapy process, since disabled offenders are more sensitive to criticism, can overreact to feedback, and are fearful of change.

Knopp (1990) recommends that a mentally retarded sex offender's history be evaluated before treatment is offered. Certain candidates may not be suitable for therapy. A risk assessment may be useful.

Such criteria may include: impulsivity; predatory behavior; prior use of physical force or a weapon; chronic substance abuse; fire setting, animal torture, and enuresis (bed-wetting); and failed specialized treatment in the past. Community safety should also be a concern if outpatient treatment is a consideration rather than an inpatient or residential setting.

In their study, Murrey, Briggs, and Davis (1992) report that victims of mentally retarded sex offenders were primarily males or females under the age of sixteen. In comparison, 88 percent of psychopathic disordered type individuals and 98 percent of mentally ill offenders selected female victims as their primary target population. However, the mentally retarded perpetrator used violence less then the psychopathic disordered or mentally ill offender, with a 51 percent report rate.

Hawk, Rosenfeld, and Warren (1993), in a Virginia study, noted that during a six-year period, more than one-fourth of mentally retarded defendants involved in a forensic evaluations were charged with a sex offense. Mentally retarded individuals constituted 13 percent of all sex offenders in the sample survey. This study also cited in a literature analysis that programs had been only recently started for the mentally retarded sex offender, with no significant research of efficacy on a global scale yet initiated.

Haaven, Little, and Petre-Miller (1990) suggest that a quality inpatient treatment program for the mentally retarded offender should include the following elements:

1. The program should be as voluntary as possible in an effort to engage the patient.
2. The treatment should use a multidiagnostic, holistic approach, individualized for the patient.
3. Use a self-help approach, which may be modified from a therapeutic community model of care, empowering patients to participate in their treatment.
4. Use cognitive restructing methods, adapted to the client's level; use categorical learning rather than inductive or deductive reasoning, which addresses personality disorders and distorted thinking.
5. Learning should be promoted as being fun, with treatment lessons presented in a dramatic format.

SERIAL SEX OFFENDERS

Sex offenders commit serial or multiple offenses. Research now indicates a number of sex offenders commit a wide range of offenses and do not fall into any one diagnostic group. However, these offenders should not be confused with serial sexual homicide offenders. Nonhomicide serial sex offenders have been largely overlooked as a specific population group. Nevertheless, certain basic disturbances meriting clinical attention may be found in this group. Therapists working with serial offenders should note the following:

1. The crime is only one in a series of sexual offenses.
2. Research indicates that most sex offenders possess two or more types of paraphilia behavior.
3. Fear of exposure impacts acknowledgment.
4. Serial offenders display a cycle of offending.
5. Masturbatory fantasies, rituals, distress, urges for sexual gratification, predatory behavior, and victim selection may differ according to availability.
6. Psychosocial stressors may include family, occupational, and social factors.
7. Reckless behavior is sometimes found.
8. Impulse control problems may be an issue.
9. Serial offenders may have multiple partners or show an inability to maintain a relationship.
10. Substance abuse may be present.
11. Other criminal behavior may or may not exist.
12. Problems of intimacy may be present.
13. Serial offenders exhibit denial.
14. Offenders often use rationalization.
15. Serial offenders tend to exhibit obsessive-compulsive features.

Treatment, in general, for a serial offender should be based on the following:

1. Acknowledgment of present and past crimes
2. A willingness to accept treatment
3. Whether the offender is awaiting adjudication on a pending charge

4. Level of risk to the community if outpatient treatment is a consideration
5. Family, social, and professional support systems
6. Whether the patient will be court ordered to treatment and on probation or parole supervision
7. The offender's desire to change
8. Offenders openness to discussion about arousal system, fantasy, and masturbatory behavior as well as victims
9. Level of victim empathy
10. Patients considered for individual or family therapies, but primary treatment model is group

STALKERS

Stalking behavior has started to receive increased interest in the criminal justice and mental health communities. This type of problem behavior has been reported for many years. Until only recently, stalking has been associated with sexual offending behavior. However, the rate of incidence between stalking behavior and sexual assault is not known. Sexual harassment is often reported in stalking cases.

Fisher, Cullen, and Turner (2000) report that a correlation was found to exist between stalking and rape. During a survey of more than 4,000 college women during the 1996 and 1997 school term, 10.3 percent who had been stalked were involved in some type of unwanted sexual activity. Either rape or an attempt to sexually harm the victim was reported.

Generally, the study found overall that 13.1 percent of all participants had been stalked, or 156.5 persons per 1,000 female students. Stalking incidents were said to last an average of sixty days. About 30 percent of those victims stalked resided off campus.

Meloy (1998) reports that a distinction exists between the legal and clinical definition for stalking. The legal definition, which may vary by state or federal statute, generally consists of three key elements: (1) a pattern of behavioral intrusion that is unwanted by the victim; (2) a direct or indirect threat as evidenced in the intrusive behavior; and (3) the intrusive behavior produces fear for a person who feels threatened.

Stalking, in clinical terms, according to literature cited by Meloy (1998), defines the behavior as (1) an abnormal or long-term pattern of threat or harassment toward a particular victim; (2) more than one overt act of unwanted pursuit by an individual directed toward a specific victim, which is viewed as harassing; and (3) obsessional following-like behavior.

In a 1997 study of 8,000 males and 8,000 females concerning stalking, approximately 8 percent of women and 2 percent of men had been stalked sometime during their lives. An estimated 1 million adult women and about 0.4 million adult men were stalked annually. Approximately 50 percent of the victims file complaints with police of which 25 percent result in arrest. About 12 percent of all reported stalking cases eventually result in criminal prosecution (Meloy, 1998; Tjaden and Thoennes, 1997).

Meloy (1998) states that research has provided some answers and direction to stalking behavior as well as which types of interventions are merited. Findings have included the following:

1. Stalking as a problem behavior is considered old; it only recently has been designated as a crime in many states.
2. Men comprise the majority of stalkers; victims are mostly female.
3. Prevalence is found mostly in the fourth decade of life.
4. Most stalkers have a prior criminal, psychiatric, or substance abuse history.
5. Axis I disorders are found in the majority of stalkers; they are most likely to include mood disorders, schizophrenia, or substance abuse diagnoses.
6. Axis II personality disorders are present in many cases.
7. Most stalkers are not psychotic at the time of the offense.
8. There is increasing empirical evidence to support a hypothesis that stalking is a pathology of attachment, with early childhood disruption and a major psychosocial stressor as an adult prior to the behavior.
9. Research suggests stalkers may be one of the most intelligent criminal groups.
10. Most stalkers are unemployed or underemployed at the time of the incidents.

11. The most common form of stalking involves males stalking women with whom they had a prior sexual relationship.
12. Threats increase the risk of violence, although most threats made are not carried out.
13. If violence occurs, usually weapons are not involved.
14. The homicide rate for stalking victims is less than 2 percent.
15. The primary motivation for stalking is not sexual, but is representative of anger, hostility toward the victim, and a need to control.
16. Defense mechanisms include denial, minimization, and projection.
17. There is a high frequency in violence associated with stalkers, as compared to other criminal groupings, with violent acts occurring in the 25 to 35 percent range.

Three separate typology groups of stalkers have been identified. These are listed as follows: simple obessionals, love obsessionals, and erotomanics. In simple obsessional stalking cases, the perpetrator has some prior history with the victim. Sometimes this relationship included sexual relations, but is not always the case. In cases involving love obsessional stalking, the victim may have not known the offender. Victims are sometimes celebrities, or the stalker somehow becomes fixated on a particular individual. Many love obsessional stalkers have a history of schizophrenia. The erotomania stalker is an individual who suffers from a delusional belief system and is of the opinion that the victim has emotional feelings for him or her that do not exist (Zona, Palarea, and Lane, 1998).

Meyer (1998) reports that a multidisciplinary approach be considered in working with stalkers. As a result, both the criminal justice and mental systems need to work in concert to limit additional incidents of stalking behavior. Each case should be evaluated carefully prior to making a decision regarding clinical treatment. A comprehensive assessment of the stalker is recommended.

Additional treatment guidelines may include:

1. Stalkers, if referred to treatment, should be court ordered and a probation officer should be assigned to the case.
2. If an Axis I disorder is found, a psychiatric evaluation is appropriate with possible medication services.
3. Individual, family, and group psychotherapy services may be appropriate.

4. Stalkers who have sexually assaulted their victims merit sex offender treatment services.
5. It is important for the stalker to acknowledge his or her crime.
6. Stalkers who are referred to outpatient treatment services may merit a potential to reoffend and/or to harm their victim.
7. Some stalkers may first be jailed or hospitalized.

SEX ADDICTS

Sex addiction is a phenomenon found among individuals who compulsively seek sexual situations in order to satisfy their (unrealistic) need for sexual gratification. Although this problem behavior is not formally recognized by the American Psychiatric Association (2000) in the DSM-IV, family, occupational-TR, and social functioning is impaired. Persons afflicted by this behavior display repeated and markedly increased interest in engaging in sexual relations. Distress is experienced if the individual is unable to obtain sex. The behavior is found in both men and women.

Kaplan and Sadock (1998c) note the following features for sexual addiction: behavior that is out of control; medical, legal, and interpersonal problems due to sexual misconduct; self-destructive or high-risk sexual behavior; repeated attempts to limit or stop; sexual obsession and fantasy as coping mechanisms; the increased need for sexual activity; severe mood change; large amounts of time spent obtaining sex, planning incidents, or recovering from episodes.

Sex addicts are known to have a potential for other addictions including chemical dependency, eating disorders, compulsive gambling, and spending sprees. Persons with this problem behavior are reported to have a high probability in having been raised in a dysfunctional family system. There can be a history of emotional, physical, and sexual abuse.

Carnes (1983) suggests that there are several levels of sex addiction. Level one behavior may be found to include excessive masturbation, affairs, pornography, involvement with a prostitute, or homosexuality. Level two behaviors are considered more intrusive and can lead to contact with the criminal justice system; they may include exhibitionism, voyeurism, obscene telephone calling, and indecent liberties. Level three sexual misconduct behavior includes rape, incest, and child molesting. (Although this information is considered important, it should not be an implication that all sexually addicted persons will offend.)

Kaplan and Sadock (1998c) recommend the following treatment models: insight-oriented psychotherapy; supportive psychotherapy; and cognitive-behavioral psychotherapy. Also, marital or couples counseling may be appropriate. Additionally, pharmacotherapy may be merited for review by a psychiatrist. Self-help groups are helpful with this problem behavior.

Chapter 15
Additional Treatment Concepts

Sexual aggression is a serious problem. The majority of victims appear to be adult women and children. Statistical data are alarming. During adulthood it is estimated that between one and four to one and ten adult women will be raped or sexually assaulted during their lifetimes. Similar figures are found for children. More than 2 million reports of child abuse and neglect situations are investigated annually. Violence is also found in domestic arrangements and can be expressed by physical, sexual, or psychological assault (O'Neill, 2000; Vallianatos, 2000; Hall, 1995; Finkelhor, 1984; Koss, 1993).

Many new interventions have been offered by those within the criminal justice, human service, and mental health community. This chapter explores these concepts, including pharmacology, risk assessment, and registration. In addition, surgical castration, relapse, and recidivism are reviewed.

PHARMACOLOGY AND SURGICAL CASTRATION

Drug therapy with sex offenders is successful in reducing recidivism rates through the reduction of arousal, deviant behavior, fantasy, and sexual drive. The success of such a treatment protocol depends upon intensive pretreatment evaluation of an individual displaying a paraphilia disturbance (American Psychiatric Association, 1999).

Abel (1989) reports that there is a considerable body of evidence indicating that sexual disturbances such as paraphilias may be improved through the use of drug therapy. There are side effects that may limit the use of such medications. Also, some sex offenders resist drug therapy in order to maintain their deviant behaviors.

Three medications have been found to lower or impact testosterone levels in persons with a paraphilia disorder. These medications are cyproterone acetate (CPA), medroxyprogesterone acetate (MPA), and leuprolide acetate (LPA). A fourth new series of medications affecting serotonin, such as serotonin reuptake inhibitors (SRIs), have demonstrated interesting results, although there are yet insufficient scientific data to endorse such medication for all paraphilias.

Berlin, Malin, and Thomas (1995) notes that CPA is an antiandrogen receptor that blocks the uptake or influence of testosterone in the brain. MPA is a synthetic progestogenic that impacts the luteinizing and follicle-stimulating hormones, reducing testicular androgen output. LPA is a synthetic nonapeptide analog hormone that suppresses serum testosterone by depleting luteinizing hormones. Currently, LPA and MPA are approved by the Food and Drug Administration (FDA) in the United States for the treatment of paraphilias. LPA is also known as Lupron. MPA is identified by the name Provera, or if injected, Depo-Provera. CPA (Androcur) is authorized for research purposes only at the present time.

Side effects for these drugs vary, but all three may include weight gain and mood liability. LPA and MPA also display possible side effects of hypertension. There are other side effects that are usually rare, but that may be harmful, including liver problems. Psychiatrists and other physicians will need to evaluate other possible reactions before using one of these medications.

Patients who consent to drug therapy report a decrease in sexual aggression or activity. Sexual fantasy, urges, and related deviant behaviors are influenced. Different medications may appear to be more effective for particular sexual disturbances. CPA and MPA as Depo-Provera have been used with persons who experience a hypersexual type of paraphilia. Examples may include compulsive sexual aggression, excessive masturbation, or sexual incidents whenever possible.

Bradford and Greenberg (1996) note that the pharmacological treatment of sex offenders has undergone dramatic changes over the past several years. In the past, pharmacological studies had been modeled on research that involved surgical castration. Recently, serotonin inhibitors (SRIs) have been advanced in the treatment of deviant sexual disturbances. Surgical castration studies have indicated a recidivism rate as low as 5 percent, with persons being followed for up to twenty years. Serotonin inhibitors may be particularly effective in the reduction of sexual aggression in individuals with obsessive-compulsive features and related impulse-control disorders. Sex offenders have wrongly been viewed in the clinical community as a population deserving humiliation with lengthy prison sentences. Instead, drug therapy may offer a new approach to the treatment of sexual deviance and offending.

First, a form of medical castration is now available by the use of antiandrogens. Second, the suppression of the sexual drive by CPA is available, through which sexual fantasy and urges can be influenced. Third, MPA is believed to offer control of problem behavior, as long as the treatment is rendered. Fourth, SRIs are revealing that there is possible hope for the treatment of paraphilias. Results appear positive with reports of recidivism and relapse in studies to be low. Additional double-blind studies are being conducted (Bradford and Greenberg, 1996). Drug therapy holds tremendous potential for the treatment of sex offenders.

RECIDIVISM AND RELAPSE

Greenberg (1998) reports that *recidivism* and *relapse* are terms that are the subject of debate. Generally, *recidivism* can be defined as a tendency to relapse or return to a previous condition and mode of behavior. *Relapse,* for a sex offender, may be seen as an incident in which an individual sexually reoffends.

However, in a major new Canadian report of 28,972 sex offenders completed by Hanson and Bussiere (1998), it was found that only 13.4 percent of sex offenders reoffended. A four- to five-year follow-up period occurred. These findings were said to contradict the more "popular view" that almost all sexual offenders reoffend. This major metaanalysis report involved 61 separate follow-up studies of sex offenders.

Overall, research data compiled found that the predictors of a nonsexual reoffense were similar to those found in research on any type of general offender population. Sexual offenders who did commit a nonsexual crime tended to be young, unmarried, and had a history of antisocial behavior. In comparison, the strongest predictor of sexual recidivism was found to be related to sexual deviance, such as prior sexual offenses, deviant interests, age, and total prior arrests. Hanson (1997b) noted that those sex offenders who were motivated for therapy were at lower risk to reoffend (8 percent), than those unmotivated or those who failed to complete a specialized program of treatment (22 percent).

RISK ASSESSMENT

Risk assessment is a major concern for any professional working with a sex offender. As a result, many excellent risk assessment scales have been developed over the years worldwide in an effort to predict reoffenses by sex offenders.

Cumming and Buell (1997) reviewed the Vermont Assessment of Sex-Offender Risk scale. The instrument is designed for evaluating adult male offenders. The findings of this scale were reported to be "encouraging," but this form of measurement is still considered only a research tool. Offenders are ranked in scoring by their potential to reoffend as being low, moderate, or high. Reportedly, offenders who test in the low range and most in the moderate range can be supervised and treated in a community setting. Those offenders found to score in the high range generally require incarceration.

The results of scoring are based on two categories: reoffense risk and violence risk. The reoffense risk includes the following groupings: a type of sexual crime; a prior adult conviction; court order violation; level of force during offense; relationship to victim; male victim or history of exhibitionism; deviant sexual fixation; alcohol abuse; drug abuse; address changes; time employed in school; reoffending during or after treatment; amenability to outpatient treatment. The violence risk section includes: prior conviction of crimes; conviction of crime using a weapon; force during current crime; sexual intrusiveness of offense; physical harm to victim; victim age (McGrath and Hoke, 1994).

Recently, the actuarial risk assessments have become increasingly popular in comparison to the guided clinical assessments. Hanson (1999) reports that the most significant difference between the two is the small number of variables that are used during measurement. Rules are very specific, explicit, and do not allow for a great deal of subjective interpretation.

One actuarial risk assessment that has gained popular acceptance within the mental health community in the United States and Canada is the Rapid Risk Assessment for Sexual Offense Recidivism (RRASOR). This assessment was developed in 1997 (Hanson, 1997a).

The RRASOR measures four categories. These groups are as follows: prior sex offense, not including the present index offense; age at release or current age; victim gender; and relationship to victim. Scoring may occur from a low of 0 to a high of 5. The scale is intended to be used only for adult males who have already been convicted of at least one prior sexual crime. This evaluation is not recommended for adolescents or female offenders. The assessment is based upon a sample survey of 2,592 offenders for evaluation over a five- to ten-year period of time. According to the Hanson (1999), the RRASOR has showed "moderate predictive accuracy." An example in scoring for sex offenses is as follows: 0 = no prior offenses; 1 = one prior conviction; 2 = two or three prior convictions; and 3 = four or more prior convictions. In addition, other variables may be used (score moderately), such as sexual preference, deviant activity, onset of offending, diverse sex crimes, criminal history, marital status, failure to complete a sex offender program, intimacy deficits, negative peer influence, attitude of sexual assault, emotional and sexual regulation, and general regulation, such as impulsiveness (Hanson and Phenix, 1999).

REGISTRATION, PUBLIC NOTICE, AND THE INTERNET

Registration for sex offenders has become a fast-growing trend across the United States. Basically, a sex offender is required to register with a local or state police or district attorney upon conviction or release from incarceration. Schwartz (1995a) reports that a least twenty-eight states now require sex offenders to notify law enforcement authorities of their presence in a local community. Also, the offender is required to update the registry upon a change of address. Registration is seen as one useful way of monitoring the location of offenders, their compliance with law, and behavior. Failure to register may serve as an alert to law enforcement staff that a problem may exist for an offender.

However, this form of monitoring has yet failed to gain nationwide acceptance. As a result, an offender may simply avoid compliance by changing his or her state of residence, particularly to border states, with different registration rules. Another problem with registration thus far is that not all sex offenders are required to register with police. In some states, only felony-level sex offenders are required to enroll in the program. Since many sex offender cases are often plea bargained, a felony is reduced to a misdemeanor, and an active pedophile is able to continue his or her active offending behavior without being monitored, if probation is not ordered.

Schwartz (1995a) reports that public notice situations are also occurring. In addition to law enforcement staff being notified of the release of a sex offender from a prison, the media may be notified. Signs, bulletins, and photos of the offender may be placed in a community. Even more alarming is the issue of the Internet, in which the names, addresses, crimes, and photographs are displayed. This form of public notice is "vigilante" in manner, and no studies have been found to prove the effectiveness of such programs. The offenders, their families, and their friends are impacted by such an approach. Some offenders are threatened, harmed, or socially separated by a community.

CONCLUSIONS

Sexual offenses continue to be reported across the United States and in other countries. Community safety and the protection of future victims is now an active concern that has impacted the visibility of this growing patient population group. Several recommendations or thoughts for the assessment, intervention, and treatment of sexual offenders may be appropriate now for review. These are listed as follows:

1. Social policy may be clinically influenced by research. Currently, there is a deficit in approved money for research on sexual aggression.
2. The majority of victims of sexual abuse are women and children. In the United States, the implications of priority may be demonstrated by social policy of those victimized.
3. Present sexual disorders are of a passive form with the exception of pedophilia and sexual sadism. Much scientific evidence supports a clinical diagnosis for sexual assault.
4. A number of outcome studies indicate a decline in reoffending occurs when treatment is used as a protocol. Yet only a minority of sexual offenders paroled are ordered into treatment.
5. Nearly 75 to 80 percent of sex offenders can be supervised and treated through a community basis.

6. Medication may soon be a major treatment intervention offered by the psychiatric community for sex offenders.
7. There is a staff shortage in most criminal justice, human service, and mental health agencies that provide services to sex offenders. Large caseloads and low to moderate salaries are cited.
8. Specialized training is merited for criminal justice, human service, and mental health professionals who work with sex offenders. Usually, funding for such training is limited.
9. There should be a revision in licensure expectations for some states, requiring specialized training for those who treat offenders.
10. Many academic institutions may desire to review curriculum requirements, adding courses on sexual abuse and sexual offenders.
11. Legislators may need to review state and federal laws regarding sex crimes. Plea bargaining, no contest arrangements, and Alfred Pleas for sexual offenses impact treatment. Courts and prosecutors should be careful in plea bargain agreements in which the offender does not admit guilt.
12. Sex offenders represent a growing population group in prison. Staff cite growing costs. Additional funding for correctional agencies is merited.
13. State parole and probation conditions merit revision. Federal probation, in most cases, requires a sex offender to remain in treatment until supervision is completed. Unfortunately, this does not always occur at the state level.
14. A national registry for convicted sex offenders with required registration. Presently, only a third of states request registration of a sex offender.
15. A strictly punitive approach to sex offenders does not appear to be effective. Evidence now exists that many sexual offenders are influenced by biomedical/psychiatric/psychological disturbances, for which treatment is appropriate.
16. Not all sex offenders respond to treatment and supervision; the protection of the community should be a major concern. There is controversy about special residential or hospital programs for offenders who have completed prison stays.

References

Abel, G.G. (1984). *The outcome of assessment treatment at the sexual behavior clinic and its relevance to the need for treatment programs for adolescent sex offenders in New York State.* Paper presented at a prison research/education/action project, Albany, NY.

Abel, G.G. (1989). Paraphilias. In H.I. Kaplan and B.J. Sadock (Eds.), *Comprehensive textbook of psychiatry/V* (pp. 1069-1085). Baltimore, MD: Williams and Wilkins.

Abel, G.G., Becker, J.V., Cunningham-Rathner, J., Mittelman, M., and Rouleau, J.L. (1988). Multiple paraphiliac diagnoses among sex offenders. *Bulletin American Academy of Psychiatry Law, 16*(2), 153-168.

Abel, G.G., Becker, J.V., Mittleman, M., Cunningham-Rathner, J., Rouleau, J.L., and Murphy, W.D. (1987). Self-reported sex crimes of nonincarcerated paraphiliacs. *Journal of Interpersonal Violence, 2*(1), 3-25.

Abel, G.G., and Osborn, C.A. (1995). Pedophilia. In G.O. Gabbard (Ed.), *Treatments of psychiatric disorders,* Second edition, Volume 2 (pp. 1959-1975). Washington, DC: American Psychiatric Press, Inc.

Abel, G.G., Osborn, C., Anthony, D., and Gardos, P. (1992). Current treatments of paraphiliacs. *Annual Review of Sex Research, 3,* 225-290.

Abel, G.G., Rouleau, J.L., and Cunningham-Rathner, J. (1986). Sexually aggressive behavior. In W.J. Curran, A.L. McGarry, and S.A. Shah (Eds.), *Forensic psychiatry and psychology: Perspectives and standards for interdisciplinary practice* (pp. 289-313). Philadelphia, PA: F.A. Davis Company.

Allen, M.G. (Ed.) (1990a). Group psychotherapy. Psychiatric Annuals, 20.

Allen, M.G. (Ed.) (1990b). Group psychotherapy—past, present and future. *Psychiatric Annuals, 20,* 358-361.

Allen, M.G. (1996). Current practice and procedures of group psychotherapy: In *The Hatherleigh guide to psychotherapy* (pp. 99-120). New York: Hatherleigh Press.

American Psychiatric Association (1987). *Diagnostic and statistical manual of mental disorders,* Third edition, revised. Washington, DC: American Psychiatric Association.

American Psychiatric Association (1994). *Diagnostic and statistical manual of mental disorders,* Fourth edition. Washington, DC: American Psychiatric Association.

American Psychiatric Association (1999). *Dangerous sex offenders: A task force report of the American Psychiatric Association.* Washington, DC: Author.

American Psychiatric Association (2000). *Diagnostic and statistical manual of mental disorders,* Fourth edition, Text revision. Washington, DC: American Psychiatric Association.

Barbaree, H.E. and Marshall, W.L. (1991). The role of male sexual arousal in rape: Six models. *Journal of Consulting and Clinical Psychology, 59*(5), 621-630.

Becker, J. (1989). The identification and treatment of the adolescent sexual offender. Conference at Portsmouth, VA, April 17.

Bengis, S.M. (1986). *A comprehensive service delivery system with a continuum of care for adolescent sexual offenders.* Orwell, VT: Safer Society Press.

Bennett, W.W. and Hess, K.M. (1998). *Criminal investigation,* Fifth edition. Belmont, CA: West/Wadsworth Publishing Co.

Bera, W.H. (1985). A preliminary investigation of a typology of adolescent sex offenders and their family systems. Unpublished master's thesis. University of Minnesota, Minneapolis, Minnesota.

Bera, W.H. (1989, April). *Adolescent sex offenders and their family systems.* Paper presented at advanced training for treatment of adolescent sex offenders, sponsored by Canadian Child Welfare Association, Toronto, Ontario, Canada.

Berger, P., Berner, W., Bolterauer, J., Gutierrez, K., and Berger, K. (1999). Sadistic personality disorder in sex offenders: Relationship to antisocial personality disorder and sexual sadism. *Journal of Personality Disorders, 13*(2), Summer, 175-186.

Berlin, F.S., Hunt, W.P., and Malin, H.M. (1991). A five-year-plus follow-up survey of criminal recidivism within a cohort of 406 pedophiles, 111 exhibitionists, and 109 sexual aggressives: Issues and outcome. *American Journal of Forensic Psychiatry, 12,* 5-28.

Berlin, F.S., Malin, H.M., and Thomas, K. (1995). Nonpedophiliac and nontransvestic paraphilias. In G.O. Gabbard (Ed.), *Treatment of psychiatric disorders,* Second edition, Volume 2 (pp. 1942-1958). Washington, DC: American Psychiatric Press.

Bloch, S. and Crouch, E. (1985). *Therapeutic factors in group psychotherapy.* New York: Oxford University Press.

Bradford, J.M.W. (1998). Treatment of men with paraphilia. *The New England Journal of Medicine, 338*(7), 464-465.

Bradford, J.M.W. and Gratzer, T.G. (1995). A treatment for impulse control disorders and paraphilia: A case report. *Canadian Journal of Psychiatry, 40,* 4-5.

Bradford, J.M.W. and Greenberg, D.M. (1996). Pharmacological treatment of deviant sexual behavior. *Annual Review of Sex Research, 7,* 283-306.

Breer, W. (1987). *The adolescent molester.* Springfield, IL: Charles C Thomas.

Breslow, N., Evans, L., and Langley, J. (1985). On the prevalence and roles of females in the sadomasochistic subculture: Report of empirical study. *Archives of Sexual Behavior, 14*(4), 303-317.

Brown, G.R. (1995). Transvestism. In G.O. Gabbard (Ed.), *Treatment of psychiatric disorders,* Second edition, Volume 2 (pp. 1977-1999). Washington, DC: American Psychiatric Press.

Burgess, A.W. and Hazelwood, R.R. (1995). The victim's perspective. In R.R. Hazelwood and A.W. Burgess (Eds.), *Practical aspects of rape investigation: A multidisciplinary approach,* Second edition (pp. 27-42). Boca Raton, FL: CRC Press.

Byard, R.W., Hucker, S.J., and Hazelwood, R.R. (1990). A comparison of typical death scene features in cases of fatal male and female autoerotic asphyxia with a review of the literature. *Forensic Science International, 48,* 113-121.

Cappelleri, J., Eckenrode, J., and Powers, J. (1993). The epidemiology of child abuse: Findings from the second national incidence and prevalence study of child abuse and neglect. *American Journal of Public Health, 83,* 1622-1624.

Carnes, P. (1983). *Out of the shadows: Understanding sexual addiction.* Minneapolis, MN: Compcare Publishers.

Chan, A., Lim, L., and Ong, S. (1997). A review of outrage of modesty offenders remanded in a state mental hospital. *Medical Science Law,* October, *37*(4), 349-352.

Cohen, F. (1995). Confidentiality, privilege, and self-incrimination. In B.K. Schwartz and H.R. Cellini (Eds.), *The sex offender: Corrections, treatment and legal practice* (pp. 26-1 to 26-16). Kingston, NJ: Civic Research Institute.

Coleman, E., Dwyer, S.M., Abel, G., Berner, W., Breiling, J., Hindman, J., Knopp, F.H., Langevin, R., and Pfafflin, F. (1996). Standards of care for the treatment of adult sex offenders. In E. Coleman, S.M. Dwyer, and N.J. Pallone (Eds.), *Sex offender treatment: Biological dysfunction, intrapsychic conflict, interpersonal violence* (pp. 5-11). New York: The Haworth Press.

Corsini, R.J. and Rosenberg, B. (1955). Mechanisms of group psychotherapy processes and dynamics. *Journal of Abnormal and Social Psychology, 51,* 406-411.

Creeden, K. and Sandford, L. (1984). The treatment of juvenile sex offenders. A preliminary description. Unpublished manuscript.

Cumming, G. and Buell, M. (1997). *Supervision of the sex offender.* Brandon, VT: The Safer Society Press.

De Young, M. (1988). The indignant page: Techniques of neutralization in the publications of pedophile organizations. *Child Abuse and Neglect, 12,* 583-591.

Dietz, P.E. (1983). Sex offenses: Behavioral aspects. In S.H. Kadish (Ed.), *Encyclopedia of crime and justice.* New York, NY: Free Press.

Dietz, P.E., Cox, D.J., and Wegener, S. (1986). Male genital exhibitionism. In W.J. Curran, A.L. McGarry, and S.A. Shah (Eds.), *Forensic psychiatry and psychology: Perspectives and standards for interdisciplinary practice* (pp. 363-385). Philadelphia, PA: F.A. Davis.

Douglas, J.E., Burgess, A.W., Burgess, A.C., and Ressler, R.K. (1992). *Crime classification manual: A standard system for investigating and classifying violent crimes.* San Francisco, CA: Jossey-Bass, Inc.

Eccles, A. and Marshall, W.L. (1999). Relapse prevention. In W.L. Marshall, D. Anderson, and Y. Fernandez (Eds.), *Cognitive behavioral treatment of sexual offenders* (pp. 127-146). Chichester, England: John Wiley and Sons, Ltd.

Ettin, M. (1989). Come on Jack, tell us about yourself: The growth spurt of group psychotherapy. *International Journal of Group Psychotherapy, 39,* 35-57.

Finkelhor, D. (1984). *Child sexual abuse: New theory and research.* New York: The Free Press.

Finkelhor, D. and Williams, L.M. (1988). *Nursery crimes.* Beverly Hills, CA: Sage Publications.

Fisher, B.S., Cullen, F.T., and Turner, M.G. (2000). *The sexual victimization of college women* (NCJ 182369). Washington, DC: U.S. Department of Justice, Bureau of Justice Statistics.

Friedman, W.H. (1983). *How to do groups.* New York: Jason Aronson.

Garland, R.J. and Dougher, M.J. (1991). Motivational intervention in the treatment of sex offenders. In W.R. Miller and S. Rollnick (Eds.), *Motivational interview-*

ing: Preparing people to change addictive behavior (pp. 303-313). New York: Guilford Press.

Gratzer, T. and Bradford, J.M.W. (1995). Offender and offense characteristics of sexual sadistics: A comparative study. *Journal of Forensic Science, 40*(3), 450-455.

Greenberg, D.M. (1998). Sexual recidivism in sex offenders. *The Canadian Journal of Psychiatry, 43* (June), 459-465.

Greenberg, D.M., Bradford, J.W., and Curry, S. (1993). A comparison of sexual victimization in the childhoods of pedophiles and hebephiles. *Journal of Forensic Science, 23*(2), 432-436.

Greenfeld, L.A. (1997). *Sex offenses and offenders: An analysis of data on rape and sexual assault.* (NCJ-163392). Washington, DC: U.S. Department of Justice, Bureau of Justice Statistics.

Groth, A.N. (1978). Pattern of sexual assault against children and adolescents. In A.W. Burgess, A.N. Groth, L.L. Holmstrom, and S.M. Sgroi (Eds.), *Sexual assault of children and adolescents* (pp. 3-24). Lexington, MA: Lexington Books.

Groth, A.N. (1990). *Men who rape: The psychology of the offender.* New York: Plenum Press.

Groth, A.N., Burgess, A., and Holmstrom, L. (1977). Rape, power, anger and sexuality. *American Journal of Psychiatry, 134*(11), 1239-1243.

Groth, A.N., et al. (1982). The child molester: Clinical observations. In J.R. Conte and D.A. Shore (Eds.), *Social work and child sexual abuse.* New York: Hawthorne Press.

Groth, A.N., Longo, R., and McFaden, J. (1982). Undetected recidivism among rapists and child molesters. *Crime and Delinquency, 128,* 450-458.

Haaven, J., Little, R., and Petre-Miller, D. (1990). *Treating intellectually disabled sex offenders: A model residential program.* Brandon, VT: The Safer Society Press.

Hall, N.C.G. (1995). Sexual offender recidivism revisited: A meta-analysis of recent treatment studies. *Journal of Consulting and Clinical Psychology, 3*(5), 802-809.

Hanson, K.R. (1997a). The development of a brief actuarial risk scale for sexual offense recidivism. Department of Solicitor General Canada. Public Works and Government Services of Canada. No. JS4-1/1997-4E, 1-31.

Hanson, K.R. (1997b, January). Predictors of sex offense recidivism. *Research Summary: Corrections Research and Development, 2*(1), 1-3.

Hanson, K.R. (1999). What do we know about risk assessment? In A. Schlank and F. Cohen (Eds.), *The sexual predator: Law, policy, evaluation, and treatment* (8-1 to 8-24). Kingston, NJ: Civic Research.

Hanson, K.R. and Bussiere M.T. (1998). Predicating release: A meta-analysis of sexual offender recidivism studies. *Journal of Consulting and Clinical Psychology, 66*(2), pp. 001-0015.

Hanson, K.R. and Phenix, A. (1999). Coding rules for scoring the RRASOR. Draft written for California laws.

Hartman, C.R., et al. (1984). Typology of collectors. In A.W. Burgess (Ed.), *Child pornography and sex rings.* Lexington, MA: Lexington Books.

Hawk, G.L., Rosenfeld, B.D., and Warren, J.I. (1993). Prevalence of sexual offenses among mentally retarded criminal defendants. *Hospital and Community Psychiatry*, *44*(8), 784-786.

Hawthorne, P. (1999). An epidemic of rape. *Time*, November 1, 59.

Hazelwood, R.R. (1995). Analyzing the rape and profiling the offender. In R.R. Hazelwood and A.W. Burgess (Eds.), *Practical aspects of rape investigation: A multidisciplinary approach*, Second edition (pp. 155-181). Boca Raton, FL: CRC Press.

Hazelwood, R.R. and Burgess, A.W. (Eds.) (1995). The behavioral-oriented interview of rape victims: The key to profiling. In R.R. Hazelwood and A.W. Burgess (Eds.), *Practical aspects of rape investigation: A multidisciplinary approach* (pp. 139-154). Boca Raton, FL: CRC Press.

Hazelwood, R.R., et al. (1992). The criminal sexual sadist. FBI Law Enforcement Bulletin, February.

Hazelwood, R.R., Ressler, R.K., Depue, R.L., and Douglas, J.E. (1995). Criminal investigative analysis: An overview. In R.R. Hazelwood and A.W. Burgess (Eds.), *Practical aspects of rape investigation: A multidisciplinary approach*, Second edition (pp. 115-126). Boca Raton, FL: CRC Press.

Hertica, N.A. (1991). Interviewing sex offenders. *The Police Chief*, February, 39-43.

Hildebran, D. and Pithers, W.D. (1989). Enhancing offender empathy for sexual abuse victims. In D.R. Laws (Ed.), *Relapse prevention with sex offenders* (pp. 236-243). New York: The Guilford Press.

Ingersoll, S.L. and Patton, S.O. (1990). *Treating perpetrators of sexual abuse.* Lexington, MA: Lexington Books.

J.J. Peters Institute (1980). *A ten-year follow-up of sex offender recidivism.* Philadelphia, PA: Author.

James, B. and Nasjleti, M. (1983). *Treating sexually abused children and their families.* Palo Alto, CA: Consulting Psychologists Press, Inc.

Johnson, T.C. and Berry, C. (1989). Children who molest: A treatment program. *Journal of Interpersonal Violence*, *4*, 185-203.

Jones, E. and McCurdy, K. (1992). The links between types of maltreatment and demographic characteristics of children. *Child Abuse and Neglect*, *16*, 201-215.

Kaplan, H.I. and Sadock, B.J. (Eds.) (1998a). Group psychotherapy, combined individual and group psychotherapy, and psychodrama. *Synopsis of psychiatry: Behavioral sciences/clinical*, Eighth edition (pp. 897-904). Baltimore, MD: Williams and Wilkins.

Kaplan, H.I. and Sadock, B.J. (Eds.) (1998b). Mental retardation. *Synopsis of psychiatry: Behavioral sciences/clinical*, Eighth edition (pp. 1137-1154). Baltimore, MD: Williams and Wilkins.

Kaplan, H.I. and Sadock, B.J. (Eds.) (1998c). Paraphilias and sexual disorder not otherwise specified. *Synopsis of psychiatry: Behavioral sciences/clinical*, Eighth edition (pp. 700-710). Baltimore, MD: Williams and Wilkins.

Kear-Colwell, J. and Pollack, P. (1997). Motivation and confrontation: Which approach to the child sex offender? *Criminal Justice and Behavior*, *24*, 20-33.

Kelman, H.C. (1963). The role of the group in the induction of therapeutic change. *International Journal of Group Psychotherapy*, *13*, 399-432.

Kennedy, W.A. (1986). The psychologist as expert witness. In W.J. Curran, A.L. McGarry, and S.A. Shad (Eds.), *Forensic psychiatry and psychology: Perspectives and standards for interdisciplinary practice* (pp. 487-511). Philadelphia, PA: F.A. Davis Company.

Knight, R.A. and Prentky, R.A. (1990). Classifying sexual offenders: The development and corroboration of taxonomic models. In W.L. Marshall, D.R. Laws, and H.E. Barbaree (Eds.), *Handbook of sexual assault: Issues, theories, and treatment of the offender* (pp. 23-24). New York: Plenum.

Knopp, F.H. (1982). *Remedial intervention in adolescent sex offenses: Nine program descriptions.* Orwell, VT: The Safer Society Press.

Knopp, F.H. (1984). *Retraining adult sex offenders: Methods and models.* Syracuse, NY: The Safer Society Press.

Knopp, F.H. (1990). Introduction. In J. Haaven, R. Little, and D. Petre-Miller (Eds.), *Treating intellectually disabled sex offenders: A model residential program* (pp. 2-9). Orwell, VT: The Safer Society Press.

Koss, M.P. (1993). Rape: Scope, impact, interventions, and public policy responses. *American Psychologist, 48,* 1062-1069.

Kottler, J.A. (1993). *On being a therapist,* Revised edition. San Francisco, CA: Jossey-Bass, Inc.

Kunjukrishnan, R., Pawlak, M.A., and Varan, L.R. (1988). The clinical and forensic psychiatric issues of retifism. *Canadian Journal of Psychiatry, 33*(December), 819-824.

Lanning, K.V. (1992). *Child molesters: A behavioral analysis for law enforcement officers investigating cases for child sexual exploitation,* Third edition. Washington, DC: National Center for Missing and Exploited Children.

Lanning, K.V. and Hazelwood, R.R. (1988). The maligned investigator of criminal sexuality. *FBI Law Enforcement Bulletin,* September.

Laws, D.R. (1999). Relapse prevention: The state of the art. *Journal of Interpersonal Violence, 14*(3), 285-302.

Madanes, C., with Keim, J.P., and Smelser, D. (1995). *The violence of men. New techniques for working with abusive families: A therapy of social action.* San Francisco, CA: Jossey-Bass, Inc.

Maletzky, B.M. (1998). The paraphilias: Research and treatment. In P.E. Nathan and J.M. Gorman (Eds.), *A guide to treatments that work* (pp. 472-500). New York: Oxford University Press.

Maletzky, B.M. and Steinhauser, C. (1998). The Portland sexual abuse clinic. In W.L. Marshall, Y.M. Fernandez, S.M. Hudson, and T. Ward (Eds.), *Sourcebook of treatment programs for sex offenders* (pp. 105-116). New York, NY: Plenum Press.

Mann, J. (1966). Evaluation of group therapy. In J.L. Moreno (Ed.), *International handbook of group psychotherapy* (pp. 129-148). New York: Philosophical Library.

Mann, M. (1996). Fantasy-based interviewing. *Law and Order,* May, 117-119.

Marshall, W.L., Anderson, D., and Fernandez, Y. (Eds.) (1999). Therapeutic processes and client self-esteem. In *Cognitive behavioral treatment of sexual offenders* (pp. 39-58). Chichester, England: John Wiley and Sons, Ltd.

Marshall, W.L. and Barrett, S. (1990). *Criminal neglect: Why sex offenders go free.* Toronto, Canada: Doubleday Canada Limited.

Marshall, W.L., Eccles, A., and Barbaree, H.E. (1991). The treatment of exhibitionists. A focus on sexual deviance versus cognitive and relationship features. *Behavioral Research Therapy, 29,* 129-135.

Marshall, W.L., Jones, R., Ward, T., Johnson, P., and Barbaree, H.E. (1991). Treatment outcome with sex offenders. *Clinical Psychology Review, 11,* 465-485.

Matthews, J.K. (1998). An 11-year perspective of working with female sex offenders. In W.L. Marshall, Y.M. Fernandez, S.M. Hudson, and T. Ward, *Sourcebook of treatment programs for sexual offenders* (pp. 259-272). New York: Plenum Press.

Mayer, A. (1992). *Women sex offenders.* Holmes Beach, FL: Learning Publications, Inc.

McGrath, R. (1990). Assessment of sexual aggressors: Practical clinical interviewing strategies. *The Journal of Interpersonal Violence,* December.

McGrath, R. (1994). *Cost effectiveness of sex offender treatment programs.* Presented at the Annual Conference for Virginia Sex Offender Treatment Providers, Hampton Beach, VA.

McGrath, R. and Hoke, S. (1994). Vermont Assessment of Sex Offender Risk. Unpublished test. In G. Cumming and M. Buell, *Supervision of the Sex Offender* (pp. 146-147). Brandon, VT: American Correctional Association.

Meloy, J.R. (Ed.) (1998). The psychology of stalking. *The psychology of stalking: Clinical and forensic perspectives* (pp. 213-223). San Diego, CA: Academic Press.

Meyer, J.K. (1995). Paraphilias. In H.I. Kaplan and B.J. Sadock (Eds.), *Comprehensive textbook of psychiatry,* Sixth edition, Volume 1 (pp. 1334-1347). Baltimore, MD: Williams and Wilkins.

Meyer, J. (1998). Cultural factors in erotomania and obsessional following. In J.R. Meloy (Ed.), *The psychology of stalking: Clinical and forensic perspectives* (pp. 213-223). San Diego, CA: Academic Press.

Minuchin, S. and Fishman, C.H. (1981). *Family therapy techniques.* Cambridge, MA: Harvard University Press.

Money, J. (1993). *Lovemaps: Clinical concepts of sexual/erotic health and pathology, paraphilia, and gender transposition in childhood, adolescence, and maturity.* New York: Irvington Publishers, Inc.

Moore, J. (1992). The worker. In J. Moore (Ed.), *The abc of child protection* (pp. 97-113). Brookfield, VT: Ashgate Publishing Company.

Moreau, D.M. and Bigbee, P.D. (1995). Concepts of physical evidence in sexual assault. In R.R. Hazelwood and A.W. Burgess (Eds.), *Practical aspects of rape investigation: A multidisciplinary approach,* Second edition (pp. 45-73). Boca Raton, FL: CRC Press.

Mullan, H., and Rosenbaum, M. (1978). *Group psychotherapy, theory and practice,* Second edition. New York: The Free Press.

Murrey, G.J., Briggs, D., and Davis, M.S. (1992). Psychopathic disordered, mentally ill, and mentally handicapped sex offenders: A comparative study. *Medical Science Law, 32*(4), 331-336.

Nadelson, C.C., Notman, M.T., and Carmen, E.H. (1986). The rape victim and the rape experience. In W.J. Curran, A.L. McGarry, and S.A. Shah (Eds.), *Forensic psychiatry and psychology: Perspectives and standards for interdisciplinary practice* (pp. 339-362). Philadelphia, PA: F.A. Davis Co.

NASW News. (2000). Caseload reduction is sought in Maryland, *45*(April), 5.

National Center for Missing and Exploited Children (1990). Case in point: Training points on the serial child molester and abductor program, Special edition, August.

O'Brien, M.J. and Bera, W.H. (1986). Adolescent sexual offenders: A descriptive typology. *Preventing Sexual Abuse, 1,* 1-4.

O'Connell, M.A., Leberg, E., and Donaldson, C.R. (1990). *Working with sex offenders: Guidelines for therapist selection.* Newbury Park, CA: Sage Publications.

O'Neill, J.V. (2000). Aid offered on reporting child abuse. *NASW News, 45*(6), 1.

Opalic, P. (1989). Existential and psychopathological evaluation of group psychotherapy of neurotic and psychotic patients. *International Journal of Group Psychotherapy, 39,* 389-422.

Pallone, N.J. (1990). Rehabilitating criminal sexual psychopaths: Legislative mandates, clinical quandaries. In E. Coleman, S.M. Dwyer, and N. Pallone (Eds.), *Sex offender treatment: Biological dysfunction, intrapsychic conflict, interpersonal violence* (pp. 5-11). Binghamton, NY: The Haworth Press.

Pattison, E.M. (1967). Evaluation studies of group psychotherapy. *International Journal of Psychiatry, 4,* 389-422.

Perry, G.P. and Orchard, J. (1989). Assessment and treatment of adolescent sex offenders. In P.A. Keller and S.R. Heyman (Eds.), *Innovations in clinical practice: A source book* (pp. 187-211). Sarasota, FL: Professional Resource Exchange.

Perry, G.P. and Orchard, J. (1992). *Assessment and treatment of adolescent sex offenders.* Sarasota, FL: Professional Resource Press.

Pessein, D., Maher, J., Cramer, E., and Prentky, R. (1998). Joseph J. Peters institute intervention program for adult sex offenders. In W.L. Marshall, Y.M., Fernandez, S.M., Hudson, and T. Ward (Eds.), *Sourcebook of treatment programs for sex offenders* (pp. 117-131). New York: Plenum Press.

Peters, J.J., Pedigo, J., Steg, J., and McKenna, J. (1968). Group psychotherapy of the sex offender. *Federal Probation, 32,* 41-46.

Peters, J.J. and Roether, H.A. (1972). Group psychotherapy for probationed sex offenders. In H.L. Resnick and M.E. Wolfgang (Eds.), *Sexual behaviors: Clinical and legal aspects.* Boston, MA: Little Brown and Co.

Peters, J.J. and Sadoff, R. (1971). Psychiatric services for sex offenders on probation. *Federal Probation, 35,* 33-37.

Phillips, S.L., Heads, T.C., Taylor, P.J., and Hill, M.G. (1999). Sexual offending and antisocial sexual behavior among patients with schizophrenia. *Journal of Clinical Psychiatry, 60*(3), March, 170-175.

Pithers, W.D. (1987). *Cost of a new sex offense and the relative cost of treatment.* Paper prepared for the Safer Society Press.

Pithers, W.D., Beal, L., Armstrong, J., and Petty, J. (1989). Identification of risk factors through clinical interviews and analysis of records. In D.R. Laws (Ed.),

Relapse prevention with sex offenders (pp. 77-87). New York: The Guilford Press.

Pithers, W.D., Becker, J.V., Kalfa, M., Morenz, B., Schlank, A., and Leombruno, T. (1995). Children with sexual behavior problems, adolescent sexual abusers, and adult sex offenders: Assessment and treatment. *Review of Psychiatry, 14,* 779-818.

Pithers, W.D. and Cumming, G.F. (1989). Can relapse be prevented? Initial outcome data from the Vermont treatment program for sexual aggression. In D.R. Laws (Ed.), *Relapse prevention with sex offenders* (pp. 313-325). New York: The Guilford Press.

Pithers, W.D., Kashima, K.M., Cumming, G.F., and Beal, L.S. (1988). Relapse prevention: A method of enhancing maintenance of change in sex offenders. In A.C. Salter, *Treating child sex offenders and victims: A practical guide* (pp. 131-170). Newbury Park, CA: Sage.

Pithers, W.D., Marques, J.K., Gibat, C.C., and Marlatt, G.A. (1983). Relapse prevention with sexual aggressives: A self-control model of treatment and maintenance of change. In J.G. Greer and I.R. Stuart (Eds.), *The sexual aggressor: Current perspectives on treatment* (pp. 214-239). New York: Van Nostrand Reinhart.

Pithers, W.D., Martin, G.R., and Cumming, G.F. (1989). Vermont treatment program for sexual aggressors. In D.R. Laws (Ed.), *Relapse prevention with sex offenders* (pp. 292-310). New York: The Guilford Press.

Poulos, T.M. and Greenfield, L.B. (1994). *Convicted sex offenders.* Richmond, VA: Criminal Justice Research Center, Commonwealth of Virginia, Department of Criminal Justice Services.

Prendergast, W.E. (1991). *Treating sex offenders in correctional institutions and outpatient clinics: A guide to clinical practice.* Binghamton, NY: The Haworth Press.

Prentky, R. and Burgess, A.W. (1990). Rehabilitation of child molesters: A cost-benefit analysis. *American Journal of Orthopsychiatry, 60,* 108-117.

Prentky, R.A. and Knight, R.A. (1993). Age of onset of sexual assault: Criminal and life history correlates. In G.C. Nagayama Hall, R. Hirschman, J.R. Graham, and M.S. Zaragoza (Eds.), *Sexual aggression: Issues in etiology, assessment, and treatment* (pp. 43-62). Washington, DC: Taylor and Francis.

Random House Dictionary of the English Language, Second edition (1987). New York: Random House.

Reid, W.H. (1997). Sexual and gender identity disorders. In W.H. Reid, G.U. Balis, and Sutton, B.J. (Eds.), *The treatment of psychiatric disorders,* Third edition, revised for DSM-IV (pp. 293-317). Bristol, PA: Brunner/Mazel Publishers.

Rooth, G. (1973). Exhibitionism, sexual violence, and paedophilia. *British Journal of Psychiatry, 122,* 705-710.

Ruegg, R.G., Haynes, C., and Frances, A. (1996). Assessment and management of antisocial personality disorder. In M. Rosenbluth and I.D. Yalom (Eds.), *Treating difficult personality disorders* (pp. 123-172). San Francisco, CA: Jossey-Bass, Inc.

Ryan, G. (1997). Sexually abusive youth: Defining the population. In G. Ryan and S. Lane (Eds.), *Juvenile sexual offending: Causes, consequences, and correction* (pp. 3-9). San Francisco, CA: Jossey-Bass Inc.

Sadock, V. (1995). Physical and sexual abuse of adult. In H.I. Kaplan and B.J. Sadock (Eds.), *Comprehensive textbook of psychiatry,* Sixth edition, Volume 2 (pp. 1729-1737). Baltimore, MD: Williams and Wilkins.

Salholz, E., Clift, E., Springen, K., and Johnson, P. (1990). Women under assault: Sex crimes finally get the media's attention. *Newsweek, 22,* July 16, 22-24.

Salter, A.C. (1988). *Treating child sex offenders and victims: A practical guide.* Newbury Park, CA: Sage Publications.

Schultz, G. (1965). *How many more victims?* Philadelphia, PA: Lippincott.

Schwartz, B.K. (1995a). Decision making with incarcerated sex offenders. In B.K. Schwartz and H.R. Cellini (Eds.), *The Sex offender: Corrections, treatment and legal practice* (pp. 8-1 to 8-18). Kingston, NJ: Civic Research Institute, Inc.

Schwartz, B.K. (1995b). Group therapy. In B.K. Schwartz and H.R. Cellini (Eds.), *The sex offender: Corrections, treatment and legal practice* (pp. 14-1 to 14-15). Kingston, NJ: Civic Research Institute.

Schwartz, B.K. (1995c). Theories of sex offenses. In B.K Schwartz and H.R. Cellini (Eds.), *The sex offender: Corrections, treatment and legal practice* (pp. 2-1 to 2-32). Kingston, NJ: Civic Research Institute.

Schwartz, B.K. and Cellini, H.R. (Eds.) (1995). Introduction. *The sex offender: Corrections, treatment and legal practice* (pp. xi-xiv). Kingston, NJ: Civic Research Institute.

Smith, R.S. (1976). Voyeurism: A review of literature. *Archives of Sexual Behavior, 5*(6), 585-608.

Smith, W.R. (1985). *Juvenile offenders and the prediction of risk.* Paper presented at adolescent perpetrator meetings arranged by Centre, Keystone, CO.

Spearly, J. and Lauderdale, M. (1983). Community characteristics and ethnicity in the prediction of child maltreatment rates. *Child Abuse and Neglect, 7,* 91-105.

Steele, N. (1995). Cost effectiveness of treatment. In B.K. Schwartz and H.R. Cellini (Eds.), *The sex offender: Corrections, treatment and legal practice* (pp. 4-1 to 4-19). Kingston, NJ: Civic Research Institute.

Sturgeon, V.H. and Taylor, J. (1980). Report of a five-year follow-up study of mentally disordered sex offenders released from Atascadero State Hospital in 1973. *Criminal Justice Journal, 4,* 31-63.

Swann, A. (1993). Recognition of abuse. In H. Owen, and J. Pritchard (Eds.), *Good practice in child protection: A manual for professionals* (pp. 38-55). Bristol, PA: Jessica Kingsley Publishers.

Time (1992). Unsettling report on an epidemic of rape. May 4, 15.

Tjaden, P. and Thoennes, N. (1997). *Stalking in America: Findings from the national violence against women survey.* Denver, CO: Center for Policy Research.

Trepper, T.S. and Barrett, M.J. (1989). *Systemic treatment of incest: A therapeutic handbook.* Bristol, PA: Brunner/Mazel.

Vallianatos, C. (2000). Summit eyes violence against women. *NASW News, 45*(6), June 1.

Virginia Statistical Abstract (1994). Summary statistics for state correctional facilities for the U.S., Virginia, and surrounding states: 1984 and 1990. University of Virginia, Center for Public Service (Table 4.10, pp. 123-124).

Waldfogel, J. (1998). *The future of child protection: How to break the cycle of abuse and neglect.* Cambridge, MA: Harvard University Press.

Wang, C.T. and Daro, D. (1997). *Current trends in child abuse reporting and fatalities: The results of the 1996 annual fifty-state survey.* Chicago, IL: National Committee to Prevent Child Abuse.

Weiss, P. (1999). Assessment and treatment of sex offenders in the Czech Republic and in Eastern Europe. *Journal of Interpersonal Violence, 14*(4), 411-421.

Werman, D.S. (1984). *The practice of supportive psychotherapy.* New York: Brunner/Mazel.

Whitaker, D.L. and Wodarski, J.S. (1989). Treatment of sexual offenders in a community mental health center: An evaluation. In J.S. Wodarski, and D.L. Whitaker (Eds.), *Treatment of sex offenders in social work and mental health settings* (pp. 49-68). Binghamton NY: The Haworth Press.

Wise, T.N. (1990). Transvestitic fetishism: Diagnoses and treatment. *Psychiatric Medicine, 8*(4), 75-84.

Yalom, I.D. (1985). *The theory and practice of group psychotherapy,* Third edtion. New York: Basic Books.

Yalom, I.D., et al. (1967). Prediction of improvement in group therapy. *Archives of General Psychiatry, 17,* 159-168.

Zona, M.A., Palarea, R.E., and Lane, J.C. (1998). Psychiatric diagnoses and the offender—Victim typology of stalking. In J.R. Meloy (Ed.), *The psychology of stalking: Clinical and forensic perspectives* (pp. 69-83). San Diego, CA: Academic Press.

Index

Order Your Own Copy of
This Important Book for Your Personal Library!

HOW TO WORK WITH SEX OFFENDERS
A Handbook for Criminal Justice, Human Service,
and Mental Health Professionals

_____in hardbound at $39.95 (ISBN: 0-7890-0733-9)

_____in softbound at $22.95 (ISBN: 0-7890-1499-8)

COST OF BOOKS_____

OUTSIDE USA/CANADA/
MEXICO: ADD 20%____

POSTAGE & HANDLING_____
(US: $4.00 for first book & $1.50
for each additional book)
Outside US: $5.00 for first book
& $2.00 for each additional book)

SUBTOTAL_____

in Canada: add 7% GST____

STATE TAX____
(NY, OH & MIN residents, please
add appropriate local sales tax)

FINAL TOTAL____
(If paying in Canadian funds,
convert using the current
exchange rate, UNESCO
coupons welcome.)

BILL ME LATER: ($5 service charge will be added)

(Bill-me option is good on US/Canada/Mexico orders only;
not good to jobbers, wholesalers, or subscription agencies.)

Check here if billing address is different from
shipping address and attach purchase order and
billing address information.

Signature_____

PAYMENT ENCLOSED: $_____

PLEASE CHARGE TO MY CREDIT CARD.

Visa   MasterCard   AmEx   Discover
Diner's Club   Eurocard   JCB

Account # _____

Exp. Date_____

Signature_____

Prices in US dollars and subject to change without notice.

NAME_____

INSTITUTION_____

ADDRESS_____

CITY_____

STATE/ZIP_____

COUNTRY_____ COUNTY (NY residents only)_____

TEL_____ FAX_____

E-MAIL_____

May we use your e-mail address for confirmations and other types of information?   Yes   No
We appreciate receiving your e-mail address and fax number. Haworth would like to e-mail or fax special discount offers to you, as a preferred customer. **We will never share, rent, or exchange your e-mail address or fax number.** We regard such actions as an invasion of your privacy.

Order From Your Local Bookstore or Directly From
The Haworth Press, Inc.
10 Alice Street, Binghamton, New York 13904-1580 • USA
TELEPHONE: 1-800-HAWORTH (1-800-429-6784) / Outside US/Canada: (607) 722-5857
FAX: 1-800-895-0582 / Outside US/Canada: (607) 722-6362
E-mail: getinfo@haworthpressinc.com
PLEASE PHOTOCOPY THIS FORM FOR YOUR PERSONAL USE.
www.HaworthPress.com